Contents

Foreword

ROD BARTON IS A RECENTLY RETIRED Australian defence scientific intelligence officer who was involved in the hunt for Iraq's weapons of mass destruction over a period of almost fifteen years. Like most people I had not heard of him until the broadcast of a *Four Corners* program in early 2005. The program led off with Barton's claim that the Minister for Defence, Senator Robert Hill, had misled the Parliament over a matter concerning him. Barton had recently been working with the Americans in Iraq. As part of his job, he had interrogated a former Iraqi minister and reorganised an entire weapons of mass destruction interrogation team. Although Barton had informed the Department of Defence of these facts, Hill had flatly claimed in Parliament that no Australian had been involved in the interrogation of Iraqi prisoners. When Barton privately complained, a Defence official helpfully explained that what he had conducted was an interview but not an interrogation.

What most interested me about the *Four Corners* program was not the charge that Senator Hill had misled Parliament – in contemporary Australia such matters are anything but rare – but the riveting stories Barton told about his experiences as a United Nations weapons inspector in Iraq; as a senior member of the Hans Blix team in New York before the invasion of Iraq; and, following the invasion, as a de facto leader of the CIA's Iraq Survey Group. It became clear Barton was able to speak about a vital chapter of contemporary history with unusual authority, vividness and precision. Following *Four Corners* I flew to

Canberra to meet Rod Barton. At the end of an absorbing interview, which took two days to complete, I suggested, like others before me had, that Rod should outline his experiences in a book. Fortunately, he agreed. *The Weapons Detective* is the result.

Before becoming entangled with Iraq, Barton was involved in some previously unknown Cold War weapons controversies and in their political fall-out. In the early 1980s the United States accused the Soviet Union of supplying its Vietnamese client with a biological weapon known as Yellow Rain for use against enemies in Laos and Cambodia. In *The Weapons Detective*, Barton reveals how a small group of Australian defence science experts, with the support of the Fraser government, defied the Americans and helped eventually prove the falsity of their claim. For Barton the Yellow Rain experience, which tarnished his reputation in Washington for a time, served as a very useful apprenticeship not only in the science but also the politics of weapons intelligence.

More positive were the consequences which flowed from Rod Barton's mid-1980s conclusion that Iraq was manufacturing mustard gas for use in its war with Iran. At first the warning was greeted in Australia with considerable scepticism. Mustard gas had, after all, not been seen on a battlefield since the First World War. When the warning proved tragically correct, the method Barton and others in Australia had pioneered – the analysis of the import orders of rogue states (the chemical ingredients for mustard gas had been imported by Iraq in the exact proportions required) – led to the creation of an informal but highly effective international arms control committee. The committee, which still exists and is known as the Australia Group, is concerned with the detection of chemical and biological weapons production and its prevention. It provides an example of fabled Australian pragmatism at its best.

Because of his expertise in the field of chemical and biological weapons, Rod Barton was offered a new job, as a United Nations weapons inspector, following Iraq's 1991 surrender at the end of the first Gulf War. Because of his taste for adventure, Barton accepted at once. He was to be one of a small handful of inspectors who remained involved in the hunt for the missing Iraqi weapons of mass destruction, from the very beginning of the process until the very end. The hunt is the main subject of this book.

A number of missing pieces of the puzzle are revealed here for the first time. Barton tells how and why the Iraqis finally admitted in 1995 that they had indeed been involved before the first Gulf War in plans for the production of biological weapons. He reveals the role played by Israeli intelligence in the eventual discovery. Barton provides a more reliable and even-handed account of the fateful collapse of the United Nations inspectorate in Iraq than any I have previously read. Following UNSCOM's collapse, Barton became involved in the work of the successor organisation, UNMOVIC. He shows why by mid-2002 most of the senior UNMOVIC staff, although not its genial head, Hans Blix, had come to think of war as an absolute inevitability. His book provides fresh detail, from the viewpoint of an insider, of the sometimes fierce pressures placed by the Americans on UNMOVIC and Blix, during the build-up to the invasion of Iraq.

After the invasion, Barton could not resist an invitation to become an adviser to David Kay, the man selected by the Americans to lead the hunt for the weapons of mass destruction which had provided the justification for the invasion. By the time Barton arrived, the once hawkish Kay had lost his faith and already quit Iraq. *The Weapons Detective* provides the only authentic account of the slightly mad atmosphere that now pervaded the camp of the invaders as the justification for their military action dissolved before their eyes. Barton's description of the visit paid by the head of the CIA, George Tenet, to the Iraq Survey Group, at a time when Washington was still in denial, is genuinely droll. Barton reveals how the head of British intelligence, John Scarlett, was still trying at this eleventh hour to "sex up" the weapons of mass destruction intelligence. Barton was a very close friend of fellow biological weapons inspector, Dr David Kelly, the man who was caught in the lethal post-invasion political cross-fire between the Blair government and the BBC over the weapons "sex up" issue. Barton writes of his suicide with a feeling that is deeper because of his restraint.

When Barton quit Iraq at this time, it was not, however, the mendacity of the official line that disturbed him most. While in occupied Iraq Barton had encountered a number of senior Iraqi figures who had been involved in one way or another in the pre-1991 weapons program, and who were still languishing, pointlessly and unlawfully, in near solitary confinement in tiny prison cells. Some are languishing there still. His book concludes with a passionate plea for their release.

The Weapons Detective is a sober and humane book by an author of unique experience, scrupulous honesty and astonishing recall, but with no political or ideological agenda of any kind. For this reason the careful verdict Barton finally delivers on the invasion of Iraq – on whether or not we went to war on the basis of a lie – carries unusual moral weight.

Because it has undermined the authority of international law, plunged occupied Iraq into a condition of almost indescribable chaos and pushed the world to the brink of the clash of civilisations of which Samuel Huntington once warned, the invasion of Iraq may well come to be seen as the most important event of the post-Cold War era. Future generations will struggle to understand all dimensions of the decision. In doing so, they will rely on the kind of honest, apolitical eyewitness testimony Rod Barton provides in this fascinating and important book about the fifteen-year-long Iraqi weapons of mass destruction wild-goose chase.

Robert Manne
March 2006

Prologue

AT THE LEISURELY HOUR OF 10 A.M., on 9 June 1991, I and twenty-four other members of the UN Special Commission boarded an ageing Romanian Airlines 727 jet at Muharraq, Bahrain's civilian and military airport. We were about to commence UNSCOM's first inspection in Iraq.

We flew up the Gulf towards Iraq and an hour later were off the coast of Kuwait. There was no doubt about this because with oil fires still raging, the country was marked by a black smudge, with an occasional orange flare bursting through the gloom. To our consternation, we noticed two F4 Phantoms of the Kuwaiti Air Force suddenly appear alongside our plane, one on either side. We felt very vulnerable: did they know we were representatives of the UN? Then, as suddenly as they had arrived, they were gone: we knew now that we were over Iraq.

Another hour and we were circling Habbiniyah military airfield, 100 kilometres to the west of Baghdad. On landing, the plane taxied towards a small concrete single-storied building. We were apprehensive: would we be welcomed, or arrested? The latter seemed a faint possibility, but then, Iraq had only with reluctance accepted the UN's ceasefire resolution and the necessity of inspections. Had there been a change of heart?

On the tarmac there was a flurry of activity, with both civilian and military vehicles pulling up alongside us. We filed out of the plane into the furnace-like heat of the Iraqi desert. A line of officials, some in uniform, some in suits, had gathered. "Welcome," an Iraqi general said, "we are pleased to have you here as guests of the Iraqi people."

For us, these were not entirely reassuring words. Western hostages, seized early in the recent war and used by Saddam's regime as human shields, were described as "guests of the Iraqi people". In fact, we were there at the instruction of the international community, and in no sense were we guests.

Our job was to inspect Iraq's chemical weapons plant, Al Muthanna. We were anxious about this, not only because this was the first time any of us had conducted an inspection, but also because we knew the place had been heavily bombed in the Gulf War and there would be damaged buildings, unexploded bombs and leaking chemicals. The Western press was later to describe this as the most dangerous place on earth.

I returned to Iraq many times in the next thirteen years. Because of intransigence and obstruction by Iraqi officials, including attempts to hide chemical and biological weapons, my work slowly, but inexorably, changed from that of an inspector to that of a weapons detective. All the skills of a detective were required: investigation, observation, analysis and deduction. The tools available were those familiar to any detective, including sampling from the "crime scene", followed by forensic analysis. And of course, interview or interrogation of the usual suspects.

In this book I have put my experiences down on paper to allow others to see, through my eyes, some of the events that shaped the world we have today. The book also tells the story of how I became a weapons detective, a job for which I had unwittingly been preparing all of my working life. It is a personal account, told in my own way. It is not an account of my personal life, nor is it intended to be a learned or comprehensive work of history. I did not have private meetings with the President of the United States or the President of Iraq. I will not write about what they said or did, except in passing. I did, however, have dealings with many individuals, from generals to general work-hands, who played key roles in the lead-up to war. Over the years I took many notes and, on occasion, kept written diaries of happenings. I have drawn heavily on these. Where there are gaps, particularly in the earlier years, I have relied on memory.

I must apologise to some of my colleagues mentioned in this book. I have not asked their permission to include them. Some would probably prefer that they were not named, particularly those with an intelligence background, such is the nature of that work. However, where they have achieved good or great things, some acknowledgment of these accomplishments should be made.

I must also apologise to those I have not included. Throughout my working life I have travelled with many who made significant contributions. For reasons of space I cannot mention them all.

Finally there are a few whom, for various reasons, I have omitted. No doubt they will be grateful for my discretion.

Rod Barton

An Accidental Intelligence Officer

IT WAS WITH GREAT EXCITEMENT AND even greater trepidation that I entered the headquarters of the Joint Intelligence Organisation in 1972. Not that I knew what I was entering, since the anonymous-looking building was not identified by any sign, even once inside the entrance. To obtain entry, I was escorted through two security checks, collecting on the way two visitor's passes. Being quick on the uptake, I figured this was probably a place where secrets were kept. This was confirmed when I was taken to the interview room, which was actually a vault on the ground floor. No windows, and a combination lock door that was blast- and fireproof. This was going to be some interview!

The vault was not that large: big enough for a desk and three chairs. I sat with my back to the door that was closed behind me, while across the table sat the interviewer and his secretary. The interviewer (or was it interrogator?) introduced himself as Robert Mathams, Director of Scientific and Technical Intelligence. This, he said, was the Joint Intelligence Organisation. Did I feel comfortable with all the security? Yes, I lied.

Mathams said there had been a terrible mistake when the job descriptions were sent out, and I had received one that related to another job. He then slid a single piece of paper across the desk, never actually releasing his grip on it, and said, "This is the correct duty statement." Stamped in red ink on the top and bottom was the word "CONFIDENTIAL" and below that, typed in capital letters, "JOINT

INTELLIGENCE ORGANISATION". I tried to read the statement quickly, but in my state of near-terror not much registered. What if this is the first test, I thought?

Bob Mathams spoke fluently and eloquently of the work of JIO, including the role of scientific and technical intelligence. He said, for example, that if a certain country developed an artificial skin for use in treating soldiers with burns, then it might give them a competitive edge in any conflict with Australia, and he needed people like me to study this. While I was musing on this rather strange example, he started to introduce, equally eloquently, what was to be the first of a series of questions. Did I think China was going to emerge as a world power? (I talked about "ping-pong diplomacy", which I had read about in the *Canberra Times*.) He then put it to me that some people argued that Japan was now doing what it could not do during World War II, that is, take over Australia, but this time was doing it peacefully by buying up chunks of real estate instead of by invasion. What did I think of this? (I said we had now moved on from World War II.) Finally he asked me to name the three most significant scientific developments of the last thirty years. I nominated "micro-electronics" (this was the age before digital watches), space technology (just three years earlier, Neil Armstrong had set foot on the moon) and the harnessing of nuclear power for peaceful purposes (Chernobyl was still fourteen years away).

I was in awe of Bob Mathams even at this first meeting. He was an imposing man in his mid-fifties, with a presence and bearing that told of his military background. He had jet-black hair, some said too jet-black, but for all that he was the genuine article. He was a scientist himself (agricultural chemistry), and his background in intelligence went back to World War II in New Guinea and to subsequent work as an officer in the Australian Army Intelligence Corps. He was the father of scientific intelligence in Australia and had built up a branch from one person (himself) to a group of about forty analysts, engineers and scientists, who looked at overseas developments in missiles, space, nuclear technology and weapons systems. Until I met Mathams, I had not contemplated a career in intelligence, but now I knew that I wanted to work for this man – and fortunately that is what happened.

It took many months for the bureaucratic wheels to turn, and I was also required, as all intelligence analysts were, to undergo a rigorous security check by ASIO before I could receive the highest-level security clearance. So it was not until June 1973 that I started my new job and became, almost by accident, an intelligence analyst.

On that first day, Bob Mathams called me into his office to tell me what my duties were to be. There had been a change of plan, he said, I was not to study the development of artificial skin by foreign powers. I can't say that I was disappointed at this news. Instead I was to work on salt. I was bewildered. In this new and exciting world, perhaps salt was some sort of strategic weapon. But how?

I had not then heard of SALT, nor, I suspect, had many Australians, but it was something with which I was to become very familiar. The Strategic Arms Limitation Treaty (SALT I) was a pact between the United States and the Soviet Union to limit the number of strategic missiles each side was permitted to have. The treaty had been signed in the year before I started work at JIO, and it was to expire in 1977. SALT I was an interim arrangement and Mathams was interested in whether a new, more permanent treaty, SALT II, could be negotiated before the expiry date arrived. My job was to follow these negotiations and assess the likely outcome.

It seemed strange to me that an Australian intelligence organisation would devote time to studying strategic treaties. My impression of intelligence, up to then largely based on James Bond films, was that it involved monitoring what our potential enemies might be up to, and although the Soviet Union might fall into this category, surely the US was an ally? Indeed, Mathams later made the point in his book *Sub Rosa*[1] that "the very word 'intelligence' still excites suspicions of clandestine behaviour and dirty tricks", going on to explain that this is a popular misconception when it comes to the majority of intelligence work.

Also disappointing was the fact that most of the "intelligence" I was to look at was not secret, but openly published material. Bob Mathams explained to me that intelligence assessments do not have to be based on "secret" information, and in fact public sources such as newspapers or official government information often form the basis of the data used for analysis and assessment. Of course, the analyst requires skill and experience to determine whether such information is reliable or accurate.

If studying treaties seemed strange work for JIO, it seemed equally strange work for me as a microbiologist; it was closer to political science than "real" science. But I tackled it with enthusiasm. In 2006, terrorism dominates the headlines, but in 1973 the pre-occupation was the threat of nuclear war: the Cuban crisis of eleven years earlier had made an indelible mark.

*

In my naivety, I thought that it was in the interest of both powers to control the numbers of their strategic nuclear weapons and that, although there were big differences in the types and numbers of weapons each side possessed, logic dictated that a new agreement would be reached. After all, even with the controls that were being envisaged, each side could annihilate the other.

Underpinning nuclear stability was the concept of MAD. This was the revealing acronym for Mutual Assured Destruction: if either side launched a pre-emptive nuclear attack, before the warheads reached their target the other side would have time to retaliate, thereby assuring the devastation of the aggressor. Hence, the theory went, this was a deterrent to both sides to initiating a nuclear war. It has sometimes been referred to as the Balance of Terror, but I prefer the acronym MAD, for mad it was. To ensure that MAD was not undermined, both sides had agreed to limit their defences against missile attack so that they remained vulnerable to nuclear attack. This was enshrined in the Antiballistic Missile Treaty that was also signed, along with SALT I, in May 1972.

I soon learned that nothing was simple in negotiations between superpowers. SALT I capped only the number of missiles permitted by each side. It did not restrict the numbers of strategic bombers or long-range nuclear cruise missiles. Nor did it restrict the number of warheads on ballistic missiles: some missiles had fourteen warheads. Controls on all these issues were to be addressed in SALT II. A major complication, however, was that these were the very systems both sides were busy developing during the period of negotiations.

Some US legislators were unhappy that the agreed numbers favoured the Soviet Union. In a US Defense Department publication entitled "Soviet Military Power",[2] it was stated that:

The decade of the 1970s, marked by the massive Soviet military build-up while the US maintained a virtually static posture, left our nation in a clearly disadvantageous position. This dangerous shift in the global balance unmistakably demonstrated Soviet intentions to attain a position of military superiority.

But the number of missiles was only one measure of strategic power and by other measures the US was clearly ahead. The US compensated for its inferiority in numbers by its vastly superior technology. For example, it put great effort into developing nuclear-powered submarines that could launch ballistic missiles against the Soviet Union from any ocean location. This capability was achieved in 1979 with the deployment on a Poseidon submarine of the first Trident 1 missile with a range of 8000 kilometres or more.

Another technological trend was the improvement in missile accuracy. The physics of explosions are such that to destroy a hardened target, such as an underground concrete missile silo, it is far more effective to increase the accuracy of the warhead than to increase the size of the blast. A "close" miss with a megaton-type bomb will be less effective than a direct hit with a little Hiroshima-sized bomb. Thus by the late 1970s the US was heading for a first-strike capability, meaning that it would eventually be able to initiate a nuclear war, destroying in the first attack the enemy's nuclear forces before the Soviet Union could retaliate. This would be the end of MAD, and the start of another kind of madness.

In my view the qualitative improvements in nuclear weapon systems were far more destabilising than the quantitative changes. Improved accuracy, for example, meant that even with a freeze on numbers, the nuclear forces of both sides were becoming far more deadly.

So the SALT negotiations seemed to me rather pointless: they had simply pushed the arms race in a different and dangerous direction. If the parties to any negotiation are only looking for loopholes to exploit for advantage, then there are no prospects for a lasting and meaningful agreement. That was a lesson that I was to carry with me years later, when I was trying to get militias in Mogadishu to disarm.

For me, the point of ultimate futility was reached in the late 1970s, when I was asked by the head of JIO's Nuclear Section, Harry Turner, to consider what would happen if the negotiations and peace failed, and the world was plunged into nuclear war. The objective of Harry's study was to determine what might be targeted in a global nuclear war, and whether there could be a winner. One of the interests in this study was the consequences for Australia. Would Sydney be hit, or – even worse from our perspective – Canberra? We carefully examined the types and numbers of Soviet warheads in an effort to work out how many of these it would take to destroy airfields and rail-marshalling yards throughout the territory of the US and its NATO allies. Similarly, we studied how a US strike might destroy the USSR. I spent many an evening with my Nuclear Weapons Effects calculator assessing the effects of nuclear strikes on cities, command centres, oil fields, missile silos …

Our conclusions were that the US had a major edge, largely because of its technological advantage. On the basis of pure statistics the US would not be totally annihilated in such a war: there were more targets than the Soviets could destroy, and so, depending on what assumptions we made, the US could be the "winner". This of course was all cloud-cuckoo-land speculation. Ours was a scientific study and did not take into consideration other, profoundly significant factors, such as the social consequences of eliminating a quarter or more of the US population, and the environmental, political, economic and myriad other consequences of a global war. There seemed to me little value in such a study.

On the consequences for Australia we concluded that the Joint Australian–US Facilities of Northwest Cape, Nurrungar and Pine Gap were likely Soviet targets because of their potential to participate in US war-fighting. However the Soviets would not have enough warheads left over, after targeting the US and various European cities, for other Australia targets. Maybe a token bomb on Sydney. So nothing much to worry about then!

Of the three Joint Facilities, we assessed that Pine Gap was the most likely target[3] and we considered in detail whether it would be taken out with a nuclear ground-burst or air-burst. We thought an air-burst the more probable and that was good because the fallout would be considerably less. Bad luck for Alice Springs, but the rest of us would be OK.

We completed this study and wrote an extensive report. I don't recall it being distributed beyond our building, probably because of its deficiencies, or perhaps because there was little we could do about the consequences it described anyway. The report may still be mouldering in a vault in a basement somewhere, a reminder of different times.

*

In 1977, Bob Mathams announced to me the good news (or so he thought) that he had managed to secure me a year-long position at Harvard University to study to improve my understanding of the complexities of superpower relations. I declined. Not only did this not suit me for personal reasons, but I had also decided I had had enough of this type of work. Mathams was not happy, but then he had not consulted with me before making the arrangements. By the end of the week, at my request, I was transferred to Harry Turner's nuclear section.

Harry was a unique individual. He belonged to a profession known as Health Physicists and in this capacity had been responsible for the safety of observers at the British nuclear weapon tests in the early 1960s at Maralinga, South Australia. He told me about his time there: plutonium fragments scattered across the desert, Aboriginal families wandering through the test zones, and other hair-raising stories. He was also interested in para-normal events and would sometimes recount personal stories of "out-of-body experiences". At the time of my joining the section, his abiding passion was the mystery of UFOs and he pursued the investigation of sightings using JIO resources. Although Bob Mathams was not happy about this, he turned a blind eye on the assumption that he could not have stopped Harry anyway. The late 1970s was a peak time for unexplained UFO sightings, and Harry collected much of the reporting that came through RAAF Intelligence. On one occasion I remember him dashing off to examine crop circles and scorch marks in a paddock near Canberra.

On my first day in the section, Harry came to me and asked what kind of work I would like to do. At that time, I had only a basic understanding of nuclear technology and was seeking something not too technical. So I told him that I had been working on treaties, and that this interested me. Good, said Harry, and left me with that. In the five years I worked for him, that was the closest I came to receiving any instruction.

Harry's nuclear section comprised five or six scientists and engineers, most of whom were in their mid-fifties. Because of the difficulty of finding Australians who knew anything about nuclear weapons, JIO had recruited these workers from the UK. While none had actually designed or built a nuclear bomb, they had had experience on the edge of this technology and what they didn't know, they could collectively deduce.

Our primary task was to monitor nuclear proliferation worldwide. The Non-Proliferation Treaty (NPT) had come into effect in 1970, with Australia acceding to it in 1972. Non-nuclear weapon powers were prohibited by the treaty from developing nuclear weapons and they agreed to inspections of their civil nuclear industry or research facilities. The five nuclear powers – the US, USSR, UK, France and China – all of whom were members, agreed *to pursue in good faith* measures to stop the arms race and eventually to disarm. At JIO, however, our real concern was those countries with nuclear ambitions – including India, Pakistan, North Korea and South Africa – that had not signed the treaty. By the year 2000, it was feared, there would be twenty or more nuclear powers, with some of them possibly on our own doorstep.

Monitoring developments in countries distant from Australia was always a challenge and we could not have done this without intelligence-sharing arrangements with close allies. Australia had (and still has) a close intelligence relationship with the US, UK, Canada and New Zealand, and under a variety of agreements shared much of the intelligence collected by a variety of sources. This gave us access to data collected by our partners from satellites, from the intercept of communications and other electronic signals, and from ordinary spying. The analysts' job was to trawl this mass of information for clues. Needless to say, we never encountered anything so obvious as *We are designing a nuclear bomb and need the following items ...*; it was more along the lines of *Please give us a price for a rotary magnetic bearing.* This might (or might not!) be a clue that a country was interested in developing centrifuge enrichment of uranium for a nuclear weapon. Assessments of scientific and technical developments went wrong when clues were dismissed because of our Western arrogance, on the assumption that *No-one would do it that way!* This led to some spectacular intelligence failings years later concerning Iraq.

From my new nuclear family in JIO, I began slowly to learn the technology of nuclear weapons. This was helped by frequent trips to the Australia Atomic Energy Commission at Lucas Heights, south of Sydney. Before ratification of the NPT, Australia's approach to nuclear research had a dual purpose. The work would not only be applicable to the peaceful use of nuclear energy but would also enhance our under-standing of technologies useful in the development of weapons, although our work fell short of actual weapons research. It is unthink-able now that Australia would contemplate a nuclear weapons option, but in the 1950s and 1960s there were concerns over whether we could defend this country with so few people. The consequence was that at Lucas Heights, all parts of the nuclear fuel cycle were examined, including enrichment of uranium and re-processing of nuclear fuel – all, of course, at a research, not production, level.

In the late 1970s, Lucas Heights still had a pilot centrifuge-enrich-ment plant capable of producing small quantities of highly enriched uranium of bomb grade. The plant was in a separate and secure enclave and many at the centre would not have been aware of its existence. However, JIO nuclear analysts were regular visitors and found the plant highly valuable in understanding the technology of uranium enrichment: we judged that the challenges faced by the Australian engineering staff in developing the plant in the 1960 and '70s would be very similar to those faced in the countries of concern to us. My guess at the time was that the magnetic bearings on the centrifuges, or the materials used for the high-speed rotors, would be the greatest techno-logical barrier. But I recall one of the engineers showing me the kilo-metres of piping in the plant and telling me that getting the "plumbing" right was their greatest difficulty. I thought it strange that something so seemingly mundane would be a problem, but experience taught me later that this sort of problem was often the greatest headache faced by countries like Iraq.

In addition to looking at nuclear proliferators, the section also expended considerable resources examining Chinese nuclear developments. Was China building a new reprocessing plant that would separate weapons grade plutonium? What was it doing about enriching uranium? These were burning questions then because, in combination with other developments, China was becoming a major nuclear power. Studying China was also part of an informal intelligence-sharing arrangement with our partners: we would put our resources into monitoring this country and our partners would concentrate on other areas, particularly of course the USSR. When I joined JIO, about half of the organisation's effort was devoted to China. This was to decline gradually in coming years, following various reviews or changes in JIO leadership.

In addition to China we also examined the nuclear developments of France. Our real interest was the nuclear explosive testing at Mururoa and Fangatuafa atolls in the South Pacific. Atmospheric testing had ceased, but underground tests continued and the Australian government was fiercely opposed to them. We were required to advise on upcoming tests and assess their effect. I was marginally involved with this work and I like to think we got most of it pretty right. Our view that the tests produced little environmental contamination – based on the depth and geology of the tests – did not provide the political ammunition that the government wanted, but we did not change it for that. Fearless advice, if you like, which was respected as such.

*

In the mid-1970s, Australia began to seek new markets for its uranium. It became a requirement of government policy (I think at Prime Minister Gough Whitlam's initiative) that JIO examine the credentials of any country that might be interested in purchasing Australian yellow cake. Our job was to produce "Nuclear Proliferation Profiles" on countries that were potential purchasers. This started off as a fairly short list but before long expanded to about forty countries.

It had not really hit me, until we started on the profiles, how important it was to find the correct wording, and what power we had to influence policy makers. By changing the emphasis, suspicion could be cast on the motives of any country. So just for fun, I decided to draft a nuclear profile on the Holy See to look at the possibilities. I wrote something like:

> While we have no firm evidence, the possibility that a nuclear reactor may be operating under St Peter's Basilica, cannot be entirely discounted.

And:

> Reportedly, "holy water" is in wide use at the Vatican; we cannot dismiss the possibility that this is really a cover for heavy water.

Very childish perhaps, but it does illustrate that statements can be made that are true and, at the same time, entirely misleading. Intelligence analysts have a grave responsibility in drafting their assessments to ensure they are objective, free of bias and accurately reflect the available intelligence. Nations have gone to war on the spin put on words.

*

By the beginning of 1979, I had carved out my own piece of turf in Harry's nuclear section: the Middle East. At the time, there wasn't a great deal of Australian interest in this part of the world: it was too far from our shores. Other countries closer to home, particularly India, Pakistan and Indonesia, excited more attention. But we argued to JIO management that nuclear developments anywhere had the potential to affect Australian interests, especially if the Non-Proliferation Treaty was undermined, as the treaty was the cornerstone of Australia's export policy on yellow cake. As the junior analyst in the group I decided that the Middle East was a niche area of study that I could move into without any opposition from other members of my nuclear family. It was also very interesting. Israel was on one side, in our view with nuclear weapons; Iraq, Iran and Libya were on the other, all (then) with nuclear ambitions.

*

My nuclear studies on the Middle East were briefly interrupted in 1979 when, on my own initiative, I went to the Strategic and International Policy Division of Defence for nine months' work experience. The building was only a short distance from ours, but in outlook it could have been a million miles away. My impression of JIO up to this time, at least in the area where I worked, was of a cross between a gentleman's club and the post office. It had a relaxed atmosphere where, by and large, we decided the approach to our work and what issues we should pursue. There never seemed to be a sense of urgency, and we worked out who was going to do what (and when). The post-office part of JIO was shuffling large quantities of paper in and out of the building, and, of course, the inevitable bureaucratic processes to which all government departments were subject.

By contrast, work in the Strategic and International Policy Division was frenetic, and directions came apace. Sir Arthur Tange was the Secretary of Defence and he had a fearsome reputation: when he wanted something, he wanted it now. One of my early jobs was to prepare answers for Parliamentary Questions (PQs) and Possible Parliamentary Questions (PPQs), and Sir Arthur vetted all these. Everything was urgent, especially questions-without-notice. Curiously, and despite their name, we were usually advised what the question-without-notice would be on the day it was to be asked. This gave us a few hours to think up an answer. In my naivety, and my desire to prepare a comprehensive response, I would do considerable research and would even try to volunteer information that had not been requested but which I thought would be of interest to the Member of Parliament asking the question. My superiors soon knocked this out of me. So a question such as, "Is the Minister aware that last financial year the Defence Department spent $1 million on toilet paper?" might simply elicit the answer, "Yes."

On one occasion my boss dropped a fat file on my desk and asked me to prepare an answer for Parliament by the end of the day. No problem, I thought. An hour went by, he returned and, throwing a file at me, told me to put aside the first task for the new, more important one. It was going to be tight, but I thought I could manage. He returned just an hour later with a new file that had priority over everything else: Sir Arthur had to have a response by lunchtime. I managed by cutting the cloth to fit the width. I was to adopt this approach for the rest of my career. If I was asked to tell the history of the world in five minutes, I could do it. Of course, what I would provide in five minutes was less than I would in five hours, or five days …

*

After my secondment to the Strategic and International Policy Division finished I returned to JIO to resume my studies of Middle East nuclear developments. The subject was still a backwater but new interest was sparked in September 1980 when Iraqi troops crossed the Iranian border, starting what became a debilitating eight-year war. If timing and relevance were the key to good intelligence assessments, then I could see no better time than now to write a major report on Iraq's nuclear program. Iraq had ratified the Non-Proliferation Treaty and its nuclear research facilities were under safeguard inspection by the International Atomic Energy Agency (IAEA). But was it obeying the rules? Might it soon have nuclear weapons? There were certain aspects of its nuclear activities that raised concern, and the scale of its research projects seemed unusually large.

It took me some time to collect all the relevant information. In the early 1980s, Iraq was purchasing equipment and technology in large quantities from Italy and France in particular. By March–April 1981, I was putting the final touches on my report when the science analyst from a relatively new organisation, the Office of National Assessments (ONA), visited me: Dr Doug Kean.

I was impressed with Doug from the start. He was a nuclear scientist and had worked at the Dounray reactor in northern Scotland. He had a sharp analytical mind and chose his words carefully. However, in 1981 he was still inexperienced and so I listened with politeness and scepticism when he gave me his assessment. He argued that Israel might view Iraq's nuclear research facility as a centre for weapons development and might try to bomb it. This seemed to me like something out of a Le Carré novel rather than a considered assessment. I was now a nuclear analyst of four years' experience, and I rather patronisingly dismissed Doug's thesis.

My report went to the JIO publications section at the end of May 1981. On 8 June we got the news that Israel had bombed Iraq's research facility at Al Tuwaitha, all but destroying a French-supplied research reactor. By this time much of my report had already been printed and although its publication could be stopped, the best course seemed simply to add an addendum recording the recent event. We stated that in due course an assessment of the damage would be issued. It was not my finest hour. But I had learned another important lesson: always keep an open mind to new ideas, no matter how unlikely they may appear. Doug had been right, and he went on to become one of Australia's finest scientific and strategic analysts. Later he was appointed Deputy Director-General of ONA.

I greatly enjoyed my years as a nuclear analyst. Those I worked with were experts in their field, and in my view it was the golden era of Australian nuclear intelligence analysis. Unfortunately, when they retired or moved on in the mid-1980s, Australia lost this expertise and has struggled since then to recruit and retain skilled personnel in this area. It was a problem I found myself trying to redress a decade later.

Yellow Rain

IN 1980, THE JOINT INTELLIGENCE Organisation started to receive a trickle of reports concerning chemical warfare attacks in Laos. These were later referred to as Yellow Rain attacks because some accounts described aircraft spraying yellow chemicals that drifted down to earth like rain. As a microbiologist and biochemist, I was interested, and since at that time no Australian analyst was monitoring either biological (BW) or chemical warfare (CW), I decided to research the subject. My boss, Harry Turner, did not seem to mind.

In the mid-to-late 1970s, according to the reports, the Lao air force had sprayed a variety of chemical warfare agents on Hmong tribesmen in the southern mountains close to the Thai border. Similar reports were later received from Cambodia (or Kampuchea, as we had learned to call it then). In Cambodia the aggressors were said to be the Vietnamese who had occupied that country a few years earlier. What began as a trickle of reports had by the early 1980s become a small flood.

The problem for the analyst was that the descriptions of the chemical attacks were very diverse. It was hard to identify a typical attack. Various types of aircraft were described, and were said by the refugees to have sometimes sprayed chemicals, sometimes to have dropped bombs, but mostly to have fired rockets which then burst to disseminate materials of various colours, often yellow, red or green. The symptoms described covered everything from mild nausea to acute internal haemorrhage, diarrhoea and death.

I approached the problem by drawing up tables and matrices and trying to discern a pattern, but with little success. The colours of the "gas" described by the victims particularly puzzled me. These were not the colours of known chemical or biological agents, but I couldn't discount the possibility that they were actually marker dyes and not the colour of the toxic component. However, there seemed to be no correlation between colour and symptom, or, for that matter, between any other recorded event. Whatever was happening was more complex than first appeared.

More information was needed, particularly samples of the chemicals, but to collect it would require resources. Any expenditure of funds would require justification, and so I decided, as an awareness-raising exercise, to write a report summarising the information collected so far and suggesting some possible explanations. One was that the refugees may have been confusing events and what they had actually seen were simply marker flares, perhaps for bombers, that would then strike the target; their symptoms may have been due to shock from blast. Chemical attacks were also a possibility, but the information we had was insufficient to confirm that. Publication of my report was scheduled for mid-September 1981. But I was gazumped.

On 13 September 1981, Alexander Haig, US Secretary of State, announced at a press conference in Berlin that the Soviet Union had been supplying chemical agents to the Laotian and Vietnamese governments and that these chemicals had been used against resistance groups. He said samples had been collected and, after analysis, found to contain trichothecene mycotoxins.

One of my nuclear colleagues came to me with the news. Grinning from ear to ear he suggested that I had better start again. Even worse, although I was a microbiologist and biochemist, I had never heard of trichothecene mycotoxins. I knew that "myco" meant fungal, and a toxin was a naturally occurring toxic substance. If that was the case, then strictly speaking Secretary Haig was referring to a biological agent rather than a chemical one. But what was a trichothecene mycotoxin? That was the least of my worries. What about my report? Was it too late to stop publication?

Fortunately the report was stopped, even though printing had finished and copies were about to be distributed. Just three copies were saved, one for me and two for the archives. Coming after the fiasco of my assessment on Iraq's nuclear program, it had not been a good year for me. Timing, as ever, was critical in the intelligence world.

*

The first step in my investigation of the US claims was to head off to the CSIRO* laboratories at Black Mountain, near the heart of Canberra. They had an extensive library and, sure enough, the organisation had researched trichothecene mycotoxins. They were a group of toxins produced by a fungus of the genus *Fusaria*, and were of some concern because they occurred very occasionally on Australian crops, particularly on wheat or other grains. If ingested they could cause a variety of symptoms including vomiting, diarrhoea and, significantly, internal haemorrhaging. I headed back to JIO thinking that the Americans, the CIA in particular, had got it right. The symptoms matched, to a large degree, those that had been reported.

Many questions needed to be answered before I could write a new report. What was the evidence that the USSR had supplied such toxins, and why? We knew that the Soviets had researched a range of chemical and biological agents, including mycotoxins, but we were not aware that they had produced these specific toxins in large quantities. Also, although the Soviets were helping the Vietnamese in a general sense to prosecute their war in Cambodia, the supply of a new range of chemicals was a step up from this. So perhaps the Soviets themselves were using the chemicals. However, this did not explain the events in Laos.

And why the choice of trichothecene mycotoxins? Other chemicals and toxins would have been much more suitable. Perhaps this group of toxins was easy and cheap to produce. Perhaps this was the testing ground for a new range of BW agent. If Indochina *was* a testing ground, this might explain the range of weapons said to have been used, and the different colours might be some sort of indicator code used to identify each test. The problem with this theory was that follow-up

---

* The Commonwealth Scientific and Industrial Research Organisation, a government-funded body that researches matter of agricultural or economic significance to Australia.

after each test would be required in order to evaluate the effectiveness of the agents. There was no evidence of this.

I examined in greater detail the nature of the toxins, of which there four main compounds. Although they were chemically related, their effects were quite different. Compared to other toxins, they were not particularly deadly, although they were quite powerful in causing nausea and vomiting. The problem, however, was that to be effective they would have to be ingested or otherwise absorbed into the body. As they were solids, absorption would not be easy: simply inhaling some, or having it land on the skin, might have no effect. But one compound, known as T-2, was very potent in producing skin necrosis resulting in lesions, even in microscopic quantities. It was also very stable and therefore would be a suitable candidate for use in biological warfare.

I soon learned through our intelligence liaison office in Washington that T-2 was indeed one of the compounds that had been found in the samples. If T-2 had been disseminated in the attacks, I figured that tiny amounts could have drifted into victims' eyes and that this would be sufficient to cause lesions, excruciating pain and probably blindness. In fact, on reflection, I thought that these should certainly be the most widely reported symptoms. A re-examination of the symptomology, however, showed only minor eye complaints. Blindness was not reported at all.

Australia now had a conservative government headed by Malcolm Fraser, and our ties with the US had become closer. Now that Haig had spoken out, there was considerable interest in the US claims, and in whether we could lend support to these views. Therefore, just a few weeks after the Haig announcement I wrote a short assessment outlining my analysis of the still very limited evidence available to us. I concluded that although the evidence supported the US allegations to some extent, the inconsistencies suggested that they were not well founded. I advised caution in accepting the US conclusions without further investigation. I referred particularly to the lack of major injuries to the eyes of the victims.

The report was distributed only to a limited audience within the bureaucracy and government. It was accepted that we needed a larger collection effort, and it was agreed that I would lead the intelligence investigation. However, I was instructed by the Director of JIO to involve as many other experts as was practical: we must be sure of our findings if we were going to disagree with our American allies.

I was new to the business of chemical and biological warfare, and although I had an appropriate background I still had a lot to learn. There is no school for workers in this field, and the only technical experts Australia had at the time worked in the Materials Research Laboratories at Maribyrnong, a northern suburb of Melbourne. I arranged for a visit there.

*

MRL was part of the Defence Science and Technology Organisation (DSTO). The complex spans over 100 hectares along Cordite Avenue, which says a lot about its origins. Some of the buildings date back to World War I, and in spite of various attempts by the government over the years to modernise and soften the surroundings, they retain an austere appearance. The chemical laboratories were a relatively small part of the complex, comprising lines of double-storey buildings built in the 1930s or '40s. The head of the chemical division was then Dr Peter Dunn, but the person with whom I was to have most contact was a member of his staff, Dr Hugh Crone, a principal research scientist.

Hugh had a reputation for being rather cranky and difficult to get on with, and first impressions seemed to confirm this. He was tall and lean, with a slight hunch to his shoulders and sharp, serious features. I soon learned, however, his crankiness was simply an expression of his scientific desire to be precise. He was an expert in his field and used his words with care. He would not hesitate to correct anyone who did not speak with the same precision. I very quickly came to like the man and respect him for both his sharp analytical mind and common sense. This was someone with whom I could work.

Hugh explained to me the basics of the chemical and physical requirements for biological and chemical agents. For example, if the agents were solids, particle size needed to be considered. Too large and the particles would be filtered out by the hairs in the nostrils; too small and they would be breathed into the lungs and then out again, in much the same way as smoke particles are exhaled. Like something out of

"Goldilocks and the Three Bears", the particles had to be just right to be retained in the lungs where they would do their damage. I found the science of biological and chemical warfare fascinating, although if I had stopped to reflect, I would have realised how morally corrupt were the scientists who develop these weapons.

We discussed the US claims and worked out a way forward: Hugh would purchase some trichothecene mycotoxins and investigate their properties. But what we really needed were some samples of Yellow Rain to examine.

Back in Canberra I decided that I needed to task the Australian Secret Intelligence Service (ASIS). Although JIO collected data, it came from open (publicly available) sources or through our overseas liaison offices. ASIS, on the other hand, had agents posted overseas, including in South-East Asia, and was well equipped to locate someone who could obtain Yellow Rain samples.

I also needed to find direct eyewitnesses to the attacks. The problem with the reports, which came mainly via the US, was that they were incomplete; many important questions seemed not to have been asked. In fact, I was not sure what the original questions had been, since all I had were summary reports, presumably prepared after interviews with refugees.

Through the Department of Immigration, I contacted Hmong refugee communities in Sydney and Melbourne to establish whether any people there had experienced a Yellow Rain attack. Sure enough, there was a Hmong man in Cabramatta who had a story to tell and I immediately arranged a visit, taking with me, as an interpreter, an army officer who spoke both Laotian and Thai.

The part of Cabramatta in which the Hmong family lived was, I imagine, very reminiscent of Vientiane. Washing was strung between the houses, smells of spices wafted from kitchens, and plucked chickens hung upside-down by their legs.

The interview itself was not easy. The man I had come to interview, Veng Suthrathong, had been in Australia less than a year and did not speak English. The Hmong language is different from Lao, but his young daughter spoke Lao, as did my interpreter, so we had a sort of three-way exchange: English to Lao to Hmong and back again. Mr

Suthrathong told a remarkable story. He had been a resistance fighter since he was thirteen; a leader since then, in fact. He was only in his late twenties now. I asked him how he had become a leader at such an early age, and he explained that when his uncle, a captain in the resistance, had decided to go back to farming, he simply passed his gun to him, and along with it his rank.

He described how his village had been attacked with Yellow Rain. The planes had flown low over their village and within a week many had fallen ill. The entire population of the village had decided to leave and they spent many weeks walking, carrying their possessions, out of the mountains; always heading south, always dodging government troops. When they reached the Mekong River, the border between Laos and Thailand, they made rafts from bamboo. Being mountain people, none could swim, and rafts broke apart in the strong currents and some were drowned. On the Thai side they were arrested by the Thai border police, who stole their gold coins, which I discovered later was the currency they used for trade in the highlands and which had been minted a century before in China.

Suthrathong could give no details of the nature of Yellow Rain: its colour, whether it was delivered by a bomb or spray, or what it looked like on the ground. The villagers had suffered mainly from fever and diarrhoea, and I asked him how he could be sure that the Yellow Rain had caused this illness. He looked at me as if I were demented. Everyone knows that aircraft delivered Yellow Rain and Yellow Rain caused illness. His people had fallen ill and therefore …

It was a story that in, various forms, I was to hear time and time again. The people from the Hmong community that I interviewed in Melbourne gave similar accounts. Sometimes the interval between the sighting of the aircraft and the onset of illness could be months. Was Yellow Rain really so slow to have an effect? What was clear was that all in the community knew about Yellow Rain and feared it, even if they had no experience of it themselves.

I wondered just what the US officials had asked the Laotian and Cambodian refugees. I discovered that the first survey had been done by State Department officials who been provided with a set of questions by the CIA. A follow-up military team had also used a standard questionnaire. This simplified their task, but led the witnesses to provide certain types of response. If asked the colour of the chemical, there was a tendency for the refugee to provide an answer of some kind, whether the individual had noticed a colour or not. Similarly, questions about whether it caused vomiting or diarrhoea would prompt a positive answer. The problem was compounded by the fact that the refugees were often seeking a new life in another country and believed that by "co-operating", their chances would be enhanced.

The US investigation seemed premised on the belief that chemical warfare had taken place. This approach seemed to me to lack objectivity and I felt, at the very least, that the inquiry should start on the basis of an open mind. Information should also be cross-checked against that provided by others in the vicinity to see whether there was consistency, something that the Americans appeared not to have done. I therefore decided simply to ask refugees to tell me their stories without interruption. Only then would I ask detailed questions, to help fill out the account.

I made up a colour card by cutting out patches from a British Paints catalogue. I would not prompt them on the colour of the Yellow Rain, but if they did mention a colour I would show them the chart. This in itself provided some surprising results: "It was yellow, like that," a refugee told me, pointing to the green patch.

Although the refugees in Australia were a legitimate source of information, their experiences were usually a year or more remote from the events they recounted and the detail they provided was sometimes fuzzy. In mid-1982 I arranged for a trip to Thailand to tour the Lao border and speak to refugees with more recent knowledge. Unfortunately because of developments in JIO, my first trip to Thailand was to be a fleeting one.

By now I was working full time on Yellow Rain and no longer participating in the work of the Nuclear Section. I went to the section head, Harry Turner, suggesting that a new job be created for me, and strongly hinted that it should be at a more senior level than my present position. He was not sympathetic to the idea. I think he realised that if a new job were to be created, he would lose not only me from his section, but also the position; after all, chemical and biological warfare research does not fit comfortably in a nuclear section. I told him I would discuss the new position with the Director of JIO, Arthur McMichael, who, as it turned out, was enthusiastic. He told me to write up a job description and asked me what section it should be in. I told him Scientific Estimates, which then was a two-person section that studied SALT. In a sense it was like going home, except that now I would be my own boss.

I defined the job at one level above my present position, wrote the duty statement and briefed the Head of Scientific Estimates on what questions he should ask at the interview. I got the job. And so, shortly after my promotion, I found myself going to London for an intelligence exchange on chemical and biological warfare. My visit to Thailand was now to be a side-trip, and, because of time constraints, it had to be brief.

Through the Australian Defence Attaché in Bangkok I arranged a visit to Ban Vinai, a refugee camp in northern Thailand. Ban Vinai was of special interest because it was where many of the refugees with stories of Yellow Rain had been interviewed by the US. From Bangkok, we flew up to Udorn Thani and then met up with an Australian Embassy Land Rover to drive the 150 kilometres or so to the camp. It was much like a Lao village, except one populated by upwards of 30,000 people. There were shops, workshops and restaurants, and the country-side for several kilometres surrounding the camp had been stripped of vegetation to provide firewood or shelter. The camp itself seemed clean and well run. Although the Thai authorities were officially in charge, real authority rested with the Hmong military leader, and so he was my first port of call for permission to conduct my investigation.

In the end, I conducted only five or six interviews, but they contributed a great deal to my understanding. The refugees' stories were like those I had heard in Australia. In some cases it seemed to me that we were dealing more with belief than actual knowledge, and this reminded me very much of my first interview with Suthrathong. Talking to other refugees in the Embassy later that week, I began to understand how differences between the Hmong and Australian cultures might explain some of what I had heard.

The Hmong are animists who believe the world is permeated with spirits. Thus if they tripped on a tree root and cut their knee, there was a spiritual reason: perhaps they had not stopped earlier that day to pray at a family shrine and were now being punished for their transgression. If they fell ill, there must have been an omen pointing to this. An unusual event such as a plane swooping low over the village the previous month could be the cause. And of course, everyone knew about Yellow Rain.

I arrived in London the following week for the intelligence exchange, which was attended by the US, Canada, and of course our hosts, the UK. I was to give an update there on the Australian findings on Yellow Rain, using the latest information gained during my trip to Thailand.

I was young and enthusiastic, and this was my first quadripartite conference. I remember approaching the podium with a sort of academic zeal, believing that I would be listened to carefully, following which there would no doubt be an intellectual discussion of the nature of the evidence. Perhaps I might even sway a few from their position of certainty to one of caution.

I was only five minutes into my presentation when a senior CIA official shouted out, "How can there be doubts? How can you question the refugees who are the victims in this?" Of course there would be inconsistencies in the evidence, he added, but I should look at the overall picture, which he asserted was an unambiguous one. I was stunned and intimidated by the outburst. It was true that I had little experience in this field, but I had conducted my investigations thoroughly. All I was suggesting was that we should be objective in our work and examine carefully all the evidence, including that which was contrary to the conventional line. I continued, but was again attacked, and my presentation turned into a shambles as I tried to counter his arguments. Time ran out and I did not finish.

At the end of this first day our hosts, the UK Defence Intelligence Staff, held welcome drinks in the main building of the Ministry of Defence. This was my opportunity to talk socially with the CIA officer and question him about his interruption. However, he turned his back on me and would not even engage me in conversation. I realised then that these intelligence meetings were not simple exchanges of academic findings – there were high-level political issues at stake. Politics and intelligence can be a poisonous mixture, as I was to experience again many years later over Iraq's weapons of mass destruction.

The CIA intelligence problem with Yellow Rain stemmed from the fact that the US Secretary of State had spoken publicly about it. Alexander Haig had given his now-famous press conference on Yellow Rain the previous September, when he had first revealed the presence of mycotoxins in the samples. Then on 22 March 1982 he had presented a special report to Congress that updated the CIA's findings:[4]

> The US Government has concluded from all the evidence that selected Lao and Vietnamese forces, under direct Soviet supervision, have employed lethal trichothecene toxins and other combinations of chemical agents against Hmong resisting government control ... since at least 1976.

On the Soviet connection the report stated that:

> The conclusion is inescapable that the toxins and other chemical warfare agents were developed in the Soviet Union.

And that:

> There is no evidence to support any alternative explanation, such as the hypothesis that the Vietnamese produce and employ toxin weapons completely on their own.

The US position was unambiguous. In that sense, it was completely unlike any intelligence assessment that I had been involved in. In the world of intelligence, certainties were a rarity. Our assessments were usually couched in terms such as *Reports from usually reliable sources suggest that ...* or *Based on the available evidence, it is probable that ...* Years later, the world would again read assessments on chemical and biological warfare similar to those the CIA was writing now. Then they would relate to Iraq and we would go to war over them. Back in 1982, all of this was new to me and I was struggling to understand.

Central to the US position was its claim that the Soviet Union was responsible. The Cold War was still on and the stakes were high. Given this, I suppose it was inevitable that when an unknown Australian, who was new to the field, questioned the US Secretary of State, his views would be summarily dismissed. Shaken as I was, however, I was not daunted; of course the CIA, great as its reputation then was, could be wrong. In any case, I believed that it was not possible for Australia to endorse the US position yet. The anomalies needed to be explored, and we needed to understand why the US had reached its very certain conclusions. Even though we had close intelligence ties with the US, it had shared very little of the intelligence on Yellow Rain with Australia. This made our own collection effort that much more important.

As it turned out, the Australian effort was going reasonably well. We had received in Bangkok a rocket-propelled grenade from Cambodia. It was a shoulder-launched device which normally had an explosive warhead, the sort of weapon favoured by militants the world over and which was used in later years to shoot down a Black Hawk helicopter in Mogadishu and to kill many Americans soldiers driving Humvees along the highways of Iraq. This one, however, appeared to be different. The warhead contained a liquid. Could it be a chemical or biological agent, perhaps even containing trichothecene mycotoxin?

A shoulder-launched chemical weapon did not seem a very likely disseminator of Yellow Rain to me; the amount it could deliver would be quite limited and cover only a small area. Nevertheless it was worth investigating. We were also compelled to receive the prize. Through a complex series of connections, the Prime Minister, Malcolm Fraser, had become involved and had authorised the payment of $10,000 for it. The question now was how to examine it. It would be difficult to bring back to Australia if it really was a dangerous chemical weapon. So we sent an ordnance team and a specialist chemist to Bangkok. As it turned out, the ordnance was nothing out of the ordinary. The liquid in the warhead was water that had seeped in as the device marinated in a swamp somewhere in the jungles of Laos.

The rocket warhead was a disappointment, but we had more success in obtaining Yellow Rain samples. These looked to be the genuine article: several samples of leaves and pebbles dotted with small yellow powdery spots. Hmong officials had given them to ASIS intelligence officers in Thailand in March 1982. We were told that they were collected from the Phu Bia mountain area in Laos, close to where a Yellow Rain attack had been reported.

Even so, the provenance of the samples was not satisfactory. There was no chain of custody and we had only a vague idea of exactly when and where they had been collected. Were they all from the same site? Were they from the same attack? Did anyone witness the attack and what was the effect of it? These were worries, but there is a difference between legal evidence and intelligence evidence. In the intelligence world the samples would be accepted with the appropriate caveats and cautions.

The examination was to be conducted by Hugh Crone at Maribyrnong. To avoid the introduction of diseases into Australia, the packages were, in accordance with quarantine regulations, irradiated to kill any living matter. This only slightly reduced their value: if they had been living biological agents, such as pathogenic bacteria, we could still have identified the organism, albeit with more difficulty.

Hugh examined the samples with forensic care and diligence. One of the difficulties he faced was how to detect trace amounts of trichothecene mycotoxins: it was a specialist field, and at the time his laboratory had no equipment capable of doing this. Instead he tested the Yellow Rain samples on the skin of rats and compared the results with those produced by other mycotoxins he had purchased. While the latter caused a severe reaction, the Yellow Rain samples caused none. Other tests established that the samples had no toxicity. To say the least, this was strange in a chemical warfare sample. The toxins were stable, and if the samples had at one time contained these substances there should surely have been some reaction.

If the yellow spots were not toxic, what were they? Examination under a microscope revealed they were made up of pollen grains loosely held together with some sort of binder. Mould was also growing over the samples, including the type of mould that sometimes produced toxins.

What to conclude? Hugh wrote:[5]

Since the samples are obvious fakes, they convey no information at all to the veracity or otherwise of the reports of chemical attacks. The reason for their fabrication can only be guessed at; monetary gain, desire to ingratiate oneself with authority, or as a disinformation campaign.

This report was issued to a select few in the Australian intelligence community at the end of April 1982. We decided that as the samples appeared not to cast any light on the Yellow Rain attacks, we should not at this stage distribute the report more widely, and certainly not to the US.

We had apparently reached a dead end. The file was now becoming thick with alleged Yellow Rain attacks, particularly in Cambodia, where they were increasing. Throughout the rest of that year I sought more samples, spoke to other experts including mycotoxin experts at CSIRO and the University of Sydney, and continued to interview refugees. As the information base grew, I would issue interim reports, always highlighting the anomalies and advising caution against accepting the US claims.

In the meantime, the US issued a further report. George Shultz had replaced Alexander Haig as Secretary of State and at the end of 1982 presented a Special Report to Congress:

> Continued analysis of prior data and newly acquired information about Soviet mycotoxin development, chemical warfare training in Vietnam, the presence of Soviet chemical warfare advisers in Laos and Vietnam, and the presence of the same unusual trichothecene toxins in samples collected from all three countries reinforce our earlier conclusion about the complicity of the Soviet Union and about its extent.[6]

Apart from the contorted phrasing, what struck me were the recurring references to the Soviets. The mention of "newly acquired information about Soviet mycotoxin development" also seemed telling. What was this information? If correct, it bolstered the US case. The report "invited others to join us in examining the evidence and in confirming the truth". This was an invitation too good to pass up, and as we had not received much information from the US to date, we decided once again to ask for all available data.

Much of what they provided concerned the Soviets. We had convincing evidence that the Soviet Union had large and active programs in both chemical and biological warfare, including large production plants. We also knew that it had now begun to research the new science of genetic engineering with the objective of making designer viruses and bacteria for biological warfare purposes. I had some direct knowledge of this after debriefing a defector from Novosibirsk in central Russia, a scientist working at one of the research facilities. Now the US shared with us information on Soviet research into trichothecene mycotoxins. There was convincing evidence that such research had taken place, but then it seemed that it had also researched almost every naturally occurring toxic substance to assess its potential for use in biological warfare. The US had done something similar in the 1950s and 1960s.

What we really needed to know was the nature of the 100 or so samples of Yellow Rain that the US collected. The information provided indicated that they contained trichothecene mycotoxins at levels allegedly many times higher than natural. I questioned that. It was true that in the scientific literature, most naturally occurring mycotoxins occurred at levels of up to ten parts per million, or 0.001% of the sample. The Yellow Rain samples had levels ten times this: up to about 100 parts per million, or 0.01%. However, there were a few instances in the literature where natural levels approached this. Furthermore, the literature usually referred to grain crops in Canada, the US or Japan where there were commercial considerations. Not surprisingly, no scientific work had been done on the occurrence of trichothecene mycotoxins in Laos or Cambodia. What might the naturally occurring levels there be?

A question that the US had not answered, in spite of numerous requests, was this: if the Yellow Rain samples contained 0.01% toxin, what was the remaining 99.99%? Was it degraded toxin, filler compound or something else? As dangerous as these toxins were, at a level of 0.01% it seemed to me that they would not be an effective weapon. Certainly you would not want to eat food contaminated to this level, but spraying it over a population is a different matter. To test this, I asked the trials division of the Defence Department to model the effect of spraying trichothecene mycotoxins over a hypothetical village. The results showed that even at full strength there would be minimal effect. The amount that an individual would inhale would be insufficient to cause any major problems.

One piece of information that the US had shared with us was an autopsy that had been conducted on a victim from Cambodia. This individual, Chan Mann (always later referred to as the *unfortunate* Chan Mann), had been a Khmer Rouge fighter who had reportedly been caught in a Yellow Rain attack early in 1982 and died a few days later in hospital. His tissues had been sectioned and found to contain levels of trichothecene mycotoxins. The result seemed to lend support to the US case, although the origin of these toxins could not be confirmed and could even have come about through consumption of naturally contaminated food. He also had high levels of another fungal toxin, aflatoxin, a common food contaminant in that part of the world. And he was suffering from Blackwater Fever and malaria, either of which might have caused his death.

By early 1983 the US had over 100 specialists working on this subject, whereas Australia had just Hugh and me. What was obviously required was a trip to the US to visit the laboratories and speak directly to the experts at the CIA and elsewhere. Given the level of interest in the subject and the increasing evidence against the US case, it was decided that the delegation should also include my boss Dr Maurice Barton, who had replaced Bob Mathams on his retirement.

*

First, though, Barton, Barton and Crone (we recognised that we sounded like a team of lawyers) went to Ottawa in Canada to attend a round-table discussion of trichothecene experts. The scientist who had analysed most of the US samples, Dr Chester Mirocha from the University of Minnesota, was there, as were specialists from Canada and France. Hugh described our samples and pointed out that they were not genuine and merely contained pollen. The Canadians stated that their samples also contained pollen. The French representative then asked if anyone had samples that did *not* contain pollen. There was an awkward silence before it was revealed that all samples contained pollen, including those collected by the US.

This was stunning news. Little wonder that the US had not told us what made up 99.99% of their samples: it was pollen! Perhaps we had had Yellow Rain samples after all, but samples without any toxin in them. We asked the US representative to tell us how many of their Yellow Rain samples had toxin and how many not. We did not receive a straight answer, and our suspicions were immediately aroused that perhaps only a few of the US samples did. These suspicions were later confirmed.

The overwhelming question was now, what did it all mean? Surely the Soviet Union could not be making chemical weapons using pollen as a carrier for toxins. And even if it was, where would it obtain the tonnes of pollen it would need? The US case was largely based on the sample evidence, and if that fell apart, so did their entire case.

Our little team headed south to the US near Washington, where we met with scientists from the US Army Medical Research Institute of Infectious Diseases, better known – for obvious reasons – by its acronym, USAMRIID. Here we learned more about the toxic effects of trichothecene mycotoxins and how they could be used as chemical warfare agents: but the conclusion was they were not very suitable for that purpose. It was a useful and open scientific discussion until the arrival of Dr Sharon Watson. Her reputation preceded her: she was the originator of the theory that trichothecene mycotoxins were the causative agent in Yellow Rain. She would have no truck with counter-arguments. I recall her cutting off in mid-sentence a USAMRIID scientist who began to discuss the natural occurrence of these toxins in Indochina.

Sharon Watson also put the case that the pollen in the samples was a deliberate addition and was being used as a carrier for the toxin. She argued that pollen grains have just the right particle size to be inhaled and retained in the lungs, where they would do maximum damage. The reason for the use of pollen and not a synthetic carrier was so that the Yellow Rain would look like a natural occurrence and would be harder to detect. She concluded that the Soviets were being both clever and devious. This all seemed like nonsense to us.

The following day saw a brief trip to the Chemical Systems Laboratory (CSL) at the Aberdeen Chemical Proving Grounds. It was the central facility for handling all the samples that arrived from overseas. It seemed to me that the scientists here were sceptical of their government's case but reluctant to go against the party line. They told us that all the pollen in the samples was from species of trees found in South-East Asia. This clearly complicated Sharon Watson's hypothesis about the incorporation of pollen as a carrier. Not only would the Soviet Union have to collect tonnes of pollen, it would also have to collect it from South-East Asia, take it back to the USSR, add the toxin and then return the resulting mixture to Vietnam. Why had all this activity not been seen?

Although the scientists at CSL would not say what they really believed, one of them gave me a clue. I was shown a photograph of a Yellow Rain sample as it appears under a microscope. There, in the middle of the pollen grains, was something that looked like a small spear. What do you think that is, she asked. I did not know and said so, but I felt that if I could only find the answer, it might solve the riddle of the samples.

Our chief meeting was in Washington. The Australian Embassy here had advised us that for political reasons we should not tell the Americans that we had reservations, but rather just listen to their case and collect information for a later assessment in Canberra. We took this to heart and even when we arrived at our Washington hotel, we were careful not to say that we had a reservation, but simply a booking.

We arrived at the State Department headquarters with several officers from the Embassy, including the JIO liaison officer, reinforcing our little delegation. Mr Gary Crocker, a senior State Department official, headed the US side, which included DIA (Defense Intelligence Agency) officials I knew through my intelligence connections and CIA people. Crocker gave a very bland presentation that merely repeated the official line. He did say, however, that Yellow Rain attacks along the Thai border were still continuing. This seemed incredible to us given all the publicity and the ease with which evidence could be collected in the area.

We kept to our game plan through several more presentations, even though by this stage it had become increasingly difficult to listen to the general assertions, twisted logic and patently wrong information with which we were being bombarded. Maurice Barton politely thanked the US side and gave a brief non-committal presentation on what future work needed to be conducted.

As the meeting was coming to a close, the First Secretary of the Australian Embassy, Paul O'Sullivan (who was appointed Director General of ASIO in 2005), innocently raised the question of natural occurrence of mycotoxins in Laos and Cambodia. It was a subject we had been trying to avoid because we fundamentally differed with the official US position. In response, Crocker responded flatly that this was not a possible explanation.

It was more than Hugh could stand. He took off his jacket and rolled up his sleeves as if entering a bar-room brawl. And that is almost what happened. Hugh was already unpopular in US government circles. His report that the Yellow Rain samples we had analysed were "fakes" had been like a ticking time bomb, which exploded in the press just as we arrived in Washington. The headlines screamed "Yellow Rain a Fake". Hugh stood by his statement: something that purports to be something it isn't is a fake.

Another Embassy official, sensing the upcoming battle, grabbed Hugh's arm to stop him standing up, but he would have none of it. He rolled out our views: the samples we had analysed were covered in mould of the types that produced toxins; such toxins were naturally occurring in that environment; toxin studies were scarce in Laos … This burst of views and findings resulted in a rapid exchange of comments including an offer by the US side to share their samples with Australia. Hugh responded that we were not interested in them as they could not be authenticated. This did little to calm the mood, and eventually an Embassy official said quietly to Hugh, "That's enough," and persuaded him to sit down.

I admired Hugh for standing up and voicing our position. Diplomacy was one thing, but it was also important to let the US know what we thought. It was interesting, too, to see the US response. It was clear that the senior officials in the State Department had little or no grasp of the technical arguments, including the very real weaknesses in the US case. Yet the US government, in its condemnation of the Soviet Union and Vietnam, was still vigorously pushing these arguments.

Perhaps the outburst had some influence, too, when Maurice Barton and I visited CIA headquarters at Langley the following day. Hugh was not invited. There the principal CIA investigator, whom I will identify only as Chris, told us that there was some extremely sensitive information that we should not really be shown, but given the circumstances we would be given a peek at. This, we were told, would convince us that the Soviets really were behind these Yellow Rain attacks. As my hands carefully opened the cover of the file, I expected to see something as profound as the meaning of life. Instead I saw an item that could almost have been lifted straight from the report that had been presented publicly to Congress a few months earlier.

We returned to Australia musing on where the investigation should go from here. The samples still seemed the key to the mystery.

The answer emerged later in 1983. Mathew Meselson, a professor of natural sciences at Harvard University, had been adviser to the US government on biological and chemical warfare during the Nixon era. He too had puzzled over the nature of the Yellow Rain samples, and in a meeting with colleagues someone had pointed out to him that they looked very much like the droppings of bees. Meselson pursued this theme and discovered what all beekeepers know well: bees often defecate in swarms, and their faeces fall to the ground like sticky drops of rain. Because pollen is a food source for bees, their droppings are yellow. He presented his findings to the American Association for the Advancement of Science in May 1983.[7]

I soon found myself becoming an expert on bee-shit. I consulted beekeepers who told me that bees will not foul their own nest. Often in windy weather they will wait for a still day before leaving the nest in swarms to fly some distance before defecating *en masse*. In fact on the south coast of New South Wales, not far from Canberra, a common cause of complaint by residents is that their cars and houses are suddenly covered in yellow spots from bees kept in nearby hives.

Hugh re-examined our samples. Under the microscope, the pollen grains looked intact, but on closer examination the outer shell in some had collapsed and the grains were empty. Apparently, in the digestive tract of a bee the cellulose outer shell is not digested, but the contents, mainly proteins and carbohydrates, are. Hugh decided on a more definitive test. A by-product of protein metabolism by insects is uric acid (in mammals it is urea). This is excreted in insect faeces, and therefore if the Yellow Rain samples contained uric acid, it had almost certainly passed through the digestive track of an insect.

All our samples contained uric acid. In other words, they were bee-shit. Hugh devised a simple screening procedure so that the other researchers could similarly test their samples. Not surprisingly, the US was not interested.

The riddle of the samples had been solved. I now recalled the clue that had been given to me in the US. The tiny "spear" in one of the US samples was a bee hair. It was evidence that the US samples were the same as ours – bee-shit. The reason why some samples contained toxins was that the wet sticky pollen grains provided the ideal growth medium for fungi, which in some cases produced toxins.

One thing was still puzzling. Why did the Hmong associate a natural phenomenon, the mass defecation of bees, with a chemical attack? Professor Meselson helped resolve this riddle too. In a literature search he found that in 1976 villagers in the Chinese province of Jiangsu had reported yellow drops falling to the ground from the sky. They were mystified by the phenomenon, which they too described as "Yellow Rain". An investigation by a Chinese scientific team concluded that it was in fact caused by the mass defecation of bees.[8] The only difference between this and the events in Laos was that the Hmong, because of their animist beliefs, had associated illness with the event even when there was a time gap of weeks or even months between falling ill and the occurrence of the Yellow Rain.

What clinched it for me was the discovery by one of my staff of a long-buried and long-forgotten CIA report. In a report, "Yellow Powder Incidents in Cambodia", dating from the late 1960s, mysterious chemical attacks against Cambodian government forces were described. The chemicals left behind yellow powdery spots and were claimed to cause similar symptoms, such as vomiting and diarrhoea, to those described a decade or more later by the Hmong and Khmer Rouge soldiers. In a strange twist, the Cambodians identified the US as the perpetrators of the attacks. So it appeared that it was not the first time in that part of the world that this phenomenon had perplexed observers.

We now had most of the answers. There were, of course, as in all intelligence investigations, some uncertainties. It was clear that the samples containing pollen had no relation to chemical warfare. They probably had been collected in good faith: they were yellow and, in many people's minds, mysterious. The explanation did not, of course, automatically rule out other chemical attacks. On the other hand, given the intensive collection effort over several years, it might have been expected that something would have been found by now.

One of the samples collected from the jungles of Cambodia in late 1983 was analysed and found to be a riot control agent, CS. This agent is not highly toxic but causes intense irritation of the eyes and nose, and, in higher doses, vomiting. The US (and Australian) forces had used large quantities of it during the Vietnam War, sometimes dropping sacks of the material to saturate jungle trails and deny territory to the Viet Cong. The CS we found in Cambodia was almost certainly of US manufacture, possibly old stock that was being "recycled" by the Vietnamese. If this was the true origin of the "Yellow Rain" stories, it was hard to avoid the irony of the situation.

I believed that by now we had enough information to write a comprehensive assessment and authoritatively debunk the US claims. Clearly the Director-General of ONA, Michael Cook, thought the same. In mid-1984 he initiated a National Assessment, a report that consolidates and reconciles the views of the different intelligence agencies. A board chaired by the Director-General of ONA and comprising the heads of the agencies scrutinises and approves the final product. At that time, few National Assessments had been written, and I understand that they are still a rarity.

In June 1984, I paid a final visit to Thailand and to the refugee camps to see if there had been any developments that would influence our comprehensive assessment. This time I stopped in a border village where a Thai woman showed me a rash on her arm that she claimed was the result of Yellow Rain. While I was examining it, our car was surrounded by other villagers with a variety of sicknesses, all of which were attributed to Yellow Rain. In discussions later with a Bangkok-based American doctor, I discovered that this was a common occurrence: the US had taken a special interest in so-called Yellow Rain victims and was providing medical care for them. But, the doctor pointed out, typically the diagnosis was of something more mundane, such as scabies.

Since we were now committed to a National Assessment, there were to be several authors. I was to be the principal, but Dr Alan Brace from ONA, Dr John Gee from Foreign Affairs and Hugh from MRL all made contributions.

The Acting Director of JIO, Garry Marshall, thought it would also be a good idea to provide the US with an outline of our arguments before finalising the assessment. This was somewhat controversial. The US had already been leaning on Australian politicians in an effort to influence them on the issue. For example, I was told that the US ambassador had cornered Malcolm Fraser at a 1982 Christmas party to persuade him of their case. To his credit Fraser replied that he had faith in his intelligence analysts.

About a week before the National Assessments board was due to meet, Garry Marshall received a letter from the CIA senior principal investigator, Chris. Clearly he was not happy. The letter was as much an attack on me as it was a reply to the arguments in the draft National Assessment. It started off by describing me as "perverse and mischievous" and continued in that vein. Chris argued that although any one stream of argument could be overturned, the US case had to be regarded in its totality: the evidence they had formed a "mosaic" that showed a pattern of Soviet complicity in Yellow Rain attacks and the use of trichothecene mycotoxins.

We mused on the letter. Taken at face value, it argued that if we found evidence contrary to only parts of their case, then we should dismiss this evidence. In our view, however, the contradictory evidence completely undermined their case. For example, the lack of serious eye injuries destroyed the argument that the trichothecene mycotoxin T-2 had been used. This was not a minor inconsistency. It was akin to arguing in a murder case that the absence of the accused's fingerprints on the gun and the presence of someone else's is trivial, a mere technicality. In any case, it was not just one element of the CIA case that was faulty, it was most of it.

There was one thing I did agree on: their case was indeed a "mosaic". A mosaic is made up of little coloured tiles put together to form a pattern. Put them together in another way and a completely different pattern results. I just did not agree with the CIA pattern.

I had one final test to undergo. Michael Cook called Hugh and me into his office. Why, he asked, should I believe you and not the hundreds of US specialists reporting something different? It was a good question. Hugh spoke first and provided some of the technical arguments. I responded by repeating something I had heard on one of the intelligence exchanges that I had attended in the US.

When Alexander Haig made his speech on Yellow Rain in September 1981, the CIA had been shocked and dismayed. They had briefed Haig on the subject, but the report was not intended for public dissemination. At that stage their explanation of Yellow Rain was no more than a theory. However, Haig was receiving a cool reception from Germany on the US proposal to deploy cruise missiles on its soil. His argument that the Russians were deploying their short-range nuclear SS20 missiles throughout Eastern Europe did not change the German position. So, in order to show the evil intent of the Soviets, he regurgitated the CIA briefing he had been given earlier. His message was that the Soviets were not to be trusted. This set off a chain of events within the CIA, and the theory was thereby transmuted into "fact". From then on, the collection effort was all in one direction, while contrary information was simply dismissed or ignored.

The CIA letter from Chris did not influence the National Assessments board. I sat quietly at the meeting and listened to the debate. I did not have a speaking part and was only there in case a query about the evidence was raised. It wasn't, and the board approved our assessment with little discussion. I believe it was a triumph for the independence of Australian intelligence assessment. On a major issue we had not merely followed the US but had conducted our own investigation to arrive at independent conclusions.

One thing still disturbed me and that was the letter sent by Chris to Garry Marshall. Was I really "perverse and mischievous"? If not, a "counter" should be put on my file. Garry said to me, "Don't worry, we don't accept it and we all understand why the US wrote this." In spite of my insistence, no counter was written, and I suppose that Chris's comment remains there to this day, unexplained and unqualified. I sometimes wonder what some future archivist will make of it – and who was this Rod Barton, anyway?

Stoichiometry

IT WAS 1983, AND I WAS BECOMING an expert in chemical and biological warfare. During the Yellow Rain investigation I had received another promotion and was now the head of a new section, Scientific Resources, which looked after CBW and other odds and ends that the other technical sections did not follow. With a total of three staff we were tiny, but the subject matter we were dealing with generated a lot of interest.

Perhaps there were no chemical or biological weapons in Laos and Cambodia, but we were becoming aware that the rest of the world was not so quiet in this regard. It appeared that about a dozen countries had CBW programs or were contemplating them. Often one country was stimulated by the belief, or in some cases the actuality, that a rival was developing such weapons. The Middle East was the classic case. Most of Israel's opponents believed that Israel had CBW weapons and accordingly a number of them responded by trying to catch up. The situation was complicated by the widespread, and accurate, belief that Israel also had nuclear weapons. The development of such weapons for many of Israel's opponents would be too much of a technical challenge, but chemical weapons were an easy alternative. Hence they were sometimes referred to as "the poor man's nuclear bomb".

My interest was brought back to Iraq. In 1981 it had started a disastrous war against Iran, and within a year the conflict had bogged down in trench warfare not dissimilar to that seen in World War I. It had become a war of attrition in which the numbers were stacked against Iraq because of its smaller population.

By 1983, some developments caught our interest in the desert near the ancient city of Samarra, 100 kilometres north-west of Baghdad. A large facility was being built and rumours coming from foreign workers who had been there suggested that it might have something to do with chemicals. Could this be a chemical weapons plant or was it simply a soap factory?

Through our intelligence-sharing arrangements with the US and the UK we were able to monitor what Iraq was importing, and early in 1983 I noticed that an Iraqi authority, the State Establishment for Pesticide Production (SEPP), had placed large orders for two chemicals* with a Dutch company. Stoichiometry is the science of chemical reactions and the quantities of chemicals used and produced in them. My knowledge of this proved useful: I realised that these two chemicals, when reacted together, would produce in a one-step process dichlorodiethyl sulphide, commonly known as mustard gas. Significantly, the chemicals were being imported in the exact proportions required for this chemical warfare agent. The conclusion was inescapable: Iraq had started a chemical warfare program. On this occasion it had made little attempt to cover its tracks; in the years to come it would not be so clumsy.

I decided I should present my findings at JIO's next Monday intelligence briefing, in front of senior military officers and policy officials. My briefing summarised the evidence and went on to speculate about whether Iraq would use mustard gas in its war against Iran. At the end I asked for questions, but the audience maintained a sceptical silence. Eventually a general commented that mustard gas had not been used since World War I and asked in a disbelieving tone, "Why would Iraq go down that track now?" I explained that the Iran–Iraq war involved trench warfare, and that Iraq might see chemicals as a way to gain a strategic edge. In addition, mustard gas is a very effective chemical agent: it is stable, persistent and causes severe blistering on contact with skin, even in small amounts. Although it can be lethal, its effectiveness is measured more in its debilitating effects and the number of soldiers it removes from the battlefield.

---

*   For the chemically-minded, the chemicals were thiodiglycol and thionyl chloride.

That day I could not dispel the scepticism of my audience, but a few months later my diagnosis was unfortunately proved correct when Iran reported the use of chemical weapons against its forces in the southern border regions. More reports followed throughout 1983, and later in that year we obtained horrific photographs of Iranian victims with massive, yellowish, fluid-filled blisters hanging off their limbs and bodies. Other parts of their skin looked as if they had been burned: they were black as the result of necrosis. These were classic symptoms of contact with mustard gas. The pictures were too graphic for some of the JIO administrative staff and I volunteered to do the cataloguing of them myself.

The heat of the battlefield is far from the cool corridors of the UN building in New York. The Security Council works slowly on these matters, and although several resolutions were passed expressing concern about the Iranian allegations and calling on both parties to cease hostilities, nothing much was actually done. However, by late 1983 the UN Secretary-General decided that he would send his own team, the first of several, to investigate the allegations. Interestingly the teams were not sent as a result of a UN resolution but on the Secretary-General's own initiative. By this technique he could bypass the long debates and indecision of the Security Council.

On the first of these missions in March 1984, a colleague whom I had met during the Yellow Rain saga, Peter Dunn, head of the Maribyrnong Defence chemical laboratories, was asked to be a member of the Secretary-General's four-man team. I recall that the request from the UN came on a Thursday evening and the mission was to start early in the next week. Peter had little background on Iraq and knew little of its chemical warfare program, so I flew down to Melbourne on the weekend with a package of sensitive material to brief him in his home. I remember meeting him on the Saturday evening when he was busy trying to work out what he might need to take: he did not expect that the UN would be able to provide respirators – or any protective gear for that matter. He was proved right on that.

Peter's mission was successful. In a desert location, just on the Iranian side of the Iraqi border, were scattered some thirty or so chemical bombs with markings stencilled in yellow paint on their side:

"BR250WP". Curiously these bombs had not detonated, and were in remarkably good condition and still filled with chemicals. It was the sort of physical evidence the team had been looking for.

Unfortunately, no member of the team had brought sampling equipment, but the ever-resourceful Iranian soldiers came to the rescue. Armed with an empty Coke bottle and a funnel, they rolled a bomb over so that the chemical poured out from a port that had been opened, and filled the bottle. Their only protection was a pair of rubber kitchen gloves. While this was happening the UN team, wearing their respirators, stood upwind, at a discreet distance. The Iranians later paid for their bravado and suffered burns to their hands and arms: kitchen gloves are not the preferred means of protection when decanting chemical warfare materials.

Analysis of the chemical showed it to be mustard gas of high purity and made by a process consistent with the chemicals Iraq had been importing from the Netherlands in the previous year. Peter also visited an Iranian hospital where survivors of another chemical attack were recovering. This time, though, a different chemical had been used. There were no signs of blisters or burns on these victims; rather, they were suffering from disorientation and central nervous system disorders. And the pupils in their eyes had contracted to pinpoints. Some had died on the battlefield and others shortly afterwards. These were unambiguous indications of nerve-gas poisoning. It seemed that the Iraqis had graduated to chemicals more sophisticated and deadly than mustard gas.

The team's findings[9] presented to the Secretary-General concluded that Iran had been attacked with chemical warfare agents and that this had resulted in injury to, and death of, Iranian soldiers. The perpetrator was not identified in the report, but, quite reasonably, the assumption was that it was Iraq.

A couple of days after Peter returned, I received his report and copies of the photographs and laboratory reports. I was puzzled by the appearance of the bombs. The casings were a little over a metre long and were made of thin steel. Yet they only had a few dents and scratches on them. Some even appeared completely undamaged. Considering the hard and rocky terrain on which they had apparently landed, this seemed, to say the least, strange. Furthermore I could not identify in any of the pictures the tail sections of the bombs. Fixed to the casing by no more than a few screws, they would probably have broken off after the bomb hit the ground, and should have been visible somewhere in the background. But nothing. My conclusion was that the bombs had not been dropped in the desert, but had been placed carefully there for the UN team to find. There were no markings to tie the bombs to Iraq, so had all this been a crude Iranian attempt to implicate the Iraqis?

I also noticed, on closer scrutiny, that a few of the bombs were encrusted with dried mud. My theory was that the bombs were actually Iraqi but had been dropped by aircraft, not on the hard desert floor but in a swampy area. This explained the minimal damage and the caked mud. The Iranians had retrieved them, minus the tail sections, to show the UN team. But why had the Iranians not just taken the team to the swamp?

The answer to that was provided by an examination of the location of recent fighting. It was in Majnoon, an area in southern Iraq. It would have been politically difficult, as well as dangerous, for the UN team to cross the border, and hence the bombs were brought to the team. This, however, somewhat compromised the evidence. Furthermore the team's report was incorrect in one important respect. The bombs had been dropped in Iraq, not Iran. In international law this makes little difference: a 1925 Geneva Protocol bans the use of chemicals as weapons of war, wherever they are used. Politically, though, the use of chemicals on Iraq's own soil to defend its territory could be considered by some to be less of a crime. I was to hear this very argument, years later, from an Iraqi general.

The publication of the findings of the Secretary-General's teams did little to stop Iraq. The UN passed further declarations condemning chemical warfare in the conflict, but reports of the use of chemicals continued. Iranian victims were sent to European hospitals and the case against Iraq was damning. In a new, worrying development, Iraq now claimed Iran was using chemicals. Was this propaganda, or had Iran developed chemical weapons too?

It was decided within the Australian intelligence community that a major examination of the proliferation of chemical weapons should be conducted, with the emphasis on Iraq and Iran. This was to result in a National Assessment and I was to be the principal author, supported by Dr Alan Brace from the Office of National Assessments.

Alan was relatively new to the intelligence business, an unconventional person and an unusual recruit for ONA. He was in his early forties, a tall lean man with a shiny bald dome. He had a penchant for wearing black T-shirts to work and leather sandals that he had made himself. He told me that he had found Australian academic life boring and had therefore gone to Taiwan, where he learnt Mandarin and taught mathematics. He returned to Australia with a Chinese wife, built a mud-brick house in the bush near Canberra, and then joined ONA for something different.

Dr John Gee, our counterpart from the Disarmament Section in the Department of Foreign Affairs, came to assist with the final drafting. The assessment was not difficult to write: we had abundant information on the developments in Iraq and we were certain of our findings. The real difficulty was deciding what was to be done. National Assessments do not contain recommendations but they can canvass policy "options", and that is what we planned to do. It seemed to me that something should be done to stop Iraq from buying raw materials to use as precursors to chemical warfare agents. Although a few countries placed limitations on the chemicals they sold to Iraq, Saddam was circumventing these by going to other suppliers, or simply buying other chemicals and using different synthesis methods to make mustard gas or nerve agent. The three of us thought that the controls could be improved. We came up with a series of suggestions: the controls should cover a comprehensive range of precursors, all countries should adopt a standard set of controls to stop Iraq (and possibly Iran) from simply switching suppliers, and international efforts in this regard should be co-ordinated.

We finished the assessment late in mid-1984 and our "options" were considered by the National Assessments board and accepted. Foreign Affairs had primary responsibility for the policy aspects and it decided that as a first step bilateral discussions should be held with those European countries, principally the Netherlands and Germany, that had been supplying Iraq. These discussions were later expanded to include other suppliers and important allies including the US and the UK. The Minister for Foreign Affairs, Gareth Evans, endorsed the initiative, which led to a meeting in June 1985 of fifteen interested parties. This first meeting was hosted by Australia in Brussels.

The Brussels meeting was successful in the sense that all parties considered it worth proceeding, but it was not smooth sailing. There was mutual suspicion that any controls could be used to gain commercial advantage, for example, to block the sales of a rival company. Another meeting was scheduled for later that same year, but Foreign Affairs decided against Brussels as the location, as it was the home of NATO and also too "public". In Paris, Australia had a large, modern embassy, a legacy of the days when France was in favour before nuclear tests in the Pacific became an issue. Our changing relationship with France meant that the envisaged increase in staff had never eventuated, and as a consequence there was room to spare in the Australian Embassy. On these grounds, the embassy was chosen as a more suitable venue. Privately, though, a senior Foreign Affairs official told me that he had suggested it because he had gone to school in Paris and since then had felt a deep attachment to the city.

I did not attend the Brussels meeting because it was considered to be entirely concerned with policy, and I was, after all, "intelligence". In Paris, however, it was felt that an intelligence exchange should be held in conjunction with the main policy meeting. This, it was hoped, would convince some of the more reluctant participants that there was a real problem with chemical proliferation and that controls should apply not just to Iraq and Iran, but much more widely. John Gee would chair the intelligence exchange and I would be Australia's representative. Dr Bob Mathews from MRL would provide advice on the science of chemical agents.

The first meeting was held in September 1985. As we gathered, it struck me that there would not have been many occasions in the history of intelligence when officers from fifteen different countries sat around a table together. Understandably, the exchange got off to a nervous start. My instructions from JIO were to say nothing and listen to the others. As John Gee tried to steer the meeting forward, calling for comment on various issues, it seemed that everyone else had received identical instructions. I decided, therefore, to heck with it, and launched into a rundown of the comprehensive evidence we had on Iraq. Such recklessness clearly stunned many of the European partici-pants, but it did break the drought, even if some participants remained tentative.

The intelligence exchange proved useful and became a regular feature of the meetings. Once countries trusted that what they provided was safeguarded, they were willing to offer up intelligence findings. What proved especially useful was information on what chemicals were being sought and what had actually been provided, including quantities. This helped us to monitor what proliferators were up to, and what chemicals should be considered for control.

Further meetings in Paris followed and I found myself visiting this wonderful city twice a year. The meetings grew in size as more and more countries saw that non-participation might disadvantage them in trade because countries within the "club" were permitted to trade in chemicals freely, while exports to non-members required permits. Japan was one country that initially was a reluctant participant. The Japanese seemed to have little interest in restricting the sale of anything, although they were interested in what other countries might propose for control. Japan, however, was also a major supplier to Libya of equipment and materials – which, probably unknown to it, were being diverted into Libya's chemical weapons program. At the 1986 meeting I decided to ask Japan what it had sold to Libya. Initially any sales were denied, but after I described a little of what we knew, the Japanese delegates provided details. This was the start of a major turnaround, and eventually it was Japan that came up with a series of new proposals, including support for the control of items relating to biological, as well as chemical, warfare.

It was also in 1986 that a name for this new control group was first discussed. The US proposed that, in honour of Australia's initiative, it should be called "The Australia Group". This suggestion was unani-mously accepted despite a small degree of pique from the French who considered that since the meeting was held in their country it should be called "The Paris Group".

Over the years, the Australia Group has become one of the most effective control mechanisms over the proliferation of chemical and biological weapons. It works because it is voluntary and, in most senses, informal: there is no secretariat or treaty. As I was to discover later, the initiative came too late to stop Iraq, but it did cause that country significant problems. On Saddam's command, a high-level Iraqi committee was established to consider ways by which the new controls might be overcome.

Today the Group has thirty-eight members and it still meets in Paris – except for one occasion, on the twentieth anniversary in April 2005, when the meeting was held in Sydney in recognition of Australia's role. It is an example of the initiatives that can be taken if only there are people with vision, as there were in Foreign Affairs at that time. It also demonstrates the value of a knowledge of stoichiometry.

The Gulf War

IN LATE 1986 I WAS ASSIGNED TO London as a liaison officer to the JIO's UK counterpart, the Defence Intelligence Staff. It was a fascinating job and gave me an insight into how British intelligence worked that proved valuable much later in my career.

I returned to Australia in October 1989 to a new job and a new organisation. Under its first military head, Major General John Baker, the Joint Intelligence Organisation was to undergo a shake-up and a name change: in 1990 we became the Defence Intelligence Organisation (DIO).

My job was director of a new section to monitor overseas developments in science and technology, particularly in regard to the proliferation of WMD and missiles. I had a staff of about twenty-five analysts, both military and civilian, and our responsibilities covered worldwide developments, but with emphasis on the local region, Asia and the Pacific. It was not long before we faced our first challenge.

On 2 August 1990, Iraq invaded Kuwait. The invasion caught DIO off-guard. Although Iraq had in the previous months accused Kuwait of stealing its oil, and there had been a build-up of Iraqi forces in the south of the country, these signs were not closely monitored by DIO. The Middle East simply was not a priority for us at the time, and few resources had been devoted to its study. Things soon changed.

On the day of the invasion, the Security Council passed a resolution[10] demanding that "Iraq withdraw immediately and unconditionally". A series of developments followed rapidly. On 6 August, sanctions[11] were placed on Iraq; on 7 August, US troops moved into Saudi Arabia; and on 8 August, Saddam announced that Kuwait was now the nineteenth province of Iraq. There was no indication that Iraq was about to back down and as it began to consolidate its position in Kuwait, the US in turn slowly and steadily escalated its own forces in the Gulf region. The Australian Prime Minister, Bob Hawke, pledged military support and Australia, by despatching three naval vessels, became the first country to complement the US forces in the Gulf.

There was now a clear possibility that Australia would be involved in a war, and the military was desperate for intelligence. My group had fairly comprehensive databases on Iraq's chemical weapon and ballistic missile capabilities, and to some degree on its nuclear capabilities, because we had followed developments throughout the Iraq–Iran War. However, there was very little intelligence on any other topic. The small section in DIO that dealt with Iraq was also responsible for the Middle East, Africa and elsewhere. It could not answer with confidence questions about the capabilities of Iraq's armed forces, the number and type of aircraft it possessed, the types of sea mines it deployed, or what anti-ship missiles it had. Information of this kind was urgently sought from our US and UK counterparts.

Even my group was struggling with the questions being posed to us. It was one thing to collect and analyse information relating to the Iraq–Iran War, but entirely a different matter if we were going to be engaged in a war in which our forces could face chemical weapons. In the assessment of the Iraq–Iran conflict, there were no consequences for Australia if we did not know the precise range of chemical agents Iraq possessed. Now it was crucial to get it absolutely right.

If it was difficult to offer assessments on chemical warfare, it was many times more so when it came to biological warfare. We had almost no information on it, and to make matters worse the US knew little more than we did. We thought it possible that Iraq had some biological weapons, but this assessment was based more on probabilities than evidence. We argued that since Iraq had developed chemical weapons, it might also have gone down the biological route. There was also a facility in Iraq, near Salman Pak, twenty kilometres south of Baghdad, that informants suggested might be associated with biological warfare.

As to the types of agents involved, the best we could advise the Australian Defence Force was that the usual ones, such as anthrax, should be anticipated.

Having chemical or biological warfare agents was one thing; being able to weaponise these and hit a target, such as one of our ships in the Gulf, was another. We knew that Iraq had long-range missiles called Al Husseins, which were basically SCUDs with an extended strike capacity, but the technology required to create WMD warheads for these was not straightforward. After launch, these missiles went out of the atmosphere and on re-entry the warheads become glowingly hot. The heat could easily destroy chemicals or biological agents when they were disseminated from the warhead. Yet, although we had doubts that Iraq had solved these problems, we advised that it "would be prudent to assume" that Iraq possessed such warheads. All serving members of the ADF in the Gulf would be issued with respirators and given refresher courses on their use.

On nuclear weapons, the starting point was my ill-fated 1981 report, which had concluded that Iraq's research program had not advanced much beyond the elementary phase. No major Australian assessment had been made since then, even though much activity had occurred at Iraq's nuclear research facility at Al Tuwaitha. We did, however, feel reasonably confident about this. Like Australia, Iraq was a signatory to the Non-Proliferation Treaty and inspectors from the International Atomic Energy Agency visited the centre every six months. To make a nuclear bomb, Iraq would have to obtain about 4 kilograms of plutonium or about 25 kilograms of enriched uranium. Plutonium is made in a nuclear reactor and the IAEA inspectors had not detected any production in Iraq's reactors. Even in the interregnum between inspections, only insignificant amounts could have been made.

To enrich uranium, Iraq would have had to build a large plant and we felt reasonably certain that this work would have been detected. Our real concern was that Iraq could seize the uranium powering its French-supplied reactors and use it for a crude bomb. We judged, however, that it would probably be a fizzer because although the uranium was highly enriched, it was not quite at a grade where it could easily be used for a weapon.

Throughout August, September, October and into November, a further nine UN resolutions were adopted condemning Iraq's invasion and demanding compliance with Security Council resolutions. On 29 November, the Council decided to give Iraq an ultimatum: quit Kuwait by 15 January 1991. After that date it authorised member states to use "all necessary means" to enforce the resolution. In other words, war.

Within DIO we were somewhat divided as to what might happen next. The US had a force of half a million men on the Gulf region and overwhelming power in its carrier fleets, close to Iraq. Over thirty countries, including, significantly, a number of Arab states, had contributed to the military build-up. Surely Iraq would back down: anything else could result in its annihilation. Others argued, however, that Saddam had already shown a propensity to miscalculate and that he might believe the US was too morally weak to start a war. They also argued that if war did start, Iraq would try to drag in Israel, in the belief that other Arab nations would then join it to oppose the US. Finally, there was even a view that Iraq could initiate war at a time of its own choosing in an attempt to gain a strategic advantage.

After 29 November, DIO notched up its activity another gear by setting up a special watch room that, if war broke out, would monitor developments as they occurred. Operating around the clock, it linked in directly with the ADF operations room and had direct links to the Minister's office and other intelligence agencies both in Australia and overseas.

I was the acting head of the Intelligence Analysis Branch, with direct involvement in the running of the Watch Office. We realised that if Iraq started the war, it would probably do so by launching its modified SCUD missiles, the Al Husseins, against Coalition forces. Any such launch would produce a very strong heat signature that would be picked up by US satellites. Through our intelligence-sharing arrangements, we could directly monitor any launch through the US–Australian joint facility located at Nurrungar in South Australia. Not only could we detect the launch point, but we could also estimate the trajectory by tracking the initial burn before the motors cut off. Consequently the Watch Office was linked directly to Nurrungar, and the missiles specialists from my group were put on round-the-clock call-in shifts. If Iraq did start the war, Australia might be the first to pick this up.

I arranged to be contacted immediately if any missile launch was detected. I did not want a junior analyst ringing alarm bells without a review. Late on Christmas Eve, 1990, I visited the Watch Office to check in and wish staff a happy Christmas. Just as I was about to leave, an infrared signal over southern Iraq was picked up by a satellite and relayed to us via Nurrungar. Was this an Al Hussein/SCUD launch? The analysts pored over the signal. The brevity of it, its location and other characteristics seemed to argue against a missile. And there was only one. After consultation, I decided not to sound the alarm; we thought it could possibly be an unusual lightning strike. But I spent a restless night. On Christmas Day we learnt from the US that a meteorite had entered the atmosphere over southern Iraq and that this was the probable explanation. They too had had a few palpitations. For those more religiously inclined, a shooting star over the Middle East at that time may have been a sign of another kind entirely.

We continued in this state of tension and readiness over the New Year period; many of the usual end-of-year celebrations were cancelled or much subdued. The deadline, 15 January, for Iraq to withdraw its forces from Kuwait came and went, and so on 17 January 1991 the US, together with other members of the Coalition, exercised their authority to use "all necessary means" to evict Iraq. Operation Desert Storm began.

Our Watch Office now buzzed with activity around the clock. Early starts became the norm. Briefing sessions for the senior management of DIO began at 6.30 a.m., but analysts and their supervisors had to begin earlier so they could prepare. From the morning briefings, the more significant of the items were selected for written briefs for the Defence Minister, Prime Minister and others. They could read these as they ate their breakfast cereal.

By the start of Desert Storm, Australia had committed significant naval and air force assets, as well as other personnel including medical teams. DIO had assigned four of its imagery analysts to a forward US photographic reconnaissance centre in Saudi Arabia. These specialists were to be involved in Bomb Damage Assessment, analysing the damage to Iraqi infrastructure after every air raid and helping to make decisions about future attacks.

Although Australia had been one of the first countries to commit military assets, we had not agreed to join in the actual fighting. This irked the US, and they tried to involve us in the action – to no avail. Even a request for a couple of F-111 reconnaissance aircraft was rejected. This decision by the Hawke government has always puzzled me. It was true that if Australian lives were lost in the war, it could be politically damaging. On the other hand, there was strong Australian public support for military action, the justification for war was clear to most, and the Coalition was operating under an unambiguous UN mandate that had the full support of the Security Council. All of this, of course, was in contrast to the 2003 war.

Iraq's immediate response to Desert Storm was the launch of eight Al Hussein missiles against Israel. Our analysts had got this bit right. We were aware that the US was talking to senior Israeli leaders in order to convince them not to enter the war. Our concern was that if Iraq used chemical or biological warheads, would US advocacy prevail? We believed it unlikely that such warheads would be effective because, with the technology Iraq possessed, any chemical payload would simply be incinerated in the bottom of the crater made by the incoming rocket. But we also judged that this would make little difference to Israel, and if attacked with chemicals it was most likely that Israel would respond.

Whether Iraq might use its chemical weapons against Coalition forces was another matter of concern. President Bush had written to Saddam Hussein on 5 January to make the US position clear:

> The United States will not tolerate the use of chemical or biological weapons, support for any kind of terrorist action, or the destruction of Kuwait's oil fields and installations. The American people would demand the strongest possible response. You, the Ba'ath Party and your country will pay a terrible price if you order unconscionable actions of this sort.

The US Secretary of State, James Baker, had met with the Iraqi Foreign Minister, Tariq Aziz, in Geneva a few days later to reinforce this message. But now the war had started, we debated whether Iraq would heed the warning. After all, it had ignored other warnings and Saddam seemed reckless. We were also concerned at what the US response might be. Would it really use nuclear weapons, as it had appeared to imply?

One week after fighting had begun, we were advised that the Prime Minister would be visiting our Watch Office. General Baker decided that we would treat this as just another visit by a senior official and brief him according to our morning ritual. Bob Hawke arrived mid-morning, a little after the appointed time and in a state of agitation. He had just had a long discussion at our rival organisation, ONA, and clearly had not liked what he heard. We were not to know this, however.

General Baker started with a short tour of the Watch Office, introducing the various personnel and their roles. Next came the brief-of-the-day, delivered in a rather uncomfortable corner of the Office. I gave an update on Iraq's WMD capability, and others spoke of recent political manoeuvrings, until we reached the main subject, which was the latest military activity. An Air Force sergeant gave this briefing. As soon as the sergeant began, I felt sorry for him: I could see Hawke's agitation and sensed something was brewing. He was fidgeting and the longer the sergeant continued, the more intense this became.

Five minutes into his talk, the sergeant mentioned that two Iraqi MiG aircraft had somehow managed to enter the north part of the Gulf but had been shot down before they could travel much further. At this point, Hawke erupted: "What the hell are you saying! I have three ships in the Gulf, and now you're saying they are not safe from attack by Iraq?" The sergeant was taken aback. (I was taken aback for another reason: *his* ships?) Trying to regain his composure, the sergeant explained that the MiGs had been flying very low and that the US had shot one of them down as soon as it was detected at the top of the Gulf; neither MiG had come close to our ships. Hawke was not pacified. "I've just come from ONA," he said, "and they told me that my ships were under threat."

At this point General Baker intervened in his careful and measured way. He explained that the Australian ships had not been at risk. The

US had taken out the first Iraqi MiG at the top of the Gulf and the second one had travelled only a little further before it too was brought down. The US had allowed the Kuwaiti Air Force to take out this second MiG for reasons of Kuwaiti pride and morale. This MiG was at all times being monitored by the US and if there had been a danger to any member of the Coalition, the US would have destroyed it earlier. This seemed to mollify Hawke and the brief continued without further incident.

I've often pondered the Hawke outburst. The MiGs did not come within cooee of our ships, and it was doubtful that they were ever a target. In any case, the ships were part of a larger US fleet with formidable missile defences against hostile aircraft, especially ageing MiGs. Hawke would have understood all this, and so I could only assume the real root of his irritation was that the advice he had received from ONA had conflicted with that from DIO. Or perhaps he was just having a bad morning.

*

The Coalition's ground war started on 22 February, led by General Colin Powell. Iraq's first response was to set fire to more than a hundred oil wells in Kuwait, thereby producing clouds of thick black acrid smoke. This created a problem that taxed the best of our technical analysts: no-one had experience with smoke on this scale. What would be its effect on military systems such as laser-guided bombs, infra-red seekers on missiles, and night-vision equipment? However, these questions soon became irrelevant: the ground war lasted just a few days. Iraq withdrew from Kuwait on 26 February and accepted a cease-fire two days later.

The end of the war left us rather stunned. First, the resistance by the Iraqi forces had evaporated remarkably rapidly in the face of superior American technology and firepower. Secondly, the halt had been called with Coalition forces still in southern Iraq. In DIO we had debated whether the US might pursue the ground war all the way to Baghdad. I personally applauded the decision to end the Coalition advance, as it seemed entirely consistent with the UN Security Council Resolution 678 demanding Iraq quit Kuwait; any military action beyond this was not mandated. Furthermore, we had all seen the horrendous carnage along the "Highway of Death", the road used by Iraqi forces to evacuate Kuwait, and I feared that continued prosecution of the war would result in more scenes like this.

With the end of the war we conducted a series of wrap-up studies. My section helped to assess what was left of Iraq's WMD capabilities. Our conclusion was, not much. The Coalition bombing campaign seemed to have had been comprehensive. The nuclear reactors at Al Tuwaitha had been hit and destroyed, and our assessment was that any nuclear ambitions had been put back by at least ten years. Bomb Damage Assessment told us that Iraq's main chemical plant near Samarra had also been all but destroyed. Of course, there were uncertainties about what might remain and what Iraq might be able to salvage, but it seemed that any WMD threat was now distant. And so I thought my involvement with Iraq was at an end. I could not have been more wrong!

Over the next few weeks the UN worked on a draft cease-fire resolution.[12] A large part of the resolution concerned the subject of WMD. Iraq was required "to unconditionally accept the destruction, removal or rendering harmless, under international supervision" of these weapons, including any support or research facilities. The emphasis on WMD surprised me. Although we had been concerned in DIO that Iraq might use chemical weapons, it had not, and in the end this had been a side issue. However, I welcomed the UN initiative, because such weapons in the hands of Saddam would only add to regional instability. The US had been the architect of the WMD provision and at that time I assumed they shared my concerns. Only many years later did I wonder whether there were other motives. The setting up of a Special Commission to monitor the elimination of any remaining WMD in Iraq also intrigued me. Who would be recruited for this?

The Most Dangerous Place on Earth

THE UN SECURITY COUNCIL APPROVED cease-fire Resolution 687 on 3 April 1991. Iraq formally accepted it a week later, and the war was officially over. Soon afterwards the Australian Deputy Secretaries of the Departments of Defence and Foreign Affairs held discussions with their counterparts in Washington. The message they brought back was that while the US appreciated the speed with which the Australian government had lent its support after the invasion of Kuwait, it was "disappointed" that Australia had not become involved in the fighting. This was mulled over in the policy areas of both departments, and a response was eventually sent back to the US: Australia would provide whatever resources were required "to contribute to the peace". This would have direct consequences for me.

One thing Australia could do was help to monitor the destruction of Iraq's WMD. My colleague Dr John Gee, who had worked with me years earlier on the National Assessment on Yellow Rain, was selected to help set up the UN Special Commission prescribed by Resolution 687. He was a natural choice. A Rhodes Scholar, he had studied chemistry at Oxford University. On returning to Australia, he joined the diplomatic corps and served in Egypt, Russia and Thailand as a senior diplomat, and later became Foreign Affairs' Director for Arms Control and Disarmament. The unusual combination of science and diplomacy made him ideally qualified for the position.

John joined the Special Commission in late April 1991 as one of its founding members. At this time, the Commission had just a handful of staff, headed by a former Swedish diplomat, Rolf Ekeus. Strangely, the US did not participate in those early days, perhaps because of anxiety over sending its nationals into a country against which it had just waged war.

The immediate problem facing Rolf Ekeus and his staff in New York was how to go about the task at hand. There were no precedents. It was easy enough to come up with a theoretical plan of action, but who would actually carry out the work in Iraq? The Special Commission had no trained inspectors, no equipment and, worst of all, no money. Unusually, the Special Commission worked for the Security Council, not the General Assembly. It was therefore not part of the existing UN structure and no provision had been made for its funding, which was contributed on an ad hoc basis by member states, mainly the US.

Given time, many of the administrative problems could have been sorted out. For political reasons, however, time was something the Commission did not have. After the Gulf War, it was expected that the UN would be in Iraq immediately to carry out the requirements of the cease-fire resolution.

The presence of the International Atomic Energy Agency contributed to the urgency. The IAEA also had a mandate under Resolution 687: whereas the Special Commission was to disarm Iraq's chemical and biological weapons and ballistic missiles, the IAEA was responsible for the nuclear aspects. As part of its routine work, the IAEA trained inspectors who travelled worldwide from their base in Geneva to inspect nuclear facilities in those countries that had signed international nuclear safeguard agreements. Iraq was one such country, and prior to the war IAEA inspectors had made regular visits to the nuclear research centre at Al Tuwaitha. By early May 1991, it was ready to send a team back there.

The Special Commission recognised that it would be embarrassing if they too did not send a team soon. The issue was further complicated by the personal rivalry between Rolf Ekeus and his countryman Dr Hans Blix, who headed the IAEA. John Gee and four of his colleagues decided to grab the bull by the horns, and met in the UN canteen one morning in early May to plan the first inspection. Their first consideration was to find people who would make good inspectors. As they were from Australia, Canada, Sweden, Germany and the UK, they selected scientists from these countries. To head the mission, the obvious choice was Peter Dunn, head of the Maribyrnong chemical laboratories and a former member of the UN Secretary-General's special teams to Iran and Iraq in 1984. Ideally these scientists would have been brought to UN headquarters for training and briefings; instead they would be sent directly to Baghdad to start work.

The first I learned of the Special Commission was when the Department of Foreign Affairs called a meeting of interested parties in mid-May 1991. To our surprise, Peter Dunn and I were asked whether we would be willing to go to Iraq on the first chemical inspection. We both said yes. "By the way," the chair of the meeting then added, "you will be leaving next week."

It was a scramble to get ready. Neither of us had any real idea what we would be doing, or what equipment might be provided. Based on Peter's previous experience, attaining a degree of self-sufficiency seemed prudent. One of my first actions was to obtain a respirator and other protective equipment from Army stores in Canberra. Since I had had little training in the use of such equipment, I arranged for a quick update at the Army's training centre at Holsworthy, just south of Sydney.

I also familiarised myself with the details of the Al Muthanna chemical weapons plant, which I assumed would be the focus of the mission. It was a very large complex covering over twenty-five square kilometrès and comprising hundreds of buildings. From satellite imagery, I knew its layout very well: I was aware, for example, that from the main gate, it was a 2.25-kilometre drive to the turn-off to the main research laboratories and then another three-quarters of a kilometre to reach them. I practised getting a feel for these distances as I drove around Canberra. But although I knew the layout, I was much less certain about the function of each building and in some cases could only guess.

Although Peter was to lead this first inspection, he was no clearer than me on how to conduct the mission. He did, however, have a letter from Rolf Ekeus setting out its objectives. The team was to conduct an exploratory inspection of Al Muthanna. We had six days at the site.

We started to plan on the plane from Australia to Bahrain, which would be our base. We faced formidable problems. We had no idea how many inspectors would be on the team, who they were or what skills they would have. We did not know what to expect from the Iraqis, or what we could demand of them. We were aware there would be serious hazards at Al Muthanna: the site had been heavily bombed and in addition to unexploded munitions there would most likely be leaking chemicals and unsafe structures. We assumed that experts on these matters would be assigned to the team, but we did not know for sure. We hoped someone had remembered to bring a first-aid kit.

At least I had with me some site drawings. I had also studied the bomb damage to structures and discussed it at length with DIO's photographic interpreters. From this, a sort of plan emerged. We decided that the team should start in the least damaged areas at Al Muthanna, which appeared to be the warehouse area in the south-west corner of the complex. From there we would progress to the administration area, which had taken some direct hits but where there were unlikely to be dangerous chemicals. Finally, we would inspect the most dangerous parts: the production plants and the storage bunkers. By the time the teams reached these areas, they would have had some experience working together and would be better prepared to identify the hazards. The plan sounded quite convincing while sipping a good Australian shiraz in the business-class section of a Qantas jet, but we recognised that the reality on the ground might be very different.

On arrival in Bahrain, our first stop was a shwarma shop where we had our first taste of the local food – only to discover later that the lamb we ate was almost certainly Australian, sold by the Australian Meat and Livestock Board. Next we checked into the Holiday Inn. It was to become almost a second home, though I did not suspect this at the time.

Over the next two days, team members drifted in from different parts of the world. Most I did not know, but one familiar face – from my London days – was Hamish Killip. He had been an analyst in the DIS chemical warfare section, and before that a staff officer to the Director General of Porton Down, Britain's centre of research into biological and chemical warfare defence. A chemical engineer by profession, he had worked in his early career for a Zambian mining company before joining the British Army. His postings included Northern Ireland, where, to ensure his survival, he developed keen powers of observation. When patrolling the streets of Belfast, Hamish later told me, "noticing a window that is now ajar when ten minutes earlier it had been closed, could be the difference between life and death." Hamish's professional qualifications, practical experience and powers of observation equipped him for an inspector's life better than anyone else I knew.

When all the team arrived, we discovered that there were in all twenty-one specialists and five support staff, including two interpreters. The planning by John Gee and the New York staff had been good: they had recruited specialists in unexploded ordnance, building structure safety, chemical detection, chemical sampling and chemical decontamination. With one exception, all the specialists were from the five countries represented by the New York staff. The exception was the medical doctor who, surprisingly, was an Iranian. This created a problem: given the bitter war between Iraq and Iran, the presence of an Iranian doctor might be provocative. On this first mission, it was a complication we could ill afford and so an early decision was made to leave him behind, much to his disappointment.

We first gathered together as a team in the Holiday Inn ballroom on the evening of 3 June. A more incongruous location was hard to imagine. The question soon arose of our security in Iraq: should we take with us UN guards, a dozen of whom had been placed on standby? Peter Dunn thought that there would be little point. If Iraq meant us harm, then a few guards would make no difference. In any case, according to Resolution 687 Iraq was responsible for our personal security. So the guards were stood down. A more immediate problem was how to get to Baghdad. Few commercial airlines were willing to fly there, but negotiations were being conducted with a Romanian company, Tarom, from which we eventually chartered a flight.

Probably the most critical part of preparation was the simulated inspection of a bombed chemical lab. We conducted these mock inspections in some derelict buildings in a corner of a Bahraini military establishment. Who of our team to send in first? When we reached

Iraq, the buildings would probably be contaminated with chemicals, so perhaps it was logical to send in the chemical detection unit. But if there were also unexploded bombs, surely the explosives experts should be first? Then again, if the building were about to fall down, the structural engineer might be a better choice. We tried a number of combinations before the obvious hit us. The answer, of course, was to work as a team.

We also anticipated another potential killer: the heat. In full chemical protective suits, including gloves, boots and respirators, operations during the summer would have to be limited to about an hour for safety reasons. Training in this gear under the Bahraini sun helped us acclimatise to the conditions we might expect in Iraq.

Back in the ballroom, medical staff spoke of heat stress, possible diseases and the toxicology of chemical warfare agents. There were other briefs on chemical decontamination, working in damaged buildings and the use of chemical protective equipment. I gave a talk on Al Muthanna itself and how we might tackle the inspection by working our way from the safest part of the site to the most dangerous.

Listening at the back of the ballroom was a small silent group who introduced themselves as US Embassy officials. They said they were there to provide US government assistance if we required it. When it came to the brief on unexploded ordnance, Peter Dunn turned to them and asked what might we be up against: what was dropped on Al Muthanna? They said they would get back to us and the following day returned with a comprehensive list. Were there any anti-personnel mines, we asked? We were assured that the use of such weapons was against US policy, so at least that was something we would not have to worry about. This group of Americans I later got to know quite well; they were, as I suspected at the time, from the CIA.

On the evening before we would leave for Baghdad, we turned to the name of the Special Commission: was there a handy acronym? John Gee said that several had been thought of, and for various reasons rejected, including one that sounded like "UNI-SCUM". He said however, that recently they had settled on UNSCOM (United Nations Special Commission). Not elegant, perhaps, but a name that I would get to know very well over the coming years.

At 10 a.m. on 9 June we left for UNSCOM's first inspection in Iraq. (It received the mission code UNSCOM 2 because the IAEA had beaten us to the first inspection by a couple of weeks. Not to be left out, UNSCOM had hastily added two observers to the IAEA mission: that mission had carried the designation UNSCOM 1.) We had wanted to fly into Saddam International Airport just south of the capital, but Iraq would not permit this. It claimed that the "American aggressors" had bombed the airport, destroying the flight-control radar and rendering it unsafe to land. UNSCOM was never to use this airport. I suspect the real reason was political. Iraq was reminding the UN that the sanctions disrupted everyday life in Iraq: if they were lifted, then repairs to the radar would be made.

Once in Iraq, we were welcomed "as guests of the Iraqi people". Despite our concerns, it was clear that the welcome was genuine and that no harm was meant us.

Iraq was then a highly bureaucratic society. In spite of the importance and historical significance of the occasion, we were immediately required to fill out the quantities of paperwork the authorities required for entry into the country. I suspect that this was mainly so that the Iraqi intelligence services could monitor who we were and what nationalities we represented. Since we all travelled on national passports, this was easy work. Later, UNSCOM inspectors would travel on special UN travel documents that gave few details: one was described simply as a "UN expert" and no nationality, place of birth or personal details were listed, much to the annoyance of Iraqi officials who often tried to elicit such information. But these were issues for the future; on this first inspection we were not concerned.

As the Iraqi bus trundled along the dusty airport roads on our way to the Palestine Hotel in central Baghdad, we saw some of the effects of the war. Concrete hangars with a single hole in their roofs showed the blast and burn marks caused by exploding smart bombs, their heavy steel doors scattered as far as 100 metres away. Bits of Iraqi planes and twisted metal were scattered everywhere, and not far from the concrete administration building was an aircraft graveyard where we saw a tangled mass of fuselages, wings and engines.

An hour later, as we sped along a modern two-lane highway, we drove past sites that were, or were to become, well known for the wrong reasons. Near Abu Ghraib, an outer-western suburb of Baghdad, the US Air Force had targeted a baby milk factory in the mistaken belief that it was a biological weapons plant. The Iraqis had taken the press there during the Gulf War to show them the split and spoilt containers of milk formula; this had been quite a propaganda coup. Close to this factory was the other place that had a certain notoriety even then: the Abu Ghraib Prison. We sat in silence and stared as we drove past, imagining the horrors to be found inside its long, sombre walls.

Soon we reached Baghdad proper. At first glance it resembled any overcrowded modern city in the Middle East. Concrete-block apartment buildings with washing flapping from balconies. Little shops with garish neon signs and steel shutters. Congested traffic, smoking buses and trucks, and everyone sounding their horns impatiently. There seemed to be little war damage, although the occasional building such as the Ministry of Telecommunications office had been neatly reduced to a pile of rubble by a smart bomb or cruise missile. Crossing the Tigris River we noticed that a bridge had also been taken out, but that construction crews had already repaired one of its spans. In contrast to all the concrete and steel, the old part of town still had a certain decayed charm, with its colonnades, balconies and wooden shuttered windows, all sullied somewhat by peeling paint and the criss-cross of power lines.

The inspection of Al Muthanna would begin on the next day. Although it was only early June, temperatures were already reaching the high thirties and we realised that this would cause us serious problems if full protective chemical gear were needed. So we decided on a 5.30 a.m. start and to knock off by about lunchtime if temperatures became too high.

Driving through the main gate of Al Muthanna was an event I could never have envisaged. It was a facility I had been studying for almost ten years; through the use of satellite imagery I knew its buildings and the layout well. It all felt very familiar and at the same time, very strange. This was no theoretical academic exercise: in the cool air of the morning, I could smell the aroma of chemicals. The bomb damage at ground level was also more severe and stark than the impression I had obtained from the photographs taken from space.

We drove around the site to become familiarised. Our Iraqi driver told us we would go first to the laboratory area, and much to his surprise I could not resist telling him to turn left when we reached the intersection 2.25 kilometres into the site. Next to the laboratories was my first surprise. Here was a large animal house with pens at the rear. Although I knew the building, our photographic interpreters had described it as an administration block. How could we have missed this? Later we passed what was clearly a vehicle repair shop: we had felt certain, based on its exterior design, that it was a mustard-gas production plant. Another building, which based on overhead imagery we had judged to be largely undamaged, had a small hole in its side where a bomb had entered, destroying all the inside structure to leave just a shell.

Other surprises were more frightening. There were two unexploded 2000 lb bombs at the site, one on top of a bunker and another in front of one of the Sarin nerve-gas plants. The Iraqis were tampering with them in an attempt to learn their secrets and we feared at any moment the bombs might explode. If this was not bad enough, we were also to discover that anti-personnel bombs had indeed been dropped. These were known as "gator" mines, after the real-life alligator's propensity to tear off limbs. Small and hard to see in the rocky and dusty desert, they fired out fine wires to a length of ten metres, ready for unsuspecting people, including inspectors, to trip and detonate the mine. It may have been politic for the US to tell us in the Holiday Inn ballroom that it was not their policy to use such weapons, but that did not cut much ice now. We made an immediate rule that no inspector was to leave a hard surface, even to retrieve a hat that had been blown off in the gusting desert winds.

We started the inspection in the warehouse area, which we had thought would be a safe zone. However, we soon came across steel shipping containers filled with drums of chemicals. As the containers baked in the heat of the Iraqi sun, the chemicals had leaked out, creating a fuming, dangerous mess. It was sign of far worse things to come.

As we drove through the plant, specialist chemical teams constantly measured the air. On the northern boundary of the site, the alarms went off and we quickly retreated upwind: the sensors had detected dangerous levels of mustard gas. On the next day we cautiously returned to the area, equipped with a strategy. The Swedish decontamination experts set up a "clean/dirty" line. Hamish and I, wearing our respirators and carrying automatic chemical detectors and two-way radios, stepped across the line to explore whatever lay beyond.

After about twenty minutes of walking through what could only be described as a chemical-drum dump, we reached the northern fence line. By this time I was sweating profusely and my respirator was sloshing around unpleasantly with perspiration. There was also a strong smell of ammonia. I knew as a biochemist that this was nothing to be alarmed about. The enzymes in my skin were breaking down components in the sweat to create the ammonia, much as babies do when they suffer nappy rash. By this time our chemical detectors were recording low levels of mustard gas and nerve agent, so I resisted the temptation to ease the mask up to let the sweat drain away.

On the boundary a line of open pits stretched as far as the eye could see in both directions. And in the pits were a variety of large containers with Arabic and English markings: GB, GF and H. These are indicators of Sarin, Cyclosarin and mustard gas. The containers were also leaking and the gas levels around the pits were dangerously high. We did not hang around too long – just enough to take a few photographs and make some notes. We followed the line of pits for a couple of hundred metres and then looped back to the "clean/dirty" line. There the Swedish team washed us down, screened for residual contamination, and only then allowed us to cross the "clean" line. It was a relief to breathe fresh air again and take a long drink of water.

Soon after this, Hamish and I returned to our assembly point for the day's wrap-up meeting. Peter Dunn was about to address the team and moved to the centre of the group. To our astonishment, before he uttered a single word he collapsed, a victim of the Iraqi heat. Although he soon recovered, it was a lesson to us all. On future inspections it would not be uncommon for a third of the team to succumb to the heat at one time or another, especially when temperatures approached or exceeded 50° C. This always had to be factored into planning so that the team could still operate without the affected members.

As well as drums of leaking chemical warfare agents, Al Muthanna also contained stacks of thousands of rockets that were leaking the nerve gas Sarin. If inhaled, the gas causes paralysis of the nervous system causing death within minutes. We discovered that the design of these rockets had a major flaw. Inside the warhead were two specially designed plastic bottles to contain the Sarin, which is actually a volatile liquid. The problem was that the stoppers for the bottles were not designed to prevent leakage when the contents were under pressure. The pressure came from two sources: the bottles did not quite fit and therefore had been rammed inside the warhead, and the rockets had then been stored in the open in the full heat of the sun. As a consequence the Sarin bubbled out of the plug to contaminate the air for hundreds of metres downwind.

Our worst nightmares, though, were the storage bunkers, particularly those that had been hit in the bombing. These bunkers were awesome in their size and construction. They had been built by an East German company and were like something from the Third Reich. They were constructed of reinforced concrete about one metre thick. Covering this was a layer of two metres of earth, which was then covered with another layer of concrete. It was this construction that made them near-impenetrable: the American smart bombs would detonate on hitting the outer concrete and the earth layer would then distribute the blast. One bunker had sustained five direct hits with 2000lb laser guided bombs and was still intact. An analyst from the US Defense Intelligence Agency later told me that he was determined that at least one be destroyed and kept authorising further hits until it was. This bunker had gone up in a spectacular manner when it was finally breached, causing a plume of smoke to rise to 2000 metres. At ground level the size of the explosion was evident by the location of one of the twenty-tonne doors that had been thrown over a hundred metres from the bunker.

Three other bunkers had been breached to some degree. Inside each was a mass of twisted reinforcing steel and falling concrete and earth.

They had stored a variety of chemical weapons, explosives and detonators. Even though our Iraqi minders followed us everywhere, here was one place they would not enter. They were wise in this because our detectors were reading maximum on the gauge and even our more modern and effective protective clothing and respirators would not have been adequate in these conditions. The bunkers were a potential deathtrap. How to clean this up would be a major problem and one that I would face again, in a different context, thirteen years later.

*

The Iraqis appeared co-operative on that first inspection. They took Peter and me into the desert surrounding the plant to show us locations where they had buried tankers of mustard gas and other chemicals. They showed us the laboratories where they volunteered they had researched the chemistry of the deadliest of all nerve gases, VX (although the head chemist quickly added that they were unsuccessful in producing it). This is a heavy oily liquid which even in the heat of Iraq will not readily disperse. One tiny drop on the skin is enough to kill: it is the most poisonous of man-made substances. They showed us the gas chamber where experiments on animals with various chemicals had taken place. And yet for all of this, some things were not right.

Outside one of the underground laboratories were little piles of burnt paper. What was this, we asked? The answer came: "Ah, it is very dark in the laboratories because of power failures, and we lit some paper to find our way around." Later I came across a much larger pile of burnt documents outside an administration building. "Just personnel records," I was told, "of no interest to UNSCOM." Of course personnel records were of interest. And then I searched in the long grass close to the fire and found that these had not been personnel records: charred remains showed that they were specifications and operating instructions for chemical processing equipment. This was of great interest, as the papers may have provided clues to what Iraq had actually made – VX, for example.

We completed the inspection in the six days allocated to us, without injury. The Iraqis, I think, also judged the process to have gone off smoothly and thought that this inspection business would soon be over and the sanctions lifted. We knew, however, that much work remained; some members of the team thought that it would take several months to finalise. I could see the problem was larger than that and thought it more likely that a year would be required to finish our work. How wrong we all were!

This first visit to Al Muthanna was the most difficult and the most memorable inspection I was ever involved with. When we returned to Bahrain, the press reported that we had visited the most dangerous place on earth. Perhaps they were right.

Gateway to Baghdad

I HAD NOT BEEN LONG BACK IN Australia when General Baker called me into his office. He explained that the CIA had an operation in Bahrain called GATEWAY. Its primary function was to provide support for UN teams entering Iraq, but there was also a spin-off for the CIA and allied agencies: the collection of intelligence from inspectors returning from the field. Already a Brit had been attached to the unit and now they wanted an Australian to join it for a three-month assignment. "I really think you should go," said General Baker. I was happy to accept the appointment.

I realised now that the gentlemen from the US Embassy sitting at the back of the ballroom in the Bahrain Holiday Inn were the GATEWAY team. They seemed nice enough, although they hadn't seen fit to tell us about the gator mines. We had mentioned this oversight on our return to Bahrain, and their response had been that the mines self-deactivate after three months so there was not really a risk to us. Of course there was the odd malfunction, but that was to be expected – presumably only the odd inspector would have been blown up.

I discovered that the Brit on GATEWAY was my colleague Hamish Killip. Strictly speaking, he wasn't a Brit at all; he was from the Isle of Man and travelled on a Manx passport. But he seemed very English to me and he shared my cynicism about international politics. I looked forward to my posting.

But there was a problem before I took it up. What would be my official status in Bahrain? Unlike the US and the UK, Australia did not have an embassy there, so I could not simply be a "first secretary". In discussions with Foreign Affairs it was decided that for my protection I should travel on a diplomatic passport and have a letter from the Secretary of that department to indicate that I was travelling on official government business. I thought that this would create difficulty, and so it did.

I arrived in Manama, the capital of Bahrain, in late August 1991. It occurred to me that if the tables were turned and a Bahraini with a diplomatic passport turned up at Sydney airport and wanted to stay for some ill-defined purpose (actually to work for a foreign intelligence agency) for three months, he would not have got far. However, the Bahraini authorities were more understanding and issued me with a three-day visa.

My first official business was at the Royal Australian Navy Liaison Office, located in a mansion complete with swimming pool and tennis court, in an outer suburb of Manama. Its role was to arrange support for the RAN ships that were still patrolling Gulf waters, but now I was seeking their assistance and local knowledge to obtain a visa of more than three days' duration. They arranged a meeting with one of their political contacts; in Bahrain, that usually meant one of the members of the royal family – in fact, a prince.

The young sheikh, resplendent in a white robe and red headscarf, met me the next day. "What is the purpose of your visit?" he asked in impeccable English. I replied that I was here to support the UN. "No problem" he said, "you are a UN official." Well, no, I said; I felt I could not tell him I was to work with the CIA. The sheikh spoke about the Australian presence in Bahrain, the trade between the two countries (Australia was then the fourth-largest trading partner with Bahrain), and how he would very much like to see an Australian embassy here one day. "So, is Australia to open an embassy here?" Well, no, I said. Eventually I decided to explain that I would be working with the Americans. Suddenly a light went on, and he said, "My dear friend, why did you not say so in the first place?" He granted me an indefinite visa.

GATEWAY headquarters was located in what was referred to as the Embassy annex, actually a rambling and ramshackle American Embassy-owned building located in a less fashionable part of town. It had its own security detachment of Marine guards, but the only occupants at present were the dozen GATEWAY staff.

After brief introductions I was shown my "office": a former conference room economically furnished with a single wooden desk and chair; there were no windows, which only added to its stark appearance. Most significantly for me, it was located outside the special "secure area" where all the CIA staff were housed. The secure area had been installed with special equipment to allow top-secret communications with CIA headquarters at Langley. Under US security rules, "aliens", Hamish and me included, were not allowed access to this area and therefore I was to be isolated in the outer room. Hamish solved the problem by simply not working there; he had got himself an office in the British Embassy. I did not have this option, but I partly solved the problem by using the RANLO office for "Australian Eyes Only" (AUSTEO) communications back to Canberra. But for access to daily intelligence reports on Iraq, I too used the British Embassy, their staff being kind enough to let me work in their secure area.

I soon settled into the new job. Hamish and I met the new inspectors as they shuffled into the Holiday Inn, tired from their journey and bewildered by Bahrain's unfamiliar sights and smells. Our CIA colleagues usually kept their distance, but neither Hamish nor I looked as though we had anything to do with intelligence and we usually got on well with the inspectors whether they were from Moscow or Manila. Over the following days we briefed the team members on Iraq and what to expect.

When there was no team in town, there was little work to do and so we explored the island. Our Friday activity was to spend the afternoon at Sheikh's Beach, complete with sand imported from Australia. This beach was actually closed to the general public, as it formed part of the grounds of one of the Emir's palaces, but the Emir was happy for us to use it one day a week. Occasionally the Emir would stop by to chat and we would have rather odd, one-sided conversations about the people he had met and the places he had been. I remember him once telling me of his meeting with the Queen (of England) and the jokes he told her. He also told me how offended he was when he came once to Sydney and Australian quarantine officials sprayed his plane.

Mainly, though, the GATEWAY work in Bahrain dominated our lives; if several teams arrived at the same time, we would work odd hours to fit in with the movement of inspectors. An important part of our work was to debrief the inspectors after they returned from Iraq. We explained to the Chief Inspector of each team that the debriefing was important because it made us better prepared to brief the next team. This argument was a bit thin, and some teams, particularly those headed by Russians or Eastern Europeans, saw through it and wanted little to do with us.

In fact, a number of inspectors from Russia, and other countries for that matter, were also in the intelligence business. We often knew through our sources who was from the First Directorate of the KGB (and after November 1991, its successor organisation, the FSB), and we assumed that in turn they knew whom we represented. None of this was directly acknowledged; rather, we danced around the subject. On this occasion we were not rivals; we were here for the same reason: the collection of intelligence on Iraq. But there was more at stake than that country's disarmament. Russia's main interest was to recover the $9 billion owed it for the military hardware, mainly MiG aircraft, that Iraq had purchased. For that to occur, Russia required the sanctions to be lifted. And there were other financial considerations: post-sanctions trade with Iraq and access to oil. For a politically changing Russia, there were also more rarefied, but no less important, matters: political influence in the Middle East and countering US policy in the Security Council. To facilitate this, Russia needed to know what was going on in Iraq.

The inspection process attracted weapons experts, scientists, engineers, intelligence officers and sometimes eccentrics from around the world. Perhaps you needed to be a little strange to want to leave your comfortable job in Germany or wherever and go to Iraq, with all its hardships, to search for hidden weapons. Almost all of the inspectors at some time came through – that is, were briefed and debriefed by – GATEWAY. Many of them I was to get to know well in subsequent years. Scott Ritter was one.

Another was David Kelly. I first met David in Chicken 69, a Chinese restaurant in the old part of Manama, on his return from leading a weapons inspection in August 1991. I liked him immediately. He seemed to me to be the quintessential Englishman, although he was actually Welsh in origin. In the heat of Bahrain he was neatly dressed in "sensible" clothes: no jeans and T-shirt for him. By profession a microbiologist, he had been a lecturer at Oxford University and then a senior scientist at Britain's biological defence research centre at Porton Down. Earlier that year he had led the British team that inspected Russia's biological warfare facilities and because of this had been chosen by UNSCOM to head the first biological team into Iraq.

David told me about the inspection, speaking softly and seriously but on occasion with a bone-dry sarcasm. The team had inspected five sites, including a key complex at Salman Pak, and had interviewed a number of senior Iraqi officials, including a female scientist, Dr Rihab Taha al Azawi, and her boss, Dr Ahmed Murthada, who was now the Minister of Transport and Telecommunications. David was convinced from what he had seen and heard that Iraq was covering up a biological weapons program. I listened carefully and with respect to his views, but realised that at present these were suspicions rather than hard evidence. In years to come, David would become a close colleague, and he and I would become part of a four-person team that would investigate these suspicions.

Even though not all of the weapons inspectors would co-operate, the GATEWAY team usually got what it was after. The US, UK and Australian members would be sidelined and grilled separately. Or we would obtain copies of photographs or documents that inspectors had collected during their visits – sometimes with their co-operation or sometimes by simply "helping" with the printing of negatives. This would often net us massive amounts of information. By far our biggest coup, however, was due to one man, Dr David Kay, who would have a significant influence on my life again more than a decade later.

On 24 September 1991, based on a tip-off, an IAEA team visited the headquarters of the Iraqi Petrochemical Company, a building known as PC-3, in downtown Baghdad. The mercurial Kay, an aggressive and determined inspector of many years' experience with the IAEA, was the head of the team. According to his source, PC-3 was a cover for a nuclear weapons program, and sure enough, in the basement the team found four trunks of nuclear documents. In a well-publicised stand-off, the team was held up in the PC-3 car park for the following four days, the Iraqi minders not allowing them to leave with the documents. In the end, over Kay's protests, a compromise was negotiated with Dr Jaffar Dhia Jaffar, the head of PC-3, who took the documents to inventory them. Kay believed that not all the documents were returned to him after this.

What Iraq was not aware of was that some of the documents were smuggled out. Team members were allowed to use toilet facilities at the building, and there they removed a few documents at a time by smuggling them in the front of their trousers. The documents were then transferred to the team's ambulance, which eventually delivered them to a waiting UNSCOM plane at Habbiniyah. The pilot later told me that Iraqi ground staff had tried to stop the take-off by driving a fuel truck in front of the plane, but he had managed to steer around it. Shortly afterwards the documents were delivered to GATEWAY at the Embassy annex – straight, in fact, to my very spacious office, followed very shortly by the trunks of nuclear information.

The documents gave us a golden opportunity to look into the Iraq's hitherto unknown and undeclared nuclear weapons program. Our fear, though, was that we would only be allowed to hold this vast collection for a brief period before being required to forward it to IAEA headquarters in Vienna. We immediately bought four photocopiers, so that we would have our own record. We also arranged for four specialist translators to be flown in from the US to supplement our translator on loan from the American Embassy. While awaiting their arrival, we pondered where best to start: translating the whole haul might take months, and at best we had days, we estimated. We could not copy everything in that time.

Although most of the documents were in Arabic, I could read numerals in that language and soon noticed that each document had a catalogue number. We organised them into piles on that basis. Then, among the mass of papers, we found a single page that I regarded to be the equivalent of the Rosetta stone: the code to the catalogue. Now we knew which documents were key and which referred to mundane administrative matters. We prioritised documents for translation and soon found reports that left us reeling.

Prior to the Gulf War, under Non-Proliferation Treaty rules, the IAEA could only inspect facilities that Iraq had declared as nuclear-related, except in exceptional circumstances. Iraq had only declared Al Tuwaitha, and the IAEA had considered there were no exceptional circumstances to visit any other facility in the country. But it was now apparent that Iraq had not been playing by the rules, and the PC-3 papers documented several facilities where weapons-related developments were being conducted. David Kay inspected some of these places in July 1991, followed shortly afterwards by another IAEA team headed by veteran inspector Demetri Perricos. Until we received the Kay documents, the real purpose of these sites had only been suspected, but now here was the proof. Uranium had been mined at Al Qaim in the north of the country, had been processed into a gaseous form at Al Jazira, and was to be enriched at two places: Ash Sharqat, and Tarmiya near Tikrit. The method Iraq used for enrichment was gaseous diffusion in calutrons, a process that had not been seen since the early days of the US nuclear program in the 1940s.

The document that really shook us, however, was a top-secret progress report from an establishment called Al Atheer. This report, which covered the period up to 30 May 1990 – seven months before the commencement of the Gulf War – described work that had been done on designing a nuclear weapon. Iraqi scientists had solved a number of problems, such as nuclear initiators, and for others they optimistically reported that a solution was near. Based on all these documents, my view was that at the start of the Gulf War, Iraq might have been only a year away from a bomb, possibly even less.

I could not help but think of the meeting I had with Prime Minister Hawke early that year, and how wrong our advice had been on Iraq's nuclear weapons program. Then we had advised him that Iraq was at least a decade away from having nuclear weapons. Now I realised that it had been on the brink. In fact, given the uncertainty in any assessment of this kind, I wondered whether the Coalition would have risked war if we had this information in January 1991.

*

GATEWAY continued throughout the entire period of UNSCOM inspections in Iraq, providing valuable assistance to inspectors but also collecting intelligence from them. It was a successful operation, but sometimes I had my doubts about its legitimacy. Certainly the UN view would have been that it was not legitimate: facilitating the collection of intelligence against one member state for the benefit of another was clearly against UN principles. Yet not only did Rolf Ekeus co-operate with GATEWAY, so too did his successor, Richard Butler. Iraq often accused UNSCOM inspectors of being spies for the US, and I suppose that this was in some cases true. On the other hand, most of the information that was gathered helped the US and others, including Australia, to assess Iraq's weapons programs. Combined with other intelligence, it was useful in suggesting to UNSCOM which targets to inspect, and which were a waste of time.

Some small amount of information gleaned from the inspectors might have been used by the US for other purposes, but I doubt whether it played any significant role given other US collection capabilities. So was GATEWAY legitimate? Probably, yes.

*

My posting to GATEWAY finished at the end of 1991, but not before another trip to Iraq. UNSCOM had put together a special team to exploit some intelligence that had been provided via US channels, with Karen Jansen, a US Army major from UNSCOM headquarters staff, as the head of the team. This created a small problem. Karen was quite junior and had not headed a team before: she would clearly require assistance. Since that first inspection to Al Muthanna, Iraq's approach to inspections had toughened up. Disruptive tricks had replaced co-operation: phone calls in the middle of the night, public demonstrations outside the inspectors' hotels, bottles thrown from windows, and even physical attacks on inspectors by "outraged citizens". On one mission Iraqi guards even fired shots over the heads of inspectors. The Iraqi intelligence services also bugged our hotel rooms and rifled through our suitcases when we were out. This new team needed experience, and Hamish and I were to provide it. We were to help plan and run the mission, with Hamish doubling as the operations officer and me as the report co-ordinator.

The GATEWAY CIA staff knew about our involvement almost before we did. The head of GATEWAY invited Hamish and me in for "discussions". What he really wanted to do was to demonstrate a new device known as a "digital camera". The senior technical officer showed us this rather bulky camera and then a small suitcase of electronics by which we could transmit the information down a phone line back to GATEWAY. To illustrate his point, he took a photo of us, plugging the camera into the suitcase, which in turn he plugged into the phone line. Lo and behold, five minutes later a picture was printed out on a fax machine. In 1991, this seemed almost magical. We were asked to take the gear into Iraq and transmit pictures back so that they could analyse them and provide us with near real-time feedback. The technician told us that they had thought of everything, including the type of electrical plugs and voltage used in Iraq, so that we could readily fire up the suitcase of electronics.

In reply, I said: "I have just one question. With the sanctions, there are no phone lines from Baghdad to the outside world. How do I dial up Bahrain?" Incredibly, he had not thought of this! My opinion of the CIA dropped a notch. In any event I had no intention of lugging the suitcase around Iraq and so this wonderful technology remained in Bahrain.

The inspection was to be conducted over three weeks, during which we would visit twenty sites, mostly airfields at which air-conditioned bunkers were located. Some of these were suspected to have stored chemical weapons during the Gulf War. One of our objectives was to determine whether they were still there. Much of the work would be routine, but we also had two very sensitive bits of intelligence. The first related to an airfield, known simply as Airfield 37, just off the road to Jordan about eighty kilometres west of Baghdad. The intelligence community knew this airfield as Muhammadi. Here, according to our information, pits had been dug to bury "biological bombs". Iraq had categorically denied ever having had a biological weapons program, so it would be a coup for UNSCOM if we could find even one weapon, as this would reveal the existence of an entirely secret program. To help find these bombs we had asked the German members of the team to bring special metal detectors that could penetrate metres of earth. To preserve the secrecy of our intelligence, however, the Germans had not been told what purpose this equipment was to be used for.

The second piece of intelligence concerned something hidden at a sugar factory in Mosul. We would leave this inspection until close to the end. And to make the mission appear routine, we decided to tuck the inspection of Airfield 37 into the middle of the trip.

We were concerned that our plans and suspicions might somehow be leaked to Iraq. This had happened on other missions: Iraq had blocked teams from entering sites or had removed incriminating evidence before the inspection. We therefore decided that only Karen, Hamish and I would share the intelligence. This caused some problems when we came to brief the team: its members needed to know where they were going and be familiar with the layout of the sites, but this was exactly the information that would tip off the Iraqis. So we provided only general descriptions and decided to hand out site diagrams when we actually reached the locations.

In late November 1991, the eighteen-person team set out. For this mission, we would use a helicopter for the first time. Our first meeting in Baghdad was with its German crew. We assumed the office in the Baghdad Sheraton had been bugged by Iraqi intelligence, and this made the briefing difficult. Sensitive discussions would usually be held in the gardens of the hotel or somewhere in the open, and even then we would be cryptic in our comments, but for this briefing we needed maps and a private space. To preserve secrecy, we intended to point to where we were going, which was all over the country including Mosul and Kirkuk. "Ah, Kirkuk!" exclaimed the navigator loudly, giving away at least one destination to any Iraqi who might have been listening. Quickly we held a finger to our lips. "Ah, don't mention Kirkuk," whispered the navigator solemnly. It felt as though we were in a sitcom.

Both Mosul and Kirkuk are north of the thirty-sixth parallel, which marked the start of the no-fly zone for Iraqi aircraft. If the Iraqi minders followed us into this zone in their helicopters, they risked being shot down. The Germans would need to liaise with the US to ensure this was not also our fate.

We were up at dawn on our first day of the inspection. There may only have been eighteen of us – including medical staff, translator, communicator, and photographer – but we were from eleven different countries. This cultural mix sometimes had amusing consequences. As we were waiting for the minibus outside the hotel in the gloom of dawn, Karen made a comment about how cold it was. Hamish said he could loan her a pullover. She did not understand the expression until Hamish explained it was something you pulled over your head, and was probably better known as a sweater to her. "No, it's my legs that are cold", she complained. "What I really need is a leg-over." Those of English background suppressed any response, and those of other nationalities continued to stare out of the window at the cold dawn.

The target on that first day was the complex of buildings at Salman Pak, about twenty-five kilometres south of Baghdad. Intelligence reports had linked it with chemical and possibly biological research. It was located in a loop of the Tigris River and as we drove into the site we could see the rows of barbed wire and chain-link fences. Many of the buildings had been badly damaged in the bombing and had an odd lean to them. One building of particular interest had, suspiciously, been completely bulldozed by Iraqi authorities and the foundations covered with earth.

We had with us a superbly qualified structural engineer from Australia, Squadron Leader Owen Hammond. He specialised in the assessment of buildings that had been damaged by fire or bombs. Earlier he had told us, among many other things, that concrete weakened by heat is recognisable by a slight pink tinge. He had been to Salman Pak before and told us how he had argued with the Chief Inspector that a bomb-damaged building there was not safe to enter. The Chief Inspector of the team would have none of it and said he was going in anyway. As they argued, their attention was caught by a low rumbling noise followed by a loud crash: the entire front of the building had just collapsed. The team made no attempt to enter what was left.

We stopped in the centre of the site and were immediately surrounded by our minders. Among this group I noticed a diminutive woman who looked a little out of place in her conservative frock and cardigan – as though she might be on a shopping trip, rather than

minding a group of international inspectors at a secret military establishment. She was introduced to us as Dr Rihab Taha. I recalled David
Kelly telling me that he had interviewed this woman on his first inspection in August. She had introduced herself as the chief scientist
involved in research into biological agents – purely for defensive
purposes, of course. Dr Taha was to accompany us for the rest of our
mission, although she largely kept to herself.

We broke up into small teams and my little group headed off to
examine a building surrounded by two rows of barbed wire and a high
concrete wall. I carefully checked to ensure there was no pink concrete.
As we entered through the outer gate that had conveniently been left
open, the reason for the high security soon became apparent: it was a
prison! Our Iraqi minders explained that it was of no interest to
UNSCOM, being only a small prison for miscreant soldiers, and now
abandoned. I thought it would be a good idea to take a look anyway.
There were only five cells; the first two were open and empty, the
remainder locked. I peered through the slit window in the door and
noticed a steel filing cabinet located in the centre of the cell. I asked the
minders to open the door. "We cannot find the key, we think it might
have been lost," came the reply, an excuse we would hear a thousand
times over the years.

Anticipating this, we had brought our own "universal key": the
largest pair of bolt-cutters a person could lift. Unfortunately they were
not much good in this case, as there was nothing to cut. Even the hinges
were recessed into the concrete. But I had to get in, and so I instructed
the minders to knock in the door with the sledgehammers we had also
brought along. Twenty minutes later I was inside the cell and eagerly
opening the filing cabinet. Perhaps here would be the smoking gun. But
no, it was empty and no-one could, or would, explain what it was doing
in there. As we wandered off to the next target, I thought how unusual
an episode this had been. Some people may boast they have broken out
of prison, but not many people can say they have broken in.

The Salman Pak complex was extensive, and our photographer
Henry Ardvisson and I conducted an aerial survey. At the rear of the
helicopter was a ramp that could be lowered to allow a vehicle to be
loaded inside, but for the reconnaissance we would half-lower it and

Henry would be strapped in to sit on the end of the ramp as the rear observer. My job was less hair-raising: I would sit between the pilots and direct where we were to fly. We circled the site a couple of times, flying low over what appeared to be a special forces camp complete with an obstacle course and an aircraft fuselage for training exercises. This camp would become of particular interest to us some years later, but on this occasion we merely took photographs.

The Salman Pak inspection set the pattern for the following days. Things would appear to be of interest, but on closer examination nothing would be found. Of course, we did not always expect to find hidden weapons, but we did hope to find clues to their existence. The real skill of the inspector is to find something that is out of place, something that doesn't quite fit. For the less-experienced inspectors this was not always easy. I remember asking a sub-team-leader who had just inspected a small concrete building, what he had seen. "Nothing," he said. "The building was empty." But what had been in the building, I asked, how long had it been empty, and what could it have been equipped for? I sent him and his team back for another look. There were always clues: the amount of dust, the type of electrical fittings, the plumbing, the size of the entrance doors, overhead gantry cranes … One technique that we developed to a high degree involved the study of bird droppings. Pigeons somehow seemed to get into many buildings and their droppings would be all over the floor. If equipment had recently been moved, then the pattern of the droppings would produce a reasonably accurate outline of that equipment.

It was observations like this that provided us with a clue at Karbala ammunition storage depot, seventy kilometres south-east of Baghdad. For a change, I had taken up Henry Ardvisson's seat on the ramp at the back, and this time Hamish was accompanying me. As we flew over a bunker surrounded by an earth barrier, I noticed that the earth next to the entry doors had been moved. We surmised that this had been done to allow large vehicles to reverse into the bunker. What could they have been carrying? Hamish, with his keen eyesight, also spotted a metal frame close to the bunker. All this required closer examination.

On the ground we discovered the bunker was empty, but tyre marks indicated that at least one large vehicle had been inside. The metal frame, which had been dumped in the scrub a short distance away, was the giveaway. About ten metres long, it had a series of semi-circular cradles along its length. We measured the curvature of a cradle and concluded that, with a diameter of just under a metre, the device had been used for transporting SCUD missiles. This was confirmed by Russian markings we found stamped into the metal. The question was, where were the SCUDs now? The Iraqis disavowed any knowledge of this but conceded that the bunker had indeed stored SCUDs at one time. Another dead-end.

At a couple of sites, there were heart-stopping moments for me. The first was at a bunker at Mansuriyah close to the Iranian border. This bunker had sustained a direct hit and now looked like a volcano: steep sides of debris with a crater at the top. Because of the danger, only the explosives expert, Master Sergeant Klaus Kessler, and I would inspect such sites. As we climbed the side of the volcano, Klaus told me in his heavily accented English, "Mr Barton, this is very, very dangerous. There are live explosives here and they have been 'cooking' in the sun. Please tread exactly where I do." So I trod carefully in the master's footsteps. When we reached the top of the volcano, we stared down into the crater below. The sides were like a fruitcake, but instead of raisins and sultanas, rocket warheads and assorted detonators were sticking out through lumps of concrete and earth. And like cake, it was very crumbly: slowly, and still upright, I found myself sliding into the pit below. Klaus grabbed my arm and stopped me before I had gathered too much momentum.

Even if I had not detonated anything on the way down, I could not imagine how I would ever have climbed out. To this day I have night-mares about the place.

On another occasion we entered a bunker that had not been bombed. We knew immediately that something was wrong when our Iraqi minders did not follow us inside. Again, only Klaus and I entered, and we soon saw the problem. Just inside the first set of doors, before entering the bunker proper, our torches shone on stacks of mines piled almost as high as the ceiling. We could see mud sticking to these mines and Klaus told me that he thought they had been recovered from the field and were still armed. "Just don't touch them," he said "and we will be safe." But as he squeezed past the first column, his backpack caught. As if in slow motion the column tipped over and Klaus and I looked at each other believing this would be the last human we would ever see. Not a pleasant sight. When nothing happened, I thought that at least I would not have to squeeze past that column of mines!

Other kinds of tensions were created by the Iraqis. At 7 a.m. one morning, as we assembled in the foyer of the Palestine Hotel ready for the day's inspection, we heard shouting outside. It was a demonstration against the UN and the US. "Down, down, Bush" and "UN equals US" were the cries, which were repeated on the banners. We politely asked the minders if they minded moving the demonstrators. "What can we do?" they replied. "This is a spontaneous demonstration of the Iraqi people." In Saddam's Iraq there were no "spontaneous" demonstrations and we had no choice but to walk the gauntlet. We could see as we walked through the chanting mass that it was largely a good-humoured rent-a-crowd; most had smiles on their faces as their organisers urged them on. Nevertheless we remained anxious that one or more individuals would take the issue more seriously and strike out at us.

Later that day I had an experience of just this. While searching yet another empty bunker, I noticed near the entrance a small chart listing the weapons that presumably it had once contained. The rest of the team filed out, but I thought it worth recording the list. We knew that Iraq's chemical bombs had certain designators: were those designators, or variants of them, on the list? Had chemical bombs once been in this bunker? Almost immediately I was surrounded by several Iraqi minders who started to jostle and push me. I protested to no avail. Fortunately, at that moment our interpreter, Samih Abou Faress, returned. Samih, a tall, distinguished Palestinian, had once been a university professor until politics overtook him. He had a certain gravitas and I noticed that the Iraqis accorded him a grudging respect. He spoke calmly but forcefully, and the minders responded as if scolded schoolboys. I resumed recording the data.

Eventually the day came for our visit to Airfield 37. But for one crater, this site had not been bombed. Most desert airfields are bleak places, but this seemed exceptionally so. Its drab appearance was compounded by the fact that it was now early winter and that morning there had been a dust storm followed by a mist settling over the desert.

We could not fly the helicopters because of poor visibility, so the entire inspection had to be done from the ground. The problem was that, although we believed our intelligence to be good, we did not know where to search. On a site covering several square kilometres, it would take weeks or even months for our little team to search every corner. And we had just one day. We therefore selected areas that seemed to show potential – for example, where relatively new concrete had been poured – but our metal detectors turned up nothing. At some pits in the ground, the earth appeared to have been disturbed recently, but our Iraqi companions claimed to know nothing about this, or what the pits had been dug for. Reluctantly we came to the conclusion that we were not going to find anything at this site either. Our hopes were now pinned on the final inspection of the sugar factory at Mosul.

Mosul is in the far north of Iraq, about 350 kilometres from Baghdad. The site in question was a sprawling complex that stretched about two kilometres along a railway line, and we decided that the search would start at the northern end and gradually work southwards.

Early on the afternoon of the first day, we struck gold. Building 73, as it was designated on our site diagram, was a large warehouse in the centre of the sugar plant complex. It had two large steel doors locked with a sturdy padlock, for which, of course, the key had been lost/stolen/could not be found. It was, however, no match for our universal key, and as we swung the doors open we saw that the warehouse was full of machinery. This corresponded exactly with our information. We asked what this equipment was. "Oh, it is just general-purpose machinery for use in the sugar factory," came the answer. We could see that lathes, presses and welders might fit that description, but there were also specially designed jigs. This machinery was for manufacturing something very specific, and we knew what that was: chemical bomb casings. On the side of many of the machines were stencil numbers that looked familiar. From our very first inspection to Al Muthanna, Hamish and I recognised the numbers as part of the same series as the equipment there. The machinery at the sugar plant had been moved from the chemical weapons factory and stored in Mosul for safekeeping during the Gulf War.

We catalogued and photographed the equipment, which comprised more than a hundred items. It was, in essence, a complete factory for the manufacture of chemical bombs – the same kind that had been filled with mustard gas and found by Peter Dunn's team in Iran years earlier. We had seen literally hundreds of these bomb casings in various states of manufacture at the Al Muthanna plant. Under UN Resolution 687, all this equipment would have to be destroyed.

The manager of the sugar factory would not budge on this. The machinery was his, he insisted. The minders were just as insistent, but had sent urgently for Brigadier Hossam Amin, the director of the National Monitoring Directorate, the organisation that Iraq had set up to handle UNSCOM. I had met Amin before and found him enigmatic. In spite of his military rank he always wore a suit and tie; he murmured his words, even though his English was good, if heavily accented; and for some reason, he always seemed uncomfortable in his job. He arrived late in the day, having flown up immediately. Perhaps he had anticipated the problem. We showed him the equipment, explaining what we thought the role of each item was; he was quiet throughout all of this. My guess was that he was trying to weigh the arguments. If he conceded, the equipment would be destroyed and lost to them. On the other hand, if he tried to maintain that it was really for use by the sugar plant, UNSCOM would report that Iraq was not complying with the cease-fire resolution and there would be consequences, including perpetuation of the sanctions.

Amin had an engineering background and realised that he could not win the argument, but he made one last try. "I agree the machinery is from Al Muthanna," he muttered, "but UNSCOM could exempt it from destruction because it would be useful in rebuilding Iraq's industries following the US aggressions." We told him that, given its previous use, exemption was unlikely. In fact UNSCOM did not exempt the equipment and over the next few weeks it was returned to Al Muthanna where it was subsequently destroyed.

We had not finished searching the sugar plant, although we had achieved our primary goal. The next day we searched the remaining structures and found, rather than WMD material, a warehouse filled with antibiotics and other drugs. From their markings it was clear that the UN itself had supplied much of this; some medicine even displayed World Health Organization labels. This warehouse belonged to the military and it was clear that the supplies were being stockpiled for its use and not for the public.

That evening we were reminded of the stockpile of pharmaceuticals. A small group of us, including the team's Australian doctor, Surgeon Commander John Parkes, were dining at a little café in central Mosul. As we were about to tuck into our kebabs, a couple of young men saw us and engaged us in conversation. It turned out that they were doctors from the local hospital and on discovering that we were from the UN, they asked us how we could justify sanctions on medical supplies: their patients were dying from the lack of even the most basic items. We explained, rather lamely, that sanctions did not cover these items. We would have dearly loved to have told them of the military warehouse full of drugs just a short distance away, but felt that this might result in riots and that we would be accused by Iraq of fomenting civil disorder. Such events would compromise UNSCOM's mission. But we vowed to ourselves to take this matter up with the authorities once we returned to Baghdad.

After Mosul, we had only a couple more sites to inspect. Kirkuk was next on the list, and for some reason our minders, who now included Hossam Amin, seemed to expect this. I was leading the little convoy and although my map reading is pretty good, the map itself was not, being ten years out of date. I took a wrong turn and, realising my mistake, stopped the car and the convoy. Hossam Amin climbed out of his vehicle and came up to my window, which I wound down. "Mr Rod, I think you are a spy. Why do you stop here?" I wondered whether he really knew that I was a spy, or whether it was just another attempt at intimidation. I shrugged off the comment and turned the vehicle around.

Our last memorable inspection of this mission was to investigate a structure located near Tikrit, the birthplace of Saddam, which had been spotted by an imaging satellite. Photographs showed what appeared to be a large underground structure with wide and well-built roads leading to it, suggesting heavy-vehicle access. Odd engineering features included pipe-work and storage tanks, partly obscured by large awnings. No-one seemed to know what this structure was.

Our Iraqi minders were very nervous, particularly when the reconnaissance team climbed into the helicopter for our usual aerial survey. They explained that on the top of the hill close by was one of Saddam's palaces; flying over it, or even near it, was prohibited. They could not permit us to take off. We could have insisted: under a new UN resolution[13] we were permitted to go anywhere, at any time and by any means. But even with these powers we could not force the issue but merely register our protests with the Iraqi government. We were the UN, not the US. Instead we reached a compromise. The pilot explained that he would keep to a height below the top of the hill and only fly over the underground structure and related roads. This seemed to satisfy the minders, who set a limit of 100 feet above the ground – actually below the safe operating height for a helicopter of the size we had.

It made for an exciting ride. At times the rotors only just seemed to be clearing the ground, especially as we moved higher up the hill. Here I saw massive air-handling units, apparently both inlets and outlets. This was no ordinary storage bunker. Other than that, it was a puzzle.

The ground inspection soon solved the mystery. It was an oil refinery, built entirely underground. The reason for the massive air handling was now apparent. Inside, it was impressive, with its towering, cracking columns enclosed by a cathedral-like ceiling. An Italian company had designed and built it, and at the time it had been state-of-the-art. The reason that it was underground was to reduce its vulnerability during the Iran–Iraq War, and its location had served it well during the Gulf War, too. It seemed obvious to me that if the intelligence community had missed an entire underground oil refinery, it could also have missed an entire underground WMD plant. Perhaps we were not as good as we thought.

If there was such a thing as a typical inspection, we had just completed one. A team of about twenty inspectors from a dozen countries had spent about three weeks checking a variety of facilities and searching for weapons or clues to their existence. Intelligence leads that at the time seemed good usually turned up little. That is the nature of intelligence: leads have to be followed for the one occasion on which they bear fruit. The discovery of the bomb-making equipment at Mosul was just such a case.

There was one last important matter to resolve. Why had the UN-supplied medical supplies we found in the Mosul warehouse not been distributed? At a wash-up meeting with Hossam Amin in the ballroom of the Palestine Hotel, John Parkes raised this. Amin explained, "You have to understand, the people of Iraq are suffering from unjust sanctions." We thought perhaps he had not understood the question. But he continued, "We cannot possibly distribute the drugs until they have been tested to Iraqi standards. And because of the sanctions, we cannot obtain the test kits." Over the years, we were to hear similarly contorted reasoning in many different contexts. We knew that ordinary Iraqis would never see the drugs, as they had been illegally purloined by the military.

The inspection ended in early December 1991, and it was my last for some time. I was not to return to Iraq for almost three years and then I was to be involved in a very different kind of inspection.

African Interlude

I RETURNED TO AUSTRALIA JUST before Christmas 1991, despite the season somewhat despondent and also somewhat unwell. The reason for my despondency was my concern over Iraq and the inspection process. I had thought on that first inspection to Al Muthanna, perhaps naively, that Iraq would co-operate and inspections would soon be over. The sanctions could be lifted and Iraq would return to more prosperous times; the people deserved this after the disastrous wars the country had been involved in almost continuously since the early 1980s. Yet now my early optimism had evaporated like Sarin on hot desert sand, and I could see the process dragging on for years.

The reason for feeling unwell was not so apparent. I thought I would leave it until the new year and see what happened. I got worse. I was losing weight and ill-defined pains wracked my body. My doctor had put me on painkillers while specialists did their usual poking and probing. I continued to deteriorate and by March was admitted to hospital. General Baker, my boss in DIO, was also concerned. Could I have succumbed to some disease in Iraq, possibly even contracted from one of the biological bombs that we had been searching for but had not found? He instructed my colleague, Surgeon Commander John Parkes, to make enquiries overseas. Had any other UNSCOM inspector fallen ill?

General Baker visited me in hospital to tell me the findings of the enquiry. By this time I was on intravenous drips of morphine and pethidine and was desperately trying to pull myself out of a euphoric haze to understand his words. It seemed, from what he was telling me, that I was on my own. Over the next few days, as more tests were conducted, I wondered whether this would be the end. I was only in my mid-forties and in my more lucid moments pondered my life so far: the things I had done, both good and bad. I decided that if I did escape this illness I would grasp any opportunity to help others that might come my way.

I did not die. The doctors detected a tumour in my spinal cord, the operation was successful and I returned home within a couple of weeks to recuperate. It took a few more months before I could return to work, which I did in mid-1992.

In April 1993, the Department of Foreign Affairs was looking for volunteers to assist the UN in Somalia. We had all seen on TV the terrible pictures of Somali villagers who seemed no more than walking skeletons; it was estimated at the time that about 300,000 Somalis had starved to death and millions more were at risk. The UN had made an attempt to provide aid in the previous year, but civil war had prevented much of that. Now the situation had grown more desperate and a second effort, called Operation Restore Hope, had been launched under the umbrella of UNOSOM (UN Operations in Somalia). Australia had provided a military contingent to provide security, but the effort was intended to form part of a more comprehensive package to rebuild the country. Would I be interested in participating? I recalled the promise I made myself while in hospital. How could I refuse? At the same time, how could I help? I was not a trained foreign officer and my experience related almost entirely to WMD and related sciences.

I registered my interest and soon received a call from an official from the UN Political Division in New York. She had read my CV and noticed that I was experienced in disarmament. Well, yes, I said, but that related to chemical and biological weapons, not AK-47s. She convinced me that this might be the job for me with a few words: "We think you might be able to help." I was hooked and agreed to go as soon as it could be arranged.

One of the advantages of having worked in Iraq was that I was ready to go anywhere at a moment's notice. Not only did I have all the equipment for survival (sleeping bag, mosquito net, medical kit, folding pliers), but I had also received immunisations against most common diseases and some uncommon ones, such as anthrax and botulinum toxin poisoning. The UN worked a little more slowly, but by early June all the necessary paperwork had been completed and I was booked to fly to Mogadishu on 7 June 1993. On 6 June I received another call from New York: the previous day had seen a surge in fighting, and twenty-four Pakistani soldiers had been ambushed and brutally murdered. The civilian aspects of UNOSOM were being suspended and the staff evacuated to Nairobi; I would have to wait until it was "safe".

After a couple more false starts, I eventually arrived in Mogadishu via Nairobi in late August 1993. As bad as war-ravaged Iraq had been, Somalia was many rungs lower on the ladder. I recorded my initial impressions in a letter to friends in Australia:

"Life and Times in Mogadishu, 9 September 1993"

After just over a week in this devastated city, I am beginning to accept as normal the lifestyle here. Life here, of course, is anything but normal by almost any standard. That it's a war zone is apparent even before the plane touches down at the airport from the long lines of Apache attack helicopters, the military transports and the security. The airport continues to be a target for mortar attacks and so many of the buildings, as elsewhere in the city, are revetted or sandbagged.

Customs, passport control or any other form of officialdom does not exist here; the fact that you arrived is the only credential needed to enter the country. On leaving the airport with luggage hopefully with you somewhere, another fact of life reveals itself: no UN official travels without a convoy and armed guards, usually Somalis toting AK-47s which look as if they have seen considerable use, and probably have.

Of course the convoys only go through the safest parts of town, which do not include the centre and therefore I've not yet seen the worst of the devastation of the city; very few buildings, I've been told, have escaped war damage. The parts of town I have seen are typical of many poor African countries – crumbling buildings, corrugated-iron shanties, food and scraps of other items being sold from open stalls or simply on the ground. Two boxes of Omo and three paw-paw here, fly-covered goat meat there. The city is still recovering from years of war but there are no starving children now, just some very under-privileged ones.

I am not living in the UN compound where most of the military is located behind high walls and coils of razor wire, but in the south part of town, the "Southern Residences". Each residence, and there are about a dozen of them (mine is 12C), are little fortresses in themselves. They are large houses of typical Arabic design, two stories with flat roofs and seemingly many internal passages to allow breezes to be channelled through, and each house surrounded by a 3 metre high wall. The gates and external doors are all made from heavy steel and judging from the scar marks on the door to my part of the house sufficient to stop a bullet from a rifle.

Security is again provided by Somali guards, who we trust are more loyal to us than any faction that may wish us harm. They are armed with a collection of weapons including, in my residence, a heavy machine gun. The Egyptian Army in tracked armoured vehicles patrols the streets outside and US attack helicopters, which often fly at rooftop level, patrol the skies above. It can be very noisy at night! On several evenings I've heard gunfire close to the house but I've been told not to worry, it's only the guards shooting at each other (but don't go on the roof!). I believe living at the residence is reasonably safe: it is part of Aideed's territory but fortunately the clan that predominantly occupies the area is a different sub-clan to his.

Getting to and from work is not simple. The office, the UN compound, is about ten kilometres away. We are picked up by minibus and taken to an assembly point where we wait until everything is organised, our security people are on board (two guns per bus) and whatever other escorts we need arrive, before we head off in twenty or so vehicles, along the least vulnerable route to the compound. A similar procedure each evening and if you miss the bus then, it's overnight in the compound – heaven knows where we would sleep. The compound itself, as mentioned above, is a fortress. It comprises the US embassy compound and the adjacent university, both of which have been taken over by UNOSOM and turned into a military camp. It is a jumble of porta-cabins, huts built out of wooden packing cases, international shipping crates, derelict buildings, generators, water tanks, coils of barbed wire and lumps of concrete and jagged metal. The embassy building itself has been converted to a headquarters by stripping it of windows (to avoid flying glass), removing false ceilings and anything else that could be dangerous, sand-bagging entrances and just generally turning into the worst kind of military accommodation. As I said earlier, the military live under not very good conditions; the civilians are much better looked after and that is a cause of some friction. The dozen or so Australian soldiers here have converted an old concrete warehouse into reasonable accommodation, naming it "Australia House" and the flag can be seen from most of the compound. I had "lunch" there today to welcome a visiting Australian general – lunch was an American field ration. I think they wanted to convince the general of the hardships they endure.

I started my work in UNOSOM as an officer in the Political Division headed by a Zimbabwean, Dr Leonard Kapungu, who, as agreed, gave me special responsibilities for disarmament. The problems faced by Somalia were mind-boggling. Through years of civil war the country had gradually torn itself apart until most organisational structures, and indeed many physical structures, had disappeared. There was no government, no councils, no legal system, no police, no schools, no hospitals … Buildings that had not been destroyed in bombing had often been looted so that everything of value – doorframes, plumbing and corrugated iron – had been stripped. Overhead power lines had been ripped down and water pipes dug up to sell as scrap over the border in Kenya to raise money for weapons or ammunition. I visited Mogadishu's power station, which had been looted; bits of electrical gear of no perceived value were scattered across the roads for hundreds of metres around.

Putting the pieces of Somalia back together was going to be a Herculean task. The UN decided that the highest priority was the re-establishment of some sort of government, without which the other institutions, including law and order, could not be rebuilt. The UN gave this task to Kapungu: he was to be the architect, or at least the construction engineer, of a new political system for Somalia. In March in Addis Ababa, a plan for this had been agreed between the major clans, led on one side by Mohammad Farah Aideed and on the other by Ali Mahdi. The plan envisaged a hierarchical structure, with a Transitional National Council at the top and below that a tier of 13 regional councils, and below that again another tier of about 80 district councils.

The clans may have supported the structure for the new political system but they did not necessarily support the way in which Kapungu decided to put it together. His approach, perhaps reflecting his Zimbabwean background, was to start at the grass-roots. District Councils would be formed first. They would nominate the members of the Regional Councils and in turn they would elect the members of the transitional government. This, however, was not the way Aideed and his entourage saw it. He believed that as the warlord who had "liberated" Somalia from its dictator, General Siad Barre, he should be appointed president and in this role he would select the lower tiers of government.

In spite of the opposition from Aideed, progress on the election of the district councils was being made, at least outside Mogadishu. UN political officers visited the districts to explain the process and rules to the local Somalis. Emphasis was always placed on the fact that we would help, but in the end it was the Somalis themselves who needed to select the twenty councillors. The elders usually did this by nominating prominent members from the community, and there were no elections. One rule sometimes caused them difficulty: there was to be at least one woman on each council. This somewhat conflicted with Somali culture, but most clan chiefs simply resolved the problem by nominating their sisters or daughters (strangely, not wives or mothers).

I was not making much progress on the disarmament front. Up to this point, disarmament had been coercive – mainly cordon-and-search operations by the US military. My approach was quite different. Given my background, I could not operate without some intelligence on the militias. Who were they? Where did they come from? What motivated them? With the help of the Somalis, I commissioned a survey and found that the vast majority were teenagers whose only skill was goat-herding. Now that Siad Barre had been overthrown, their political motivation was not high and although they were loyal to their clans and their leaders, the survey suggested that given an alternative, they would surrender their weapons. So an obvious course suggested itself: I would provide incentives for disarmament.

I found that my ideas were greeted with little enthusiasm by Kapungu, who in any case gave disarmament a low priority and few resources. This difficulty was soon solved when a new UNOSOM division, Disarmament, Demobilization and Demining (3D), was created on 17 September 1993. I was to head the first two Ds and a former US Marines colonel, Murphey McCloy, was given the latter.

While I now had my own division (or at least two Ds of it), I had no staff and no money. Kapungu indicated that he could help with the staffing. I was immediately suspicious: this man never gave away anything. But I was desperate, and he transferred two of his staff. One had been the former Sudanese Ambassador to the UN, Abdul Gadir El Sheikh. He had impeccable manners and was the encyclopaedia on protocol. The other was Mohammad Ismael, a retired Egyptian general who had a love of the relaxed life and Cuban cigars. Neither knew anything about disarmament, nor seemed initially to have much interest in it, but in due course they became valuable team members. Later I was also assigned an Italian army officer, Major Francesco Andreani, a diminutive man who always carried a small Beretta pistol strapped to his belt. He had some experience in disarmament, and proved to be a great asset in this former Italian colony.

On funding, the UN promised that financial mechanisms had been put into place in New York and voting on these would occur within a month or two. I could see that I would have to find my own funds. Surprisingly, Kapungu came to my aid here, too. He was going to a conference in Kenya to talk with some aid organisations and asked whether I would like to come and perhaps raise some money for my projects. The next week, he and I were on a UN Learjet (such were the contradictions in UN spending) to Nairobi. There I spoke with passion about the projects that I had in mind and the funds that I would need. The presentation was a great success and in a couple of days about $1.5 million was pledged for my demobilisation projects. I felt at last things were moving.

I had come to the conclusion that disarmament in Mogadishu was a lost cause until there was some sort of political settlement. Curiously. Kapungu seemed to think that it was the other way around; without disarmament, he argued, there could be no political settlement. But my sense of the situation was confirmed at a meeting of militia leaders that I organised through my Somali political contacts.

The meeting was held late in September in an old UNOSOM office, now abandoned because it was on the boundary between the two warring factions and had become too dangerous. We chose it in the hope that Aideed's militia leaders might feel safer at this location. They may have felt safer but I did not. I organised our little convoy of three four-wheel drive vehicles. The first and last carried armed guards and I was in the middle car with armed Somalis sitting on either side. Even leaving the UN compound was difficult as there had recently been riots outside the gates and shots fired. The heavy steel gates were opened up just long enough for us to race out, and slammed shut as soon as we hit the street outside. I crouched down as we sped along the road bounding the compound, past burning barricades of tyres and off to the wild side of town. More shots were fired, but it was hard to ascertain whether they were aimed at us or not, as by this time I was almost on the floor of the car.

I reached the meeting place, which had been secured by a Pakistani contingent of UN guards. The colonels from Ali Mahdi's militias were already sitting around the table and I decided we should not start the meeting until Aideed's representative arrived. After ten minutes I heard a ruckus and Aideed's political spokesman entered the room. I began the meeting with some brief introductory comments setting out its purpose, and then invited Aideed's man to speak. He started by noting that he was there only as an observer, but then proceeded to speak for almost an hour. Apart from tirades against Ali Mahdi, the UN and the US, he surprised me by saying that Aideed was prepared to disarm immediately. But, he continued, "This is conditional on our enemies disarming first." He then quickly folded his papers and left the meeting.

The outcome of the meeting with the militias had not been a surprise and I had already decided that my major work would be outside the capital. I had my eye on the region of Baidoa because it was one of the most politically stable in the country, albeit still with security problems because the young militiamen there were using their skills to hold up UN convoys and sometimes the locals too. The head of UNOSOM was a retired US admiral, Jonathan Howe, so I went to see him with my plan. He was pleased with what I had done so far and liked what I had in mind, but asked, why Baidoa? I explained about political stability, but thought it might be prudent to keep from him my other reason. Baidoa had been an area where the Australian forces had been operating earlier in the year and I thought as an Australian I might be welcomed by the locals.

*

The night of 2 October was a little noisier than usual, but this did not particularly concern me: every night I went to sleep to the sound of gunfire or explosions and was now almost immune to such things. During the day it was much worse. The UN compound was mortared almost every twenty-four hours – hit-and-run exercises in which a volley of – usually – three mortars would be fired before the US helicopters were up in the air hunting down the perpetrators. One morning, from inside my metal porta-cabin office, I had heard a first mortar land about 100 metres away, followed by a second much closer and a third hitting the corner of my building with a deafening crash, followed by the screams of the workers inside. I went into the corridor and people were crouching or lying on the floor. More angry than afraid, I walked around the prone bodies to see if anyone needed help. At the same time, in another part of my mind, I was hoping there would not be a fourth mortar.

So there was nothing especially alarming about the noise on the night of 2 October. The next morning, however, we realised that the attack had been serious: two US helicopters had been shot down and there had been a major battle in Bukara market, not so far from where I had my meeting just a few days earlier. The UN closed all roads that day, so I could not get to the UN compound and spent the day at my residence.

Only on the following day, however, did I learn the full extent of the battle. Without informing the UN, a US Ranger team had attempted to capture Aideed or his lieutenants, but a Somali RPG had hit their Blackhawk helicopter. This caused a firefight that resulted in about 100 US casualties, including eighteen dead, and possibly thousands of Somali casualties. We were all greatly saddened and it was apparent to me that Howe also felt despair. He later confided to me that the UN should never again allow two different military commands (in this case the UN and the US) to operate independently in the same area. He said that even he had not been informed of the Ranger operation. If we had known, we could have put in place a rescue plan to extract injured Americans, and the tragedy might have been largely averted.

*

The "Blackhawk down" incident spurred me on to move my activities out of Mogadishu. Two days later, Major Andreani and I were in an ageing and noisy Russian MI-8 helicopter flying low, westwards across the desert, with the Indian Ocean behind us. After an hour in the air, we reached Baidoa, where we were met by the UN District Commissioner, who took us to our accommodation at the "palace", ironically the former residence of the dictator, Siad Barre.

Now that I was in Baidoa, I was not quite sure where we should begin, but thought that taking a walk through the marketplace might be a good start. This would familiarise us with the layout of the town and, more importantly, let the people know that something new was happening. In a country without newspapers or radios, it was the best means of publicity available to us. We stopped the cars a short distance from the marketplace and instructed the guards to stay with the vehicles; I was here to disarm the militias and it did not seem appropriate to march heavily armed through a crowded marketplace. Major Andreani was clearly very nervous at this prospect, but dutifully walked behind me, clutching the Beretta in his holster. He need not have worried. An unarmed white man walking through the marketplace was not a sight many had seen for a long time; they were more curious than hostile. A leading local approached and, pointing a finger at my chest, said "You American?" "No," I replied "Australian." There was a buzz through the gathering crowd and I could hear it running ahead of me: "Australia! Australia!" Someone asked, "Is Australia coming back to Baidoa?" I explained no, and gave a little of my purpose there, but added gently that the people would have to want that, too.

I met with councillors in the palace the next morning. I spoke about the militias in the area and who they were. I explained that if we could provide some vocational training for these young men they might be induced to give up their weapons in return. I thought something like a carpentry shop might work well; there was certainly a need to replace doors, windows, roof trusses and school desks that had been looted during the civil war. The council leader, Musse Hussein, an elderly and distinguished man in traditional Somali dress, welcomed the initiative but said that what they would really like was for us to build a farm on the edge of town and impound the militiamen on that.

I pointed out that we would help them build a farm but could not "impound" the militiamen. If we built a farm, it would belong to the Council, not the UN: the Council would be responsible for its running and also for the young men who worked there. I told him that it was a Somali problem that required a Somali solution. The UN was only there to help. For example, we could provide tools, fences, sheds, seed and so on, and we could also provide food for the workers for an initial period, say six months. It would be a pilot scheme but if they could get it to work, we would help with similar projects.

Musse Hussein accepted my offer somewhat reluctantly. It was clear that he would rather have the UN take on the project entirely in order to get rid of these militiamen, who were now no more than bandits. We then discussed where the farm could be built: there was a site at Bong'kai to the west of Baidoa, which I agreed to inspect.

The meeting with the colonels of the militia was not so easily arranged. Six militia groups representing about 2000 men were scattered within a 100-kilometre radius of Baidoa. Word of my visit had got around and they were willing to talk, but they were wary of a trap designed to round up the leadership. They said that I must go on my own and I would be led to the meeting place by one of their own. Now I was wary of a trap, but decided to take the risk: the leaders were known within the community and the advice I received from the District Commissioner was that it was "probably" OK.

I met my guide at the prearranged location, and we walked through the heat of the early afternoon, my canvas hat protecting me from the fierce equatorial sun. I was led between small concrete block buildings, down a small alleyway with chickens scurrying away in front of us. Suddenly he stopped before a wooden door, gestured for me to enter, and I did.

I stepped inside and after the blinding light of the street it took a few seconds for my eyes to adjust to the gloom. Eventually a table came into focus around which sat seven or eight men, most of whom seemed to be in their mid-thirties to mid-forties. They did not look as if they were going to murder or kidnap me, so I sat down. We talked for about an hour. As the District Commissioner had predicted, they were interested but cautious. They did not trust the UN, nor did they trust the Council, but at the same time, with the number of successful raids now diminishing, they realised that this was an opportunity for a different future.

The following morning I visited the brigadier of the Indian contingent that now provided the security for the area; the Indians had taken over from the French, who in turn had taken over from the Australians. Over a cup of sweet white tea, I told him that there were two matters I needed to discuss. The first was water. I knew that Indian engineers had sunk a bore near to the farm site and wondered whether we too were likely to find water. The brigadier invited me to talk to his colonel engineer. The other matter was to do with disarmament itself. My plan was to ask the militiamen to hand in their weapons in return for admission to training on the farm. Would the Indian Army set up procedures for receiving these weapons? He assured me they would be delighted: he could see that disarmament might make his job easier. Business over, we talked about an equally important matter: cricket.

Before leaving, the brigadier told me that he had few visitors out in this distant province, and would be grateful if I returned for dinner. I told him I would be honoured. That evening I attended an Indian banquet that had been set up in a marquis adjacent to the parade ground. We sipped gin and tonics under the stars while an Indian Army band played "The Hills are Alive with the Sound of Music", with not a hill in sight. I thought, what a strange world it is.

As the evening wore on, the brigadier turned to me and asked, "Do you mind if I ask you a question? Why was the Australian Army so popular when they were here? I can understand why the French were not liked, but most of my soldiers are peasants like the Somalis, and we are not as well-favoured as the Australians." I suggested it might have something to do with the fact that the Australian contingent arrived when people were starving (Baidoa had been called the "City of Death"), and had managed to save many from that fate. Privately, though, I thought that it had more to do with the way Australians treated the locals – with respect, and as equals. His soldiers may have come from similar backgrounds, but they seemed to regard the Somalis as inferior and this was resented.

*

I was pleased to get back to the sanctuary and relative sanity of Residence 12C in south Mogadishu. Here was my little international family, a cross-section of the UN: eight people aged twenty-two to sixty-two, equally divided between men and women, hailing from five different countries. Life might have not been normal by outside standards, but in here it seemed so, in spite of all the strange circumstances with which we had to contend: rat plagues, food poisoning, fights between our Somali staff, leaking pipes and, of course, complex security measures. After the Blackhawk incident we had implemented a roster system at night to check on our Somali guards, who were supposed to patrol our grounds to ensure that insurgents were not climbing over the walls. Once, on my turn at three in the morning, I watched the strange sight of the guards in our little courtyard dutifully marching in their greatcoats despite the heat of the night.

Back at work in Mogadishu, I noticed a change. By mid-October 1993, the US military no longer conducted patrols, instead hunkering down in their bases. There were rumours that an understanding had been reached between Aideed and the US, a sort of cease-fire: you don't fire on us and we won't fire on you. It was also apparent that our own security situation had changed and now it was not uncommon to see on the streets the occasional militiaman standing around with an AK-47 slung over his shoulder. On one morning someone took pot-shots at our convoy on the way to the UN–US compound. The situation was also not good for our Somali staff. We paid these people in the local currency, which because of inflation had become almost worthless, so that a week's wages was taken away in a plastic garbage bag. Within sight of the UN–US compound, these workers would often be robbed and the US guards would now just watch while this occurred. Shortly after such an incident, the Somali woman who cleaned my office asked me for duct tape. I did not ask what it was for, but gathered later that she and others took their pay home in small amounts strapped to the inside of their thighs in the hope that Muslim norms would prevail and their cache (or perhaps more accurately, cash) would not be discovered by the robbers.

The change in the security situation also affected me. I discovered that Aideed's militia had placed a price on my head. I was a little embarrassed to discover that the sum in question was only $100, although in Somali terms that was still quite a fortune. I was asked whether I wanted a gun and the training to go with it. I decided that as head of disarmament, arming myself would not look good.

My colleague Murphey, however, hired a security force of seventeen Somali guards to protect us as we drove around Mogadishu, as we did frequently. I suspected that these guards were all former militiamen. It was a depressing thought that as head of disarmament I had not yet disarmed one Somali, but had approved the arming of seventeen. Later, when I briefed the head of the UN Peacekeeping Operations, Kofi Annan, who was visiting from New York, I did not mention the ledger of armed versus disarmed; I thought my career might otherwise be cut short. Perhaps I needed not have worried, but at that time I did not know this softly spoken, amiable man.

*

I did not have much time to enjoy the pleasures of Mogadishu. El Sheikh, a couple of our local 3D staff and I boarded a UN-chartered plane to fly to Hargeisa in the north. The aircraft was a DC3 of World War II vintage, but the South African crew assured me that it had been regularly serviced. My confidence was not boosted when shortly into the flight the right engine streaked oil over the wing.

Although the journey took about two hours, the pilot told me that he would not be stopping for a break or re-fuel in Hargeisa; he simply would put the plane down to drop us off and be on his way. In fact, at Hargeisa we got off the aircraft with the engines still running; we had barely cleared the tail wings when the plane spun around and sped along the runway to take off. The reason for this hasty departure soon became clear. Five young Somali militiamen approached, AK-47s pointing at us. None of them would have been older than seventeen or eighteen, and the guns they carried seemed very large in their hands. "Landing tax ten dollar," they said. A new, crudely painted sign on the dilapidated terminal behind them read "Welcom to Hargheysa Internationale Aerporte". "Internationale" explained all: the money they were demanding was in their eyes justified because we had just entered another country.

I was more angry than intimidated by their demands. As El Sheikh and my Somali staff fumbled for their money, I pushed the guns aside and told the others to put away their cash. We were UN officials here to help the local people. If they wanted, they could take up the issue with our local office, but we were not paying. The militiamen, looking rather dejected, wandered off back to the terminal.

The next morning I was on a plane with El Sheikh to Berbera to look at a demobilisation camp set up by the local Somalis. We landed at the massive airbase there. In earlier times it had been a Soviet military base intended to provide a strategic foothold at the entrance to the Red Sea, much to the concern of the US. Now it was abandoned and had an eerie feel to it. The runway was so large that our little singled-engined Pilatus could just about have landed across the width of it.

The disarmament camp was a dusty sprawl of tents huddled under clumps of trees. It was overcrowded with young former militiamen who seemed to be short of everything from food to shoes. A parade was quickly organised and from a low platform we watched as about a thousand of them marched past, arms swinging high as they chanted some kind of war song. I found it all highly disturbing. Far from gaining new skills to allow their reintegration into Somali society, this group of men was isolated and the only training they were receiving was military-related.

*

I was keen to get back to Baidoa to get the farm project rolling. Arriving in early November, my first task was to call a meeting between the Council and the heads of the militias. I explained that funding had been approved and that I had also arranged for the World Food

Programme to provide food for six months to the former militiamen, and for the Food and Agriculture Association to provide tools and seed. With the agreement of the Council I would also find a Somali manager for the farm and the UN would pay his wages. But I needed something from them within a week: a list of names of the first fifty-five militiamen to work on the farm. Since the farm would belong to the Council, it would be the Council who would need to approve the list.

The head of the Council, Musse, thanked me and added that this meeting with the militias who had been terrorising the town was a strange one, but he would work with them to provide me with the list I had requested. I thanked him and told the gathering that it was now their meeting, then stood up and left.

I envisaged a farm that would produce both chickens and crops, and eventually support about 300 militiamen. I knew, though, that providing the list of the first fifty-five was not going to be easy. There were six militias of differing sizes and influence, and there would be many disputes in settling on the names. For me, therefore, it was a matter of survival to give the Council the job of approving the list.

Finding a manager for the farm turned out to be easier than I thought. There was in Baidoa a well-respected Somali agronomist, Hussein Moalim Iman. I was greatly impressed with this man. He had a degree in agriculture from a US university and had run various farms in Somalia before the civil war disrupted all activities.

At the site of the new farm, Colonel Sooch thought water could be found within 100 metres of the surface. In fact, there was even an abandoned drilling rig nearby, although on closer examination it was evident it was never going to drill another hole: it had been burnt out entirely. Moalim explained that the locals had burnt it to get the reinforcing wire from its tyres to tie their huts together. A half-million dollar rig had been sacrificed for $5 of wire! Better news was just around the corner: Colonel Sooch knew of a Texan drilling crew working on another project down the road, and after a short drive we met up with them. Sure, they said, they would be happy to take up a contract, and since they already had the rig in the area they could offer a discount. Sometimes you just get lucky.

Moalim and I planned the farm in detail. He borrowed my calculator and within minutes had produced rough estimates of the quantities of timber, corrugated iron and other building materials required to turn the ruined buildings into chicken runs. He also said we needed to buy chickens from Kenya – not from Nairobi which, because of its elevation, is a cool climate – preferably from Mombasa. As luck would have it, I was to go to Mombasa next week on leave; I would investigate a supplier when I was there. I was beginning to enjoy life here.

*

On 13 November I was up earlier than usual to head for the airport for my flight to Mombasa. I was looking forward to the trip very much, not only because, as a young child, Mombasa had been one of the most exotic places imaginable, but also because after working seven days a week for the last few months I needed a break and a decent shower with hot water. Meanwhile my friends from 12C started their usual morning journey north along Dead Cow Road to the UN–US complex.

At the airport, I received a message over my radio that there had been an "incident", and the last thing I heard before boarding the plane was that "it does not look good for 12C." Radio security procedure precluded more detail, but I learned more on my return a couple of days later.

Our four-wheel drive, with four of my housemates from 12C, had been ambushed on the way to work. The Somali guards, following in another vehicle, had suddenly abandoned them, and they found themselves confronted by four Somalis armed with AK-47s. Another five were behind them. Lars, a Norwegian UN guard who had been driving the car, got out with his hands in the air, yelling at the Somalis not to shoot – they were unarmed. Lars assessed that all they wanted was to steal the car which, if sold across the border, would be worth several Somali lifetimes of wages. Unfortunately, Kai Lincoln, a 22-year-old American who was in the back of the car, did not see the situation in the same way as Lars. He grabbed an M16 rifle from the back; almost immediately a rather one-sided firefight broke out. Lars felt a bullet go harmlessly through his shirt but another slammed into his leg and he fell to the ground. Shirley Brownell, from Ghana, who had been on the backseat, stumbled out of the vehicle with a shoulder wound. Kai was hit twice in the chest, and the injury was fatal.

The Somalis jumped into the car and drove off, not noticing that one person remained in the vehicle. This was Carole Ray, a young Englishwoman who, as the shots rang out, had sunk down lower and lower in the front of the car until she was almost under the dashboard. She and Lars were romantically involved, so it was with particular anguish and passion that Lars called out to let her go, which thankfully they did. Meanwhile another gunman had come up to Lars, put a gun to his head and pulled the trigger. The weapon failed to discharge. Lars told me later that when he realised what his fate would be, he was quite calm and, for some unknown reason, removed his blue UN cap so that the bullet would not damage it.

Then it was over. Over 100 shots had been fired, including the rounds fired by Kai. As well as the 12C workers, two Somalis had been injured, one fatally.

My return to 12C was very emotional, with many hugs and tears, even from our Somali staff. Kai, who had been working for the UN Children's Fund (UNICEF), had told me during the many evenings we had spent together that he had come to Somalia for adventure and to do something worthwhile. His death shattered our lives, too; it personalised the death and destruction that was a daily event in Mogadishu. I also could not help but feel that as head of disarmament I had some responsibility for what had happened, irrational though that was. Kai's death made me even more determined to establish the demobilisation farm at Baidoa. If the pilot scheme worked there, it could be replicated throughout the country, and perhaps there was hope. Quietly, too, I decided subtly to change the name of the farm from Bong'kai to Bon Kai as a silent tribute to my friend.

*

I was soon back in Baidoa to receive the list of the first fifty-five militia-men. I had been pushing for some time on this matter, and the list was now well overdue. But after several meetings of the militia and Council, it still was not settled. It seemed to me that if they could not resolve an issue like this one, then the outlook for the farm was not good. I therefore gave them an ultimatum. Tomorrow morning at ten o'clock the helicopter would arrive to take me back to Mogadishu: unless I had the list by then I would start a pilot scheme elsewhere.

That morning I went out to the airport. I was sitting glumly next to the area of runway where I expected my helicopter to land, my hat shading my eyes, when I noticed in the distance a cloud of dust approaching. The cloud became larger and I realised that it was a vehicle approaching rapidly in a direct line across the surrounding desert. In it was Musse, the Council chairman, and he had in his hand the list. After greeting me, he quickly added that it still lacked the final three names but they were negotiating this. Would it do? I thanked him and said it was satisfactory and reminded him once again that it was he, not I, who approved the list.

Over the coming weeks the construction of the farm got underway. By early New Year, the construction material arrived and the first mili-tiamen, who were to be the advance workers, handed in their weapons to the Indian Army. They built fences, repaired sheds, put in roads and dug irrigation ditches. Even more importantly, the Texas oilmen drilled for water and, as predicted by the Indian engineer, found it at about 100 metres. I had arranged for a pump and pipes to be delivered and these were soon connected. The Council decided to sell some of the water to the locals and therefore they now had a source of income to pay for the diesel used by the pump.

I decided I would announce at Admiral Howe's morning briefing that the farm was now underway. My opening words were, "The chicken has landed." At least it caught the attention of the gathering, which was more used to hearing about the increasingly grim news of the latest shootings.

At about this time, I thought I would chase up the money that had been promised by the aid agencies. I went to Kapungu and asked after it. After some evasiveness, he eventually said, "Well, the money has been allocated, but it was given to my Division. I need it to help estab-lish the Councils in Mogadishu, the last ones at the District level." I was puzzled that over $1 million was required for this: surely political insti-tutions can be established through sweat and toil, rather than money? He explained that it would be used to build council chambers and provide other instruments of office. He characterised some of this as incentives for Councillors to agree to nomination. I could not help but wonder whether the "incentives" might be more than simply the symbols of office. But whatever it was to be used for, it was clear that my division was not going to see a cent of it. I would have to find another source of funding for my future projects.

*

In late 1993 I had become, almost by default, the chairman of the UN Reconstruction of Mogadishu Committee that co-ordinated the efforts of all agencies rebuilding the capital; given the impossible security situation, it was a task that no-one else wanted.

My involvement with the Committee took me to some interesting meetings. One in particular stood out, in January 1994; it was called by a US general who shall remain nameless. He told the committee that before he left, he wanted his engineering unit to do something for the Somalis. I welcomed this. Then he said:

> I'm gonna build a goddamn school across the road [from his base], and before you know it, the kids will be singin' "God Bless America".

I was stunned by his arrogance: his "gift" was nothing to do with the Somalis and everything to do with his own narrow concerns. His logic was that if a school was built next to his base, the militias would stop their attacks on his base as it would endanger the children. I happened to know that part of Mogadishu quite well and also knew that it already had a school in the area. What the locals really wanted were desks and benches for the school. I gently suggested that it might be wise to ask the local community what their priorities were.

By January 1994, the US had begun to wind down its military presence and this manifested itself many ways. The most dramatic effect of the US pull-out was the deterioration in security, despite the continuing presence of UN multinational forces. The militias could see that it might not be long before UNOSOM also left and had begun jockeying for positions in a post-UN Somalia. Furthermore, banditry increased and shootings and hold-ups were becoming more common. Even the UN–US compound was not immune. In February 1994, one of the biggest heists of the twentieth century occurred when the militias stole over $3 million in cash from the UNOSOM pay office. Even getting to and from the UN–US compound from our residences in southern Mogadishu was now extremely hazardous, and early in 1994 there were several ambushes where UN personnel were shot. On a few occasions, the only way I could get to work was by Blackhawk helicopter, which I boarded at the nearby airport to be whisked the eight kilometres to the compound.

I was now beginning to contemplate my future in Somalia. I liked the work and I liked the people, who I felt needed a chance to recover from years of war. But if the UN effort was likely to collapse, were the risks worth it? My six-month contract would finish at the end of February and Admiral Howe was urging me to stay on. I could not decide what to do. At the end of January, I had also received an interesting fax from UNSCOM. They were seeking experts to head both the biological and chemical monitoring groups in New York: would I be interested in coming there immediately to take up one of these roles? I replied that I had not yet finished in Mogadishu, and I needed some time back in Australia, so I could not contemplate going to New York before September. But the biological position interested me. New York said they would get back to me.

*

The farm was now nearing completion and I thought we needed a little official opening ceremony, so I returned to Bon Kai on 12 February. That morning, as I inspected the progress at the farm before the dignitaries arrived, there was shouting and a commotion near the gate. A small flatbed truck with several Somalis on the back sped up the road towards me. "Man shot!" someone yelled in English, and as the truck pulled level, I could see two men lying in a pool of blood on the tray at the back.

The first had been shot in the head, with only a small wound in his right cheek, but I could also see the left rear of his skull was missing, blasted away by the exiting bullet. His companion was still alive but, with a wound to his left thigh, he was in shock and bleeding profusely. In the history of Somalia's civil war, it was just another incident, an everyday occurrence, but I had not seen death close-up like this before. I pushed the scene out of my mind and tried to concentrate on the living.

I always carried my backpack, a habit that I had learnt in my UNSCOM days, and from it I pulled out my pocket-knife and some duct tape. I had been a boy scout and had learnt a little first aid, although treating bullet wounds had not been part of that. Nevertheless, I knew the man would die without a tourniquet, so I cut away his trousers and, using the only thing I could find in my pack – a spare pair of underpants – as a pressure pad, taped it tightly over the wound. It stopped the bleeding. I also recovered the man's wallet and noticed that the bullet had passed cleanly through a stack of Somali notes. Before the truck drove off to the Baidoa hospital, I tucked the wallet back in his pocket with a ten-dollar note, hoping that he would find it later. I was not quite sure what he would make of my underpants!

The Council members, leaders of the militia, clan elders and members of the 3D team started to arrive and I quickly washed the blood off my hands to greet them. Musse shook my hand and also shook his head. "I am so sorry," he said. I wondered what the crisis was now. "I am so sorry," he repeated, "Australia is on fire." I was still puzzled until I realised he was referring to recent bushfires near Sydney, which he had heard about on the BBC international news service. He added, "When Australia is on fire, it is like Somalia is on fire." I was deeply touched by his comment; it seemed to me a genuine reflection of the gratitude he felt towards Australia, which dated from the time when the ADF had come to the rescue of the "City of Death".

After Musse and I had made short speeches, I announced that I would give a demonstration of boomerang throwing. There were looks of puzzlement all round. I removed the boomerang from my pack and, although a little out of practice, threw four near-perfect loops to the applause of the crowd. Major Andreani then asked me for a try, but he could only throw it into the ground. Then it was El Sheikh's turn. He put all his shoulder into the throw, and it was a good one, except for the direction: it spun into the gathered crowd, scything down dignitaries as it went. I thought we had better leave quickly before another clan war broke out. However, I did say a few hasty words of farewell and presented the boomerang to Musse.

I knew then that this would be my last trip to Bon Kai, and that unfortunately I would not see the project's completion. The shooting of the two Somalis earlier that morning had been the decider: one day that would be my fate, too. At the same time, I felt I was abandoning people who had come to rely on me for help; it was not an easy decision. But I could not really see the UN experiment in Somalia working; I think Admiral Howe also realised this, as he tendered his resignation later that month.

Moalim and others from 3D carried on the work at the farm, where around three hundred Somali militiamen eventually received training, handing in their weapons in the process. The ledger of Somalis armed versus those disarmed had finally swung in the right direction, and the project showed that, given the right circumstances, disarmament and demobilisation could work. UNOSOM finally pulled its forces out a year later and fighting resumed between the factions. The farm, however, continued on with the Council in control. There had been critics who told me that I could not just "give" the farm to the Somalis: they would run off with everything. The fact that it continued when almost all other UNOSOM efforts crumbled, demonstrated to me that this was the only way to go. The Somalis had to be in control of their own future, for better or worse.

How I felt about my contribution, and the UN's, was summarised in a letter I wrote to friends in Australia just before I left Mogadishu:

Please forgive me if I've told you this, but our residence, 12C, has a pet tortoise ("din-din" in Somali) and we have become close friends. (You can form some peculiar relationships in this sort of environment!) I discovered it had no name, so I named it Jonathan (after Admiral Jonathan Howe); the Somalis think this is very funny, immediately picking up the connection. The tortoise is now about eight years old and will probably live to 108 and if the name sticks, I fear it could be the only lasting memory of UNOSOM. And of my contribution to the country.

From UNOSOM to UNSCOM

ON MY RETURN FROM MOGADISHU AT the end of February 1994, a friend met me at Sydney airport, and as I got into his car I felt decidedly uncomfortable. Then it hit me: this was the first time in six months in which I had been in a car without an escort of at least two guards armed with AK-47s. I saw that it was going to take time to return to ordinary life. I was mentally exhausted from all the killings, hold-ups and UN corruption that had characterised my time in Somalia.

Once home in Canberra, I was immediately contacted by UNSCOM who again offered me a position with the New York staff. After the initial burst of biological inspections in 1991, interest had waned and there had been no dedicated biological inspections in 1992 and only one in 1993. Furthermore, there was no inspector on the New York staff with qualifications in the biological sciences. It was almost as if UNSCOM had given up on the subject. This was strange given the suspicions raised by the top British inspector, David Kelly, after the inspection of Al Hakam in September 1991. David had reported then: "There was something extremely curious about the site. It was inconsistent with the Western appreciation of a site to be developed for civilian purposes." David even doubted the credentials of the person said to be the director of Al Hakam, Dr Nassir Al-Hindawi: he "lacked credibility as the site Director".

It was true that Iraq had denied ever having a biological weapons program, but this did not seem to me to be an adequate reason for UNSCOM not to investigate; just the opposite, in fact. Under the cease-fire Resolution 687 and a subsequent resolution,[14] Iraq was required to declare all biological activities, civilian and military, that might be relevant to a weapons program, but it was not until May 1992 that it lodged such a declaration. That declaration emphasised that only biological defensive work had been conducted and nothing had "been converted to military offensive purposes".

It was not until March 1993 that the earlier suspicions concerning Al Hakam were investigated by UNSCOM. A team headed by top US inspector Colonel David Franz concluded that there was "no evidence of participation in a BW weapons program" at Al Hakam. His report made no mention of the site being "extremely curious" or of any of the other anomalies that had been noted in 1991. To him, the site did not resemble a biological warfare production facility, and he believed that it would have been unsafe to produce BW agents there because the "level of containment is inadequate to protect workers or the environment from agents such as anthrax".

It was hard to reconcile the Kelly version of Al Hakam with the Franz version. What seemed clear was that more investigation was desperately required, and this was largely my motivation for accepting the job in New York.

UNSCOM had started a new inspection phase in 1994. It was termed "monitoring" or, to use UNSCOM-speak, "Ongoing Monitoring and Verification". From the start of the inspection process, the UN envisaged that Iraq's industries and research institutes would be monitored to ensure that they were not misused for WMD purposes. To this end, the Security Council adopted a new resolution[15] in October 1991. Iraq vehemently opposed the resolution, describing it as "a gross intervention in [its] internal affairs" and an excuse to "direct accusations against Iraq of non-cooperation with the United Nations and ... consequently, permit the continued impositions of the economic embargo against the people of Iraq and to use it to threaten armed aggression at any moment."[16]

Although Iraq had continued its opposition throughout 1992 and 1993, it realised that sanctions would not be lifted until it had complied with the monitoring provisions. But, as always with Iraq, if it was to accept monitoring, it wanted something in return. Late in 1993, the executive Chairman of UNSCOM, Rolf Ekeus, offered a deal to Iraq's Deputy Prime Minister, Tariq Aziz*: he would provide Iraq with a clean report card on disarmament in return for Iraq's agreement to monitoring. Iraq thought it could see the light at the end of the tunnel on sanctions and formally agreed to monitoring on 26 November 1993.[17]

Monitoring involved inspectors checking sites in Iraq on a routine basis to ensure that they were not being converted for weapons purposes. Thus inspectors might go to a dairy to check on yoghurt fermenters to see if they had been modified to produce anthrax. To prepare for this, about a dozen such inspections were planned for 1994, each lasting from three weeks to three months to build up a database on some 200 sites, ranging from vaccine plants to university laboratories. Planning and co-ordinating this was to be part of my job.

I had very little preparation in Australia for the UNSCOM job. However, the Australian Army thought it would be a good idea to "kit me out". At the Randwick barracks in Sydney I did a quick tour through the Army store, picking out respirator, filters, sleeping bag, thermal underwear, sunglasses and so on. The major looking after me then said, "You're going to New York and we need to kit you out for that, too." Although I knew New York could be dangerous, I wondered what special kit he had in mind. We went off to David Jones and, with my plane to Canberra about to leave, very quickly bought a suit, several shirts, ties and other clothing. The astonished salesman asked, "How would you like to pay, sir?" I responded that I did not know. "Please ask him," I said, pointing to the Major, who quickly produced a credit card. I knew then what it might be like to be an eccentric millionaire.

*

I arrived in New York on 6 September 1994. My first day at work was rather bewildering. The co-ordinator of the biological group, Annick Paul-Henriot, a French international lawyer in her mid-thirties, greeted me and hurried me around for a tour of the UNSCOM offices on the thirtieth and thirty-first floors of the UN building. As we

---

* Saddam Hussein was both the President and Prime Minister; Tariq Aziz was therefore Deputy Prime Minister.

breezed through the crowded workspaces, she rapidly introduced me to the people that we bumped into along the way, and then just as quickly dashed off to a meeting.

I was left wondering how I fitted into the organisation – or for that matter, just what was the organisation, for there seemed to be none. I posed the latter question to an inspector to whom I had just been introduced, a Frenchman, Didier, who was UNSCOM's photographic interpreter. He explained, "It is blurb management." I thought he was perhaps referring to management by rumour-mongering, but it turned out his English was good but his accent was not; he actually meant "blob management". "Blurb management," he elaborated, drawing a picture with his hands, "involves a centre, Ekeus, and round him a blurb. The closer to the centre, the more influence. When the centre moves, the blurb moves," and he slid his hands across the desk to illustrate the concept. I was trying to understand and digest this valuable piece of information when a stocky man somewhere in his early sixties interrupted us. I assumed by his demeanour that he must be in the inner part of the blob.

This was Dr Dick Spertzel. His reputation had preceded him. One of my Australian GATEWAY colleagues had described him as a cantankerous bugger who was obstinate and argumentative. Based on my previous experience in Iraq, I thought these might be useful qualities in an inspector. But today he seemed quite gentlemanly. I had also been briefed that Dick was a veterinarian, a retired US Army colonel, and that he had been the deputy director of the US Army Medical Research Institute of Infectious Diseases (USAMRIID) at Fort Detrick before his retirement.

Dick told me that he had been recruited by UNSCOM with little notice and had started at the end of March that year. I noted to myself that this was shortly after I had declined Annick's offer to come to New York. He introduced me to the two other experts in the biological section – Amelia Jones from the UK and Ray Zilinskas from the US – and although he did not say it, he made it clear that he was in charge. I wondered where this left me, as I had agreed to come to New York in the belief that I was to head the group. I decided not to try out his reputation by challenging him; I would wait to see the lay of the land.

I was then shown my work "space". With the imminent advent of monitoring, the staff of UNSCOM had grown steadily throughout 1994, but the space had not. Inspectors occupied the northern end of the thirtieth floor of the UN Secretariat building and there were now about 100 people occupying an area that really would have been crowded with even half that number. It was a jumble of little cubicles, filing cabinets, and miscellaneous cupboards and boxes. New York standards of occupational health and safety did not apply here: *we* were the UN!

The four biologists, including Dick and me, had a sort of shared cubicle. It was so crowded in there that for Dick to leave his metre of bench space, I had to stand up. After securing my metre space, I thought I would start by looking at UNSCOM's evidence concerning a possible Iraqi BW program. The file was depressingly thin. Virtually nothing had been collected since David Kelly's inspections in 1991. I turned to Dick and asked him where he thought I should begin. Perhaps misunderstanding me, but probably not, he suggested that there was some filing to do and gave me some papers to put away. It was a depressing beginning.

*

A week later I was back in Iraq, as part of a "baseline" inspection. It was intriguing to see the changes that had occurred after a two-and-a-half year absence. At first glance Baghdad appeared much the same, with its bustling noisy streets reeking of diesel fumes, but there were differences. Now there were a few new trucks and buses, the markets had more goods than before, and a decent cup of coffee (not made from dates) could be obtained. While the sanctions were obviously taking their toll, ways to get around them had been found. It seemed that the members of the middle class were hardest hit and in the markets, items such as second-hand furniture, jewellery and used refrigerators were in ready supply, as they gradually turned their possessions into cash.

The greatest impact of the sanctions had been on the currency. On that first inspection of Al Muthanna in 1991, three US dollars bought one Iraqi dinar; now one dollar bought over a thousand dinars. We could fill up our four-wheel-drives for the equivalent of eight cents. In

1991 we could not afford restaurants, but now we could dine in the best restaurants for a few dollars. However, finding a good one was not easy; many had to close as their middle-class clientele gradually became poorer.

UNSCOM was now much more organised. We had our headquarters at the former Canal Hotel, which was also being used by other UN organisations operating in Baghdad. There we had all the support facilities required to run an operation of this kind: an operations and communications room, offices, canteen, a chemical analysis laboratory, medical treatment room and car maintenance workshop. We were also in the process of setting up a monitoring room with TV screens that were directly linked to cameras at key Iraqi facilities. That way we could monitor these places on a 24-hour basis, although physical inspections would still have to be carried out occasionally.

Inspectors no longer stayed at the large tourist hotels, the Palestine and Sheraton, but at a string of lesser hotels that had been approved by the Iraqi authorities. Most visiting teams stayed at the Hyatt – named not after the famous chain of luxury hotels, but for the Arabic word "hyatt", meaning "life". And there certainly was a lot of life at the hotel: mainly giant cockroaches and rats. I was told, too, that bugs of the electronic variety had occasionally been found in the rooms of inspectors.

My overall impression of the UNSCOM operation in 1994 was that, compared to three years earlier, it was a slick and professional outfit. At any one time there might be four or five teams in Iraq, involving as many as a hundred inspectors heading off on different missions to all parts of the country. And although the work could never really be described as routine, it seemed to run very smoothly.

I soon learned what "baselining" was all about. Over the next two or three weeks we inspected thirty-four biological sites around Iraq, recording as we went what equipment was where and what it was being used for. We drew up site diagrams and recorded details of key workers and projects. To keep track of pieces of equipment we would stick barcodes on them so that some time in the future we would be able to scan these codes into a computer and electronically keep track; we called this "tagging". All of this information would form a database of Iraq's entire industry and research capabilities. If there were any changes in the future – any attempt to use civilian facilities for WMD purposes – we would know about it very quickly.

One of the industrial sites we were to inspect was Al Hakam. Our first stop was at Dr Rihab Taha's office, just a short drive from the entrance, and she greeted us with an embarrassed and resigned smile; inspectors now regularly turned up at her door and we were just another group she had to endure. I had not seen her for more than two years, but she had changed little – perhaps she was slightly wearier and her short hair was a little greyer. She still looked out of place, dressed in an orange floral blouse and calf-length black skirt with, as one of my colleagues remarked, Minnie Mouse shoes.

I was particularly interested in the production area at Al Hakam because if there had been a biological warfare program, this is where the agent would have been made. Heading a small sub-team I drove off to this area with Dr Taha following a short distance behind in her old green Mercedes. As David Kelly had said all those years earlier, there was "something extremely curious about the site". After a three-kilometre drive through the desert we reached a cluster of ordinary-looking shed-like buildings that housed production equipment. Inside were two rows of smallish fermenters, eight in all, standing three metres tall and connected to other tanks by gleaming pipe-work.

Iraq had declared this site to be a pilot plant for the production of yeast, referred to as Single Cell Protein, intended as animal feed. I turned to Dr Taha and asked her how production was going. She was evasive and started talking about quality control and problems with getting the right strain of yeast. I already knew the answer from earlier UNSCOM inspection reports. Dr Taha had in fact been unable to produce any significant quantities of yeast. At Al Hakam they kept twenty or thirty chickens as experimental animals and they would all have starved if they had had to rely on the feed produced in these fermenters.

From there we drove the two kilometres to "Area D", where two large warehouse-type buildings were nearing completion. Dr Taha explained that these buildings would house three 50,000-litre fermenters in a scale-up of the process we had just seen. Apparently their lack of success in the small-scale operations had not deterred them from investing further. I asked Dr Taha about this and she coyly responded with "a child has to learn to walk before running." An odd response, I thought, since this child had not yet learned to walk.

Four kilometres away was "the southern production area", again a small cluster of buildings. Here they had apparently had more success, not with yeast but with the production of a bacterium, *Bacillus thuringiensis* (BT), which infected insects and could therefore be used as an insecticide. In one hall was a large cylindrical machine with an inverted cone at its lower end and a dusting of white powder on the floor. I recognised it as a spray-dryer. It was a new development and Dr Taha proudly explained that they had perfected a way of drying the bacteria by mixing it with slurry of a type of clay, bentonite, and then spray-drying the product. The resulting powder could be dusted onto crops to kill caterpillars and other insect pests.

The BT process was of considerable concern to UNSCOM. The bacterium is almost identical to *Bacillus anthracis* (anthrax), but produces different toxins that are harmless – unless you are an insect. The process of its production and, even more importantly, the process of its drying are almost identical to the procedures for producing anthrax as a dry biological warfare agent. The only difference would be that greater precautions would have to be taken with anthrax; white powdered anthrax on the floor would be a hazard for workers even if they wore protective clothing. But we believed that safety could readily be achieved to an acceptable level: for example, by simply shrouding the dryer in plastic sheeting. But in spite of our concerns we could not close Dr Taha's BT plant, so we just photographed and tagged the drying machine and other equipment.

*

I returned to New York from that inspection still quite undecided about Al Hakam. The place was indeed "extremely curious", and it was not the way industrialised countries would go about producing Single Cell Protein. But were we just arrogantly judging by Western standards? As a director of intelligence in DIO, one lesson I had emphasised to all new analysts was that they must understand not just the technical aspects of their work, but the people in the country they were studying.

I was reminded of this lesson when I was at GATEWAY. Two US inspectors, chemical engineers, told me after inspecting the chemical weapons plant at Al Muthanna that the place was "shit". One of them said: "They have the best chemical equipment money can buy, but hell, there's stuff leaking all over the place. They could never produce anything there!" I gently reminded them that this plant had produced thousands of litres of chemical agent that had killed or maimed thousands of Iranians.

The difference in standards was also demonstrated in work practices at Al Muthanna. The Iraqi doctor there told me that out of a workforce of 700 he would treat about 100 casualties a year. When I criticised the safety standards, he simply told me that in Iraq they did things their own way. Perhaps Al Hakam too had produced deadly agents in unsafe conditions with casualties accepted as the price of obtaining WMD.

*

On 26 October 1994, Ekeus invited the biologists for a meeting in the "bunker", our secure and windowless meeting room adjacent to the inspectors' work area on the thirtieth floor. The purpose of the meeting was to discuss our progress towards monitoring, and to hear our views on a possible Iraqi biological weapons program.

Annick and Dick were convinced that Iraq was covering up such a program. Ray Zilinskas, however, sat in silence, staring at his hands and looking tense. I knew from the heated discussions he had with Dick that he thought all this was nonsense. In his view Iraq had never had a biological weapons program. I also sat in silence. I was not convinced, but believed that we had no choice but to investigate. I looked at Ekeus, and from his studied expression surmised that he was uncertain about the validity of Dick's argument. He then asked, somewhat rhetorically, "What makes you think that after all these years of inspections you will find any evidence now?"

The outcome of the meeting was that Rolf Ekeus decided to give us a chance to uncover the evidence, although it was expressed more in the terms of "Put up or shut up." He gave us no time-frame for the investigation, but it was evident that we had to move quickly: his patience was not going to last forever.

Now the pressure was on Dick and me to achieve something, and rapidly. I had a few ideas. We had been fortunate that a number of countries had provided us with intelligence. Israeli intelligence services had recently provided us with two assessments and other information on Iraq's biological weapons program. In themselves they did not say much, but they suggested a few leads to follow up. Most importantly, the Israelis had also listed some suppliers of equipment and materials to Iraq. Whether the purchases in question were related to biological weapons was another matter, but I thought I could at least write to the governments asking about these companies. Early in November I prepared letters for Ekeus to sign, hoping that in due course they would yield something.

We also arranged for a briefing from the CIA and they visited us on 28 October for a meeting in the bunker. Although the two officers who briefed us were quite forthcoming, they had little to say that was really new – except for a few snippets. We learned a little more about a "Project 324" for which HEPA* filters had been ordered, but they had no idea what the project was or even where. HEPA filters are used to produce clean air and would be relevant to a number of industries such as electronics, but they might also be useful in a biological weapons plant to ensure that any pathogenic bacteria produced did not escape into the environment.

The best news we received also arrived on that day. Nikita Smido-vitch, a tall, brooding Russian inspector, had just returned from discussions in Baghdad with General Amer Rashid. Nikita, more because of his country of origin than his engineering ability, was UNSCOM's senior missile inspector; Amer, who had once headed Iraq's SCUD program, was his counterpart. These two were a good match. Nikita, in a former life, had been a tough Russian negotiator on arms control and a diplomat; Amer, on the other hand, was an ill-tempered, bullying general and Iraq's senior representative on UNSCOM matters. Nikita's news from General Amer was that, "in the spirit of co-operation" promised by Tariq Aziz, UNSCOM would be allowed to interview the scientists who had once been involved with

---

* HEPA filters, an acronym for High Efficiency Particle Air filters.

Iraq's defensive biological program. Previous requests had been turned down as irrelevant, beyond UNSCOM's mandate, or, more usually, because "the scientists are all now driving taxis and cannot be found."

Dick and I were not sure what the interviews would yield, but it was an exciting opportunity that we had to make the most of. We decided a small team was best and thought we would invite David Kelly because of his experience and expertise, and Hamish Killip, my colleague from the Defence Intelligence Staff, GATEWAY and the first inspection of Al Muthanna. Both David and Hamish had spent several months on baseline inspections throughout 1994 and were more familiar with Iraq's facilities and scientists than any other UNSCOM inspectors. We also thought it would be useful to have Ken Johnson, an experienced Canadian, join the team, and he would stay on in Baghdad to start interim monitoring. Dick would head the team, with Annick remaining in New York to set up future inspections.

We needed to plan the interviews carefully and decide on approach and style. It might be our only opportunity to talk to these people, as the mood in Iraq could easily swing the other way and access be denied again. I drew up a list of those we should interview and some provisional questions. The list started with the ten scientists and workers who had been involved in the "defensive" program, including Dr Taha, but I also included the names of a few other senior Iraqi scientists. The logic here was that in Iraq's small academic community many scientists would know each other and we might just glean something from them. I also had a list of Iraqi names that the CIA had compiled as possible suspects in a BW program. I had no idea how the CIA had selected these names. Some were familiar, others were just "Mohamad Ali?" and therefore not particularly useful. But I thought it was worth a go, and I picked some names from this list almost at random, in case we got lucky.

We now had everything in place; the scene was set for what was to become UNSCOM's biggest coup. We would meet up with David and Hamish in Bahrain on 13 November for detailed planning, before the interviews commenced in Baghdad on 16 November. We did not know it then, but this was the start of the end for Iraq's biological weapons program. Even so, it was going to be a bumpy ride.

Uncovering Iraq's Biological Weapons Program

ON 14 NOVEMBER 1994, SIX OF US making up a new team, UNSCOM 104, were waiting in the foyer of the Holiday Inn. There had been a subtle change in us. Officially we were "UN weapons inspectors", but none of us had ever seen an Iraqi biological weapon to inspect: Iraq was denying their existence. We had become weapons detectives, employing the tradecraft of any detective: investigation, observation, analysis and deduction. To assist in this, we collected intelligence and used forensics science in the examination of samples. Soon we would be boarding a noisy and uncomfortable C160 transport aircraft for Baghdad to conduct UNSCOM's first set of interviews of Iraqi biological scientists.

What was taxing the team's collective mind was the question of whom to interview. We were restricted by time – just a week in Baghdad – and therefore had to tailor the program carefully. Iraq had told us ten individuals were involved in the biological "defensive" program at Salman Pak, and we would be given their names once we reached Baghdad; we only knew that Dr Taha was one of these and the leader of the group. We decided to allocate a day to Taha, leaving her until last: that way we could use the information from the others and perhaps get more out of her. This left six days and we figured that we could interview four or five people a day, which meant a total of about thirty. It was going to be an exhausting week.

On our first day in Baghdad, we assembled in a conference room of the Rashid Hotel. Hossam Amin, the head of the National Monitoring Directorate (UNSCOM's counterpart), had selected this as a "neutral" interview location in spite of the fact that it was well known to be a Ba'ath Party hotel. We did not object, as we felt that in Baghdad there was no such thing as a neutral location: the Rashid was just less neutral than others. As if in confirmation of our views, the main entrance displayed a large mosaic of a snarling President Bush, with the words "Bush is criminal" gracing its border. Although walking across the face of the US President did not particularly bother us, we understood that it was a great insult in the Arab world.

Amin had assembled eight of the workers from the former "defensive" biological program, and the first, a junior scientist, was asked in. He sat between Amin and Dr Taha. David Kelly started the interview with a brief introduction and the questions: "You were employed at Salman Pak?"

"Yes."

"Did you work for the research team headed by Dr Taha?"

"Yes."

David proceeded in a careful and methodical fashion. At times, progress seemed excruciatingly slow but it was essential to build up layers and layers of background before coming to more pertinent questions. The line of questioning resembled that employed by a detective interviewing a suspect, its purpose being to establish a base that left little wriggle room for later inventions. For example, it would be difficult for the Iraqis to deny a certain type of biological experiment because of lack of equipment if it had already been established that the equipment was there and fully functional.

After David had finished, we took it in turns to ask our questions, covering details of experiments, personnel, locations, dates, achievements, imports, security, military connections, and even where they had lunch. We completed the eight interviews in three sessions, knocking off late in the evening.

Over dinner, which we managed to squeeze in just before midnight, we reviewed the results. It was apparent that they had all been well coached. Apparently no-one knew who worked in the next laboratory, no-one had discussed his work with anyone else (and hence could not comment on others' work), and no-one had kept notebooks.

We debated whether we had really made any progress; at first glance it seemed as if we knew little more than before. The stories we had heard obviously could not be true. No scientist works in a vacuum and it was inconceivable that no-one knew what others were doing, especially as their work had a common purpose: allegedly, research into defence against biological agents. If the work really was innocent, there was no reason not to be more open with us. So, in a sense, we had advanced: clearly there was more to their work than they had revealed. I was starting to become a believer in the existence of an Iraqi biological weapons program.

The following morning we were back in the Rashid. The first person up was Adel Nafi Salman, one of my "wildcards". We really had no idea who he was, except that somehow he was connected with Salman Pak. David began as usual: "You worked at Salman Pak?"

"No."

David looked puzzled: who was this person? "You worked for Dr Taha?"

"No."

"Where did you work then?"

"The Ministry of Trade."

Turning to me, David said, "My colleague, Mr Barton, has some questions for you." The mention of my name shook me out of a daze; apparently I had some things to ask.

It was always good to start with a question about work history, and while he was answering this I got my wits about me. This man had been the chief purchasing clerk for the Technical and Scientific Materials Import Division, TSMID. As the name implied, it was involved in importing technology items for Iraq. He told us that TSMID imported only for the Technical Research Centre at Salman Pak, with the main items purchased being electronic components, but some "chemical" equipment and materials were also acquired. Since he was not a scientist he did not know what this material was.

When I asked him for the records of the purchases, he told us that in 1992 the staff were given instruction to destroy them all. This story of destruction was a consistent line of the Iraqis, but the date was new. Immediately Amin intervened, suggesting that Salman was mistaken, he had really meant 1991. This was the first instance, but not the last, when the "observers" made a comment during an interview. We objected, but the damage was done: Salman told us he had been mistaken and "corrected" his account.

The other "wildcard", Ahmed Khudayyer, also turned out to be connected with TSMID: in fact, he had been its director. He confirmed what Salman had told us – that TSMID only imported for Salman Pak. It seemed to me that the establishment of a special division for foreign purchases was significant, and I mentally filed away this snippet of information.

As the days passed we steadily ploughed through the list, which included two former directors-general of the Al Muthanna chemical weapons plant. Finally we reached Dr Taha herself. As usual, David began the interview with questions about her background. She told us that she had wanted to be a medical doctor, but her marks were not high enough, so she had decided instead to become a microbiologist, studying in the UK from 1980 to 1984. In 1985 and 1986 she worked part-time at Al Muthanna on bacterial pesticides and during this time a 150-litre fermenter was bought from the Swiss company Chemap. She said she did not achieve very much at Al Muthanna and there was no encouragement or interest from others working there.

It had taken us over two hours to get this far, so we took a short break before returning to discuss her time at Salman Pak. It was then that things started to get rocky. She said that in 1986 she was recruited to Salman Pak to work on the detection of microbial contamination of foodstuffs required for the protection of high-ranking officials (I assumed by this she meant she was Saddam's food tester). Then she tried to explain how this work somehow transformed into research into defence against biological warfare agents:

Originally the work was designed to protect high Iraqi officials. Then the Iran–Iraq War was at its apex and so I thought, why only focus on high-ranking personnel? It should be on protecting all the Iraqi people. For example, in 1986, we had a cholera epidemic, which was attributed to water coming from Iran. So if we received contaminated water or meat, how would we detect this? We must have the basics. So it was decided to have a defence against this and we studied the characteristics of pathogenic organisms. It started simple and kept building up.

David could not see how the transition took place. He commented: "But there is a fundamental difference between the defensive purpose of BW and the situation you describe for the detection of contamination in foodstuffs." He also tried to elicit who had authorised this change in direction. By now, Taha had become evasive, claiming that because there was no real change in policy, no authorisation was required. "It wasn't a change," she argued, "just an expansion of trends."

The atmosphere was now tense and Taha was quite agitated. But David did not relent. Before returning to the question of what the research program was and who organised it, he remarked, "Your accounts have changed over the past four years." There was an explosion from Taha: "I am trying to tell you what happened and you don't believe me! This is the way it was! I did it and others were not needed. It's up to you to accept or not!"

Her voice was shrill and her arguments disjointed.

David decided to move on, and asked whether her program was the only one in Iraq involved in defensive biological research. For a little while calm prevailed, although Dr Taha was still evasive, giving long circular responses but not really answering any of David's questions. I now found her very difficult to understand and it was clear that David, too, was having difficulty making any sense of anything she said. Finally he had had enough, and quietly but purposefully said, "Dr Taha, please stop!" There was no explosion this time, just a fizzle. I recall her trying to pick up a glass of water, but her hand was shaking so much, the water was spilling out. She stood up and tried to speak but no words came. Then, to our astonishment, she burst into tears and ran out of the room.

I think that Hossam Amin, too, was stunned, although he soon recovered. He accused David of insulting Dr Taha, and added for good measure that David had insulted others too and (I think) impugned the dignity of Iraqi womanhood in general. With feelings running high, it was obvious that we were not going to get anywhere. In the absence of Taha, we agreed to a recess until after lunch.

That afternoon we were waiting in the conference room when Amin walked in. Dr Taha was not to be seen. "She's in the next room," Amin explained, "but I found it difficult convincing her to return." He added obliquely, "You have to consider she is a woman." Amin then suggested a solution to the impasse. "You can continue, but without the presence of Dr Kelly." Dick told him that this was not acceptable. Amin proposed a compromise: "Dr Kelly could write his questions down and then pass them into the room for others to ask." Now it was getting absurd. Dick hung on and his stubbornness was now his strength. We were either going to proceed with David or not at all; our mission would end and we would report Iraq's lack of co-operation.

It took another hour of negotiations, and further threats by Dick to terminate the mission, but eventually Dr Taha did return to the conference room. David asked her, "Will you listen to me?" and Taha grudgingly responded with, "If I see you walking a certain way, I will go another. But for the sake of my country I will listen." And for the sake of peace, David proffered an apology:

I never, ever had any intention of insulting you. I have a high personal regard for you. I hope we can work together to solve the problem. Inevitably we are locked together because of your association with the past program and my involvement with UNSCOM.

It was not a comfortable afternoon, with David inhibited by what he thought he could ask and the rest of us feeling as though we were treading on eggshells. In any case, Dr Taha had now regained her composure and it seemed unlikely that we would extract any more useful information from her. And with that, the mission was over.

*

A week later in New York we briefed Rolf Ekeus on what we had found and described the incident with Dr Taha. While we had not uncovered dramatic new information, we had learned things, such as dates and locations, that contradicted – if only in detail – Iraq's earlier stories. Most importantly, Iraq's approach to the interviews demonstrated that it was covering up something, although just what we did not know. We also discussed the significance of Taha's breakdown: it had not resulted from any insult from David, but we could not be certain just what had triggered it. Our report recommended that we have another round of interviews in January. Ekeus listened politely and although he was not convinced, he was willing to go along with us – for now.

*

The new year, 1995, brought with it new opportunities. We were to have a three-day visit by Israeli intelligence officials on 5 January, the same day on which we were to meet General Amer Rashid and his entourage, including Hossam Amin. Having the Israelis and the Iraqis at the same time would require juggling.

The Israelis were the first to turn up. That morning an Israeli Embassy first secretary escorted two military intelligence officers into the UNSCOM offices to introduce them to Annick, Dick and me. The senior officer, whom I will call Aaron, was a Lieutenant Colonel in his mid-thirties. He was someone I immediately felt I could relate to; perhaps it was that we were both in the same business. We apologised for not having more time to chat. The first secretary suggested that we meet up in the UN canteen at lunchtime.

While we were greeting the Israelis, directly above us on the thirty-first floor Rolf Ekeus was greeting General Amer Rashid, the former head of Iraq's missile program and now Iraq's senior representative on UNSCOM matters. Later, Ekeus told us that when Amer entered his modest office, he remarked, "This would not be allowed in my country – it's not even large enough to shout in." We would learn later that Amer knew a lot about shouting.

The main meeting with the Iraqis was held in one of the UN conference rooms in the basement. It was attended by most of the UNSCOM inspectors, including David Kelly, who had flown in from London. Rolf Ekeus opened with a lengthy presentation on UNSCOM's work to date, including the problems we needed to resolve before we could proceed much further with monitoring. The few Swedish diplomats whom I have met have impressed me with their style, which is both diplomatic and direct. Ekeus was no exception. On the problems we faced with Iraq's past programs, he told Amer Rashid:

Iraq has tried to put the blame on the Commission. The Commission has been successful in getting some supporting information but this is the wrong approach. We search and search and only in the end do we find this confirmation. It is up to Iraq to provide us with the information. We recognise that some documents have been destroyed but we do not accept that it is all. I encourage Iraq to co-operate, to be more forthcoming. We take this opportunity to be blunt but we do so in a constructive fashion.

General Amer Rashid was also in good form:

We came with open minds to settle all outstanding issues and think that we have exceeded our requirements. However, after one year we feel we are in a worse situation, even after our full co-operation. Some of us feel that UNSCOM has exceeded its mandate ... From Iraq's point of view it would be pointless to retain anything.

He continued on in this fashion before coming to how he believed UNSCOM could solve the problems it claimed to have:

How to handle outstanding issues? To really resolve it you should keep two things in mind. The first is that a thousand interviews will not resolve it. You should first get rid of scepticism from your minds because it colours your perception of the facts. I am talking here mainly of chemical and biological inspectors. Even if we showed you all the documents, you still would not be satisfied.

Secondly, you should stick to your mandate in the resolution, and not go beyond it. We understand your difficulties with influential members of the Security Council. Some of the interviewees look down on you because they wonder why you are asking trivial questions – this applies mainly to biological [inspectors].

Amer was not finished. He expanded on his theme:

We have never had a [biological weapons program] and I, General Amer, will prove this myself. In my judgment, your dealings with foreign governments and international intelligence communities are wrong. You should not believe them. You should get the green light to go to the companies directly and this will be enlightening to you. It's unjustifiable that our people suffer because of minor matters.

Rolf Ekeus had the last words before lunch:

Our people are scientists, General Amer. They come with open minds, and develop their own scepticism. None of us have another agenda. Small bits of information may be significant to us and that is why they ask detailed questions which may not seem important to Iraqi workers.

It had been an interesting exchange, not because it resolved any of the issues but because it made clear what Iraq's approach would be. We already knew from experience that Iraq would not co-operate with our investigation of its biological program, but from now on we could expect active opposition. Amer Rashid, however, did give us one good suggestion: we "should get the green light to go to the companies directly". A little unusual in a bureaucratic UN, but what a good idea, I thought.

As Dick and I made our way to the canteen to meet Aaron, I could not but think of Amer's warning about foreign intelligence services. What did he know? Of course we would not accept at face value the information passed to us, but rather use it as a lead in our investigations. In the end, if we were to prove an Iraqi biological weapons program, it would be on evidence that was plain and transparent, not on whispers and rumours.

The UN canteen is not renowned for its food, but it does boast views of the broad expanse of the East River to Queens. The arrangement was that Aaron would be at a table near the picture windows at the back of the canteen. However, as we wound our way through the tables, sitting directly in front of us was Hossam Amin with some of the officials from the Iraqi Embassy. We politely nodded in recognition, continued to the windows and indicated to Aaron that he should follow at a discreet distance. It was a close call: being seen at lunch with Israeli intelligence after General Amer's diatribe might leave him tut-tutting, or worse.

Juggling the Israelis and Iraqis required some thought. David Ezekiel, our support officer, came up with a solution. He offered the use of his apartment, just a short walk from the UN building. In the morning we could meet the Israelis there, and in the afternoons the Iraqis at the UN.

Aaron's information was almost overwhelming in its detail and scope. He spoke from his notebook while Dick, David Kelly and I occasionally interrupted, but just mainly listened, scribbling notes all the while. On that first morning, he referred to projects we had heard about such as Project 85 and Project 324. He also had details of purchases of a range of equipment and materials including the dates, people and companies involved. The following morning, just to play it safe, we switched to my apartment on the corner of Fortieth Street and Second Avenue, again just a short distance from UN headquarters. Aaron continued with his details along the same lines as before. It was a touch surreal to sit in my apartment with the imposingly graceful Manhattan skyline in the background and listen to the details of what could be an Iraqi biological weapons program.

None of what Aaron told us gave us definitive answers, but it did provide hundreds of leads to follow up. There was the problem of what was relevant and what was not. Might not some imported equipment just be for a vaccine plant or a hospital, or nothing to do with the biological sciences at all? And although we learnt more detail of Project 324, including the HEPA filters for buildings E and H, we still did not know what this project was, where it was, or even what it was. The situation was the same as that faced by all intelligence analysts. It resembles putting together the picture of a jigsaw puzzle, complicated by the fact that some pieces do not belong to your puzzle and other pieces are missing and may never be found.

Among the vast array of intelligence Aaron had given us was one piece of information that all three of us considered significant. Iraq had imported from a British company, Oxoid (a subsidiary of UNILEVER), several tonnes of bacterial growth media. Growth media are nutrients, such as casein extracted from milk, that are mixed with water to allow bacteria to multiply in a fermenter. There are many legitimate uses for this material – for example, in the production of vaccines or antibiotics – but we knew from our extensive baseline inspections that Iraq had only limited industries in this area. What caught our eye in particular was the fact that this material had been imported into Iraq by TSMID. I recalled what we had been told the previous November: TSMID only imported for Salman Pak. What was Salman Pak doing with tonnes of growth media? Unless …

After our second day with Aaron we had a chance to question the visiting Iraqis. We began with the standard, invariably pointless discussion of inadequate declarations and lack of supporting documentation before turning to the real issues at hand. David then said:

> We have deep suspicions of the roles of both Al Muthanna and Al Hakam. It would be a useful start to have additional candour about the biological program, including its origins: what was the perceived threat, what was the role of the military, and what was Iraq thinking at the time? We cannot accept that the program was limited to just ten people at Salman Pak. Until we have a better understanding of the past program we will have difficulty in monitoring.

We had to be careful in asking questions relating to the information given to us by Aaron. This was in part not to compromise our source, but also because we were still uncertain how solid or relevant it was; the information on suppliers needed to be cross-checked with the companies themselves. However, we wove in elements, sometimes obliquely, into our discussions with Amin. For example, Dick asked if Iraq had imported any HEPA filters and, if so, what these were for. I raised the question of bacterial growth media that had been noted during an inspection of Al Hakam, but which had not been declared. David asked about the import of fermenters.

We received no real response to our questions, but no doubt they alerted Amin to the possibility that we were onto something and that Iraq had a real problem. We hoped, perhaps optimistically, that Iraq might modify its position slightly and concede some more ground; another piece of the jigsaw puzzle might then be revealed to us. To emphasise our concerns, Annick finished with the observation that compared to UNSCOM's investigations in other areas, the biological inquiry was only at its beginning. Amin looked surprised and asked, "What percentage do you believe you still have to go?" David, leaning forward across the table and looking at Amin squarely, answered for all of us: "95%." Now Amin was annoyed:

What is the value of UNSCOM if over these years you have had inspections, interviews, declarations etc. … if you start from zero now? We feel you have gone outside the context of [Security Council Resolution] 687 in the biological field. Your questions are not in the context of 687. Iraq has met its obligations.

We may have got a buzz from rattling Amin, but we were brought down to earth the next day when we were briefed on the latest meeting of the sanctions review committee. At the meeting, Tariq Aziz had dismissed the problems of the past biological program with a wave of a hand and a statement that "the outstanding issues are trivial." The Russian delegate, Sergei Lavrov, reinforced this view and argued that perhaps the time had come to start easing the sanctions. The French delegate said now that Iraq had recognised Kuwait, the review was "taking place in a profoundly different environment," and added that UNSCOM "could not expect perfection in Iraq's account of the past program". Even though other countries did not support these views, it seemed to us that time might be running out for our investigations.

Before going home on Friday 13 January, I prepared a series of letters to the French, German, Swiss, Italian and British ambassadors to the UN. Using the information that Aaron had given us, I asked specifically about the companies we had been told exported equipment and materials to Iraq. Breaking with the usual UN protocol, I also asked for their governments' permission to deal directly with the companies, giving my name as a point of contact, as I thought this would expedite the process. Rolf Ekeus seemed happy enough with this approach, and signed the letters. Yes, General Amer's suggestion had been a good one.

In just over a week Dick, David, Hamish and I would be leaving for the next interview mission, but this time we would be better armed. Although it seemed unlikely the suppliers would reply to us by then, we felt much more optimistic about the next set of interviews because we now had Aaron's intelligence information.

*

It was not long into our return encounter with Dr Taha that we struck paydirt. Although Iraq claimed it had destroyed all documentation relating to the past biological "defensive" program, we felt that documentation relating to Al Hakam should still be available. After all, Iraq claimed that Al Hakam had nothing to do with a biological program. Trapped by its own argument, Iraq provided the documents. Hamish, the engineer on the team, questioned Dr Taha about it: "Regarding Al Hakam, and the name of the design project, what was it first called?"

Dr Taha replied:

Within my group, the Technical Research Centre, it was just called "Industrial Protein". But I now know the whole history and the engineering company had a number, "Number 324", which was the Al Faw Engineering company's name for Al Hakam. But I don't know if Al Faw or TRC gave it this number.

With those few words a mystery had been solved. Both US and Israeli intelligence had connected Project 324 with a biological warfare program; now we knew it actually referred to Al Hakam. More significantly, we knew that HEPA filters had been ordered for Project 324, and one thing we were certain of was that a yeast plant, which was what Al Hakam was purported to be, had no use for air filtration to that standard.

Hamish continued: "What do you understand by an 'absolute filter'?"

"It means 100% fresh air, devoid of any particles or chemical dust," Dr Taha responded.

"Why is there an absolute filter in the exhaust system?"

"Because when you are dealing with animals they may contract a disease, for example, chickens can catch Newcastle virus, so you have to protect the environment."

Absolute filters might filter the air absolutely, but we had just heard unfiltered absolute nonsense. If the chicken house at Al Hakam had filtered exhaust air to this standard, then it would have been the only commercial facility in Iraq, and probably the world, with such containment. In fact, the plans that Hamish had in his hands showed that the chicken house, "Building E", was not designed for that purpose, but as a laboratory. Dr Taha simply dismissed this as a change of plan.

The revelations regarding Project 324 and Al Hakam were followed the next day by other stunning admissions during a seminar meeting at the National Monitoring Directorate. With Aaron's information at the back of my mind, I asked about the tonnes of bacterial growth media Iraq had imported. Why did TSMID, the organisation exclusively importing for Salman Pak, purchase so much growth media? What need did Salman Pak, allegedly a research organisation, have for tonnes of bacterial growth media?

Dr Taha explained:

> It was not for Salman Pak ... TSMID imported them for the Drugs and Medical Appliances Company, in the Ministry of Health. They needed it for diagnostic testing, to check for diseases. What you received is the closest to the truth regarding actual imports.

I could recognise a lie when I heard it – diagnostic testing might consume a few kilograms at most, not tonnes. But I decided to move on. Why had TSMID imported for the Ministry of Health? – this was contrary to what we had been told before.

Ahmed Khudayyer, the former director of TSMID, answered:

> They [the Health Ministry] did not have the foreign exchange: it had expired. Therefore, they resorted to another way via TSMID

(we had foreign allocations). A request was made to TSMID and we would provide, through our foreign exchange. This also happens now and then. This is not an unusual occurrence.

The explanation did not gel with previous ones, but I thought we could follow up on that later. What I really wanted to know was the quantity imported. Aaron had given us some figures and Iraq was admitting to a few tonnes, but just how much more was there?

I said:

The quantities imported are large, whereas what Iraq has declared is small. For example, regarding casein, over eleven tonnes were delivered – this is specific information. Regarding yeast extract, Iraq said there were no imports, yet information available to UNSCOM shows that at least eleven tonnes were also imported, mainly in 1988–89. For peptone, Iraq says only a few kilograms yet our information says more than 3000 kilograms ... How much media did Iraq import?

Dr Taha did not deny any of this but became defensive about the total quantities: "TSMID can answer that. This is the closest to the truth that we could find ... We will check into the eleven tonnes of casein with the company and TSMID and we hope to reach that figure. We will try to verify the figures."

Dick picked up the theme of the quantities and Taha's claim that it was to be used for diagnostic testing. He asked the representative from State Company for Drugs and Medical Appliances (Marketing) why they needed tonnes of growth media. The SCDMAM representative explained:

Iraqi orders are bigger due to supply uncertainty, so please keep this in mind. We always ask for five years' supply of any item, such as spare parts. Suppliers always ask, why so much? Iraq is in an abnormal situation. During the Iran–Iraq war, we always made big orders for disposable items. Again, this is an unusual situation. We have no other recourse.

Dick could not help but remark: "You must admit that these media quantities are astronomical even for five years."

Looking slightly uncomfortable, the company representative shrugged: "Let us verify the quantities. This was the same quantity to be used for the entire medical spectrum."

I did not want to leave the meeting without trying to get more out of Iraq on the quantity of media they had imported. No doubt the figure they would eventually provide us with after "checking" their records would depend on how much they thought we already knew. I had two reference numbers for letters of credit, the promissory notes that banks pay out on delivery of the goods. I tried a bluff: "Perhaps it might help if I could give you some references to the letters of credit?"

This really caught their interest. I riffled through the pages in my folder as if it were stuffed with copies of letters of credit. "Ah, here is one!" I said, looking at my Bahrain Holiday Inn receipt. I read the number of one letter of credit that related to a purchase of growth media from Oxoid. For a moment I contemplated whether to give them the only other reference I had, or hold it back as a check when they came back with a list. It was like holding a weak poker hand but I decided to go for it. "Here is another." I read out the other reference and asked for the complete record of their letters of credit.

The bluff worked. Although Hossam Amin could not be sure exactly what intelligence we had, he decided to play safe: he knew that it would not go down well with the Security Council if we could prove that Iraq had imported media which it refused to declare. On the last day of the mission, Hossam Amin provided me with references to other bacterial growth media purchases. This revealed that another twelve tonnes had been acquired, on top of what we already knew. It also revealed another major supplier: Fluka, a Swiss company. In all, about thirty-seven tonnes of growth media had been purchased in 1988 and 1989, coincidently at the same time that Al Hakam was being built.

We wanted to know what had happened to all this material; as Dick had already pointed out, it was an absurdly large amount to acquire for diagnostic purposes. Hossam Amin had an answer for that as well. He told us that about half the media had been sent to pathology laboratories at seven regional hospitals, where there had been riots and the media stolen – approximately twenty tonnes in all. The remainder was still in the Department of Health stores in Baghdad. In confirmation of this he offered to provide us with Department of Health documentation, but these would take a few days to find and collate.

*

We returned to New York in early February, jubilant at the success of our mission. We now had evidence that Al Hakam was designed for a purpose that was more consistent with biological warfare agent production than with yeast production. We also had evidence that at least thirty-seven tonnes of bacterial growth media been imported by Iraq in 1988 and 1989, about half of which was now missing. To make matters worse for Iraq, it had given us an unbelievable story to account for the missing media. The coincidence of media being sent only to hospitals where riots had occurred, and the image of the theft of every single drum, led us to refer cynically to the episode as "The Great Media Riots of 1991". Rolf Ekeus accepted that we were onto something, although he thought that convincing some of the sceptical members of the Security Council would require even more evidence. But now we had many leads.

To increase the pressure on Iraq, Ekeus decided some publicity for our findings would be useful, and agreed to an interview with noted *New York Times* journalist William Safire; I was invited to participate. Safire seemed as much interested in the language of scientists as he was in the growth media, and we entered into a lengthy discussion about whether one referred to "media" as "medium" when it was in the singular. Once over that hurdle, he rather threw me with a question about whether Dr Taha was beautiful! In fact she was rather a dowdy, mousy sort of person but I was not about to tell Safire this and simply responded by saying that it was completely irrelevant what she looked like. But Safire was not finished with Taha and asked me whether we called her something like "Dr Germ". Now I could see tomorrow's headline: "The Beautiful Dr Germ: Iraq's Bio-Queen". I told him that I had never heard her called this, but in the *New York Times* the following day he referred to Taha as Dr Germ – a name that stuck in the popular press. We, the Gang of Four, never called her this. David had invented a far more romantic epithet: the "Desert Rose".

Safire did, however, capture the essence of our argument and wrote:[18] "Rod Barton, the commission's top bio-war expert, tells me that 'for research you need grams, not tons. This much cannot be for research. It was for production.'"

While we had been in Baghdad, Oxoid had replied to my letter, providing me with information about what it had sold to Iraq. I was interested also in what had been requested, even if it had not actually been provided. Perhaps Iraq had found another supplier, and this might give us an insight into what it had been planning. I called the contact number on the letter to speak to the sales manager. He was very helpful; although it was a number of years ago, he recalled the order because of its size. He said there might be more paperwork around somewhere and invited me to visit the company for further discussions. I readily accepted the offer.

Dick returned from Baghdad with the purported original growth media purchase documents at the end of February. If I had not already been certain these Department of Health documents were fakes, I was now. Apart from their pristine appearance, the serial numbers were all in sequence and the same ink appeared to have been used throughout, even though the entries were months apart: the documents were fakes, and clumsy ones at that. But in accordance with Ekeus's requirement for "solid evidence", I decided to apply a more definitive test. I sent some to the FBI forensic division to see if they could tell how old the ink was. If I was right, the ink would still be drying, or to be more precise, oxidising.

The initial results came back from the FBI within a couple of weeks. Without a sample of the original ink it was difficult for them to be certain, but they believed the documents could not be more than two or three years old. That put their writing after 1992, yet the imports of the media had been in 1988 and 1989. The FBI would do more sophisticated tests in an attempt to pinpoint the date, but this would take a few weeks. But even from the preliminary findings, the documents had to be fakes.

Later that morning Rolf Ekeus was to address the Security Council on the status of disarmament of Iraq, so I immediately went to see him, documents in hand. I explained to him what I had just learned and handed him the documents, suggesting that he strengthen his presentation on Iraq's BW program by holding them up, declaring them to be fakes. I could see he was weighing the pros and cons of this theatre, but took them anyway into the Council. In the event, he grabbed the newspaper headlines by telling the Council that seventeen tonnes of bacterial growth media had not been accounted for by Iraq, but he decided against using the documents. We should wait for the final FBI report, he suggested.

*

The pressure was mounting on Iraq. On 25 March, Rolf Ekeus returned to Baghdad to hammer out the major outstanding issue, Iraq's biological weapons program, with his Iraqi counterparts. Waiting in the conference room on that day were General Amer Rashid, Dr Taha and an assortment of other officials, including Dr Riyadh Al Qaysi, who was then the deputy Foreign Minister. We all sat down, the Iraqis on one side of a long conference table, with Amer in the centre and Taha to his left; and UNSCOM on the other, with Ekeus in the centre. Amer opened the meeting with a short statement saying that Iraq would look seriously at the issues and he hoped outstanding matters could be resolved.

Rolf Ekeus was blunt. He said that the atmosphere in the Security Council was hardening and there was increasing nervousness, especially now that the sanctions end game loomed. He emphasised that UNSCOM's approach was factual and scientific, but that doubts remained concerning the biological issue. After dangling the prospect of the lifting of sanctions, he countered with "there can be no thought of lifting the sanctions while the issues in BW remain."

Nikita Smidovitch presented our assessment of Iraq's biological program, listing as he went the information that conflicted with Iraq's declaration. He highlighted the problems we had with Iraq's accounting for the bacterial growth media and listed the difficulties we had with accepting Iraq's claim that Al Hakam was a yeast plant. He concluded by stating that the purpose of Al Hakam was to produce biological warfare agents, and that based on the missing media, "significant" quantities could have been produced.

Taha looked as if she had been eating sour lemons. Amer was clearly agitated and shouted:

> You should not listen to the lies that countries tell you. The intelligence you have been given has misled you – you should use Iraqi information to support your conclusions ... I tell you, there is no evidence that is contrary to our declaration.

With regard to the media, he said:

> You know, this media was ordered for one year for all the hospitals in Iraq. This was one tonne. Then his boss said, let's make that five years. So now it was five tonnes. And then that man's boss said, let's play safe and double it. So, ten tonnes. Then his boss, and his boss, doubled it again, so through these idiots we finished up with forty tonnes. It was a one-off mistake.

He then promised that everything would be made clear by Dr Taha's presentation on the following evening: "She will demolish all Mr Nikita's arguments."

The evening arrived and Dr Taha started her lengthy presentation. She argued that there had been a shortage of media for diagnostic purposes and gave figures for the numbers of diagnostic tests: "In 1989 the total number of tests in Iraq were 1,800,000." She went on, "The amount ordered was for five years. There was an exaggeration in the amount, not because of an 'idiot' but because of priorities and instructions from the World Health Organization." It seemed she had now debunked Amer's explanation and was arguing that it was really the fault of the WHO, a UN body.

Taha then went up to the whiteboard behind the seated row of Iraqi officials to explain that there was no way that Al Hakam could have consumed seventeen tonnes of media. "We just do not have the fermenters for that," she claimed. "With our equipment it would take 26.6 years to consume seventeen tonnes of growth media." She starting drawing up the calculations to substantiate her figures, while Dick and I, the only biologists in the room, followed her reasoning. I noticed that Al Qaysi was watching her intensely.

Dr Taha then moved on to the other issues that Nikita had raised. She argued that while HEPA filters may have been planned for the chicken house, they were never installed. She dismissed Nikita's argument that Al Hakam could have produced biological agents: "Where is the biological containment? Where are the double windows, airlocks, negative pressure? Your argument is totally unscientific!" She claimed that all of the other equipment that had been imported for Al Hakam, such as the dryers, was required for yeast production. She even argued that the filling machines that had been imported (but somehow now lost) were to be used to fill containers with biopesticide. I thought this latter argument was particularly creative since the "biopesticide" produced at Al Hakam was a powder, while the filling machines were pumps for liquid.

Dick addressed Taha's argument that the media was required for diagnostic purposes. He showed that the most Iraq could have used were kilograms and that this was supported by Iraq's own Department of Health figures. He pointed out that the types of media ordered were unsuitable for diagnostic purposes. Finally, he argued that growth media ordered for hospitals is normally supplied in small jars, not in the twenty-five or even 100-kilogram containers Iraq had imported.

We concluded at 11.30 that evening with a deliberate understatement by Rolf Ekeus: "There are still doubts in our hearts."

The next evening it was our turn to address the points raised by Dr Taha. I had the task of countering her statement that Al Hakam could not have consumed the missing seventeen tonnes of media. Dick and I had been working on this and we had agreed on a set of figures. I thought that it was important not to become too technical so that everyone could follow the arguments, particularly Al Qaysi. Ekeus believed he was attending as a sort of umpire who would weigh up the relative merits of the arguments, to see what, if anything, Iraq had to answer in the Security Council.

Just as Dr Taha had used the whiteboard, so did I. I walked around to the "Iraqi side" and began working through some very simple figures showing the number of fermenters available at Al Hakam. From this I calculated the amount of anthrax and botulinum toxin that could have been produced in them and the amount of media this would consume.

I had not got very far into my presentation when behind me I heard Dr Taha raising objections. I assumed it was another disruptive tactic and decided to ignore her. My presentation lasted about fifteen minutes and Taha kept up her objections to the end. When I was finished, I turned around to face her and to my shock, she had tears streaming down her face. I was puzzled and even somewhat upset at her reaction. Had I, in someway, offended her? I did not have long to contemplate the puzzle before General Amer Rashid directed a stream of invective at me – a mixture of threats and allegations of lies.

I scurried around to the relative safety of the UNSCOM side of the table and resumed my seat, which I figured was just out of reach of the fists of General Amer. While Amer poked his finger at me, berating me with claims of "outrageous" and "lies", I conjectured as to the nerve I had hit. Surely my presentation could not have been that much of a surprise? After all, Nikita had just yesterday explained our assessment and Dick had more than amply backed him up. It was to be a couple of months before the answer to this question became apparent.

Eventually Rolf Ekeus intervened and called for calm. He looked stunned; although we had told him of Dr Taha's previous breakdown in response to David Kelly's questioning, this was the first time he had witnessed such behaviour himself. Calm did return. General Amer, after a short consultation with Dr Taha, who was sitting next to him, said to me, "You claim that we have many fermenters at Al Hakam. They are not fermenters, they are mixing tanks." Dick and I had anticipated this, and I responded that we had experts who had inspected the tanks: there was no question they were fermenters and could produce the bacteria I had claimed. "In any case," I said, "Iraq has declared that these are fermenters." This elicited another outburst from Amer, "Who would dare say this! Tell me, who would say such a thing!"

We had also anticipated this rejoinder. As part of the monitoring arrangements, Iraq was required to declare the equipment present at each facility and we had copied the declaration for Al Hakam. It clearly identified the "tanks" as fermenters, and better still, Dr Taha had signed it. I looked at Amer and said quietly, "Dr Taha said they are fermenters. She signed the declaration." I slid a copy over the table to Amer, whose hands were shaking with fury. Dr Taha was now looking very stressed and cried out, "They made me sign it. UNSCOM forced me to do it!"

On that note the meeting wound up. It had been valuable because if Iraq had not previously appreciated that it had a problem, it certainly did now. We felt that if we kept the pressure on, it would only be a matter of time before Iraq confessed to a biological weapons program. But as it turned out, there were still a few bumps in the road.

*

Back in New York the reality of our stance hit me. We had accused Iraq of covering up a biological weapons program, but what if we were wrong? Although the evidence seemed overwhelming, could we be 100% certain? The stakes were high here: unless Iraq blinked, the sanctions, and all the suffering they entailed, would continue. I asked Dick whether he had ever woken up in the middle of the night with doubts. He said that he had momentarily entertained such thoughts, but he was certain that Iraq had had a biological weapons program. In this regard we were of one mind.

*

My priority now was a visit to Oxoid. A few days later, on 5 April 1995, I was on a plane to England to meet the company's Customer Services Manager, who for privacy reasons I will identify as Paul. I made it clear to him that we were not investigating the company, but rather Iraq's pattern of purchases. He then showed me a file that established that the company had sold twenty-two tonnes of bacterial growth media to Iraq in 1988. Normally the files would have been shredded after five years, but the orders were so unusual that he had kept them.

Paul also showed me the other sales the company had made during the years around 1988. Interestingly, Iraq's Department of Health was also making regular purchases of diagnostic media in amounts that might be expected for medical reasons. This seemed to demolish Iraq's stories that it had run out of foreign exchange and that there was a shortage of diagnostic media because of the war with Iran. Paul took me on a tour of the plant and when I reached the technical section I asked about the lifespan of the media. Almost indefinite was the

◁ Alleged Yellow Rain victim, showing marks on arm. June 1984, Thailand.

◁ On the Yellow Rain trail: the Ban Vinai camp for Hmong refugees in June 1984.

◁ Major Andreani, Colonel Sooch and Rod Barton at Bon Kai demobilisation farm, Somalia, in November 1993. Burnt-out drill rig in background.

Muharraq airfield, Bahrain, 1991.

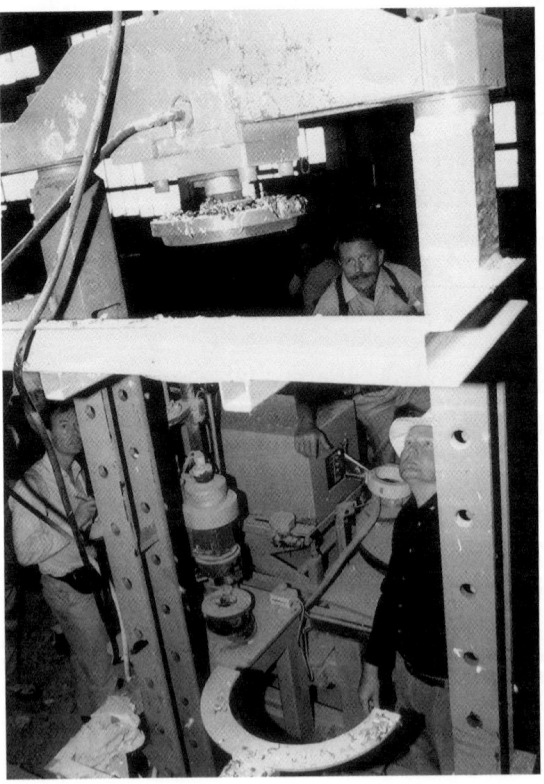

◁ Mosul sugar plant: the discovery of chemical bomb-making equipment hidden in a warehouse in 1991. From left: Rod Barton, Klaus Kessler, Hamish Killip. (UNSCOM)

◁ Al Muthanna chemical weapons plant, 1991. Leaking chemicals from mustard-gas production plant. (UNSCOM)

▷ Al Muthanna chemical weapons bomb factory, 1991.

◁ Rod Barton at Al
Muthanna in June
1991, holding a
Sarin rocket insert.

▷ Al Muthanna, 1992:
R-400 bombs (empty)
destroyed under UN
supervision. In 1995,
Iraq acknowledged
that these were bio-
logical bombs.
(UNSCOM)

▷ David Kelly and Rihab Taha at the Palestine Hotel in 1994.

Main entrance to Al Hakam biological weapons plant, 1995.

Rod Barton at the Oxoid bacterial growth media plant in 1995, examining media of the type sent to Iraq.

The 'Bunker' at UN headquarters in New York, mid-1999. From left: Dick Spertzel, Rod Barton, Oleg Ignatiev, Gabrielle Kraatz-Wadsack, Christian Seelos, interpreter, Ken Johnson, David Kelly, Hamish Killip.

Rod Barton at UN headquarters in New York, 2003.

Hans Blix (right) and Mohamed El Baradei speak to reporters as they leave the UN Security Council chambers on 19 December 2002. (AFP: Don Emmert)

Iraq Survey Group members entering Al Muthanna chemical weapons bunker in January 2004.

◁ Camp Slayer, the Iraq Survey Group headquarters. February 2004, Baghdad.

answer, provided the drums were stored undercover and were not opened or exposed to air or moisture. That was important information: any media that was still being retained could at some time in the future be used to produce biological warfare agents.

The trip had been well worthwhile. Now I had actual documentation that constituted "solid evidence" of the sort Rolf Ekeus insisted on: it showed not only the amounts that Iraq had reluctantly admitted but also smaller quantities that it had not yet acknowledged.

I felt I could not leave without asking Paul a question that was gnawing at me. What did *he* think Iraq was buying the media for? He answered that he assumed Iraq had started an antibiotic production plant or something similar, but admitted that he had conducted no checks. The answer did not surprise me. Although I had been studying Iraq for years and would have been highly suspicious of the reason for such purchases, I could imagine that to the company it was just another order, albeit a little larger than usual.

By the time I returned to New York, other companies had also replied to my enquiries. The Swiss company Fluka had provided us with the documentation of their sales of media to Iraq. Together with Oxoid, the total supply was just on forty tonnes, purchased from 1988 to 1990. This also debunked General Amer's claim that the purchase was a "one-off" mistake by a bunch of idiots. Also, by this time the monitoring team in Baghdad had completed a detailed audit of how much was in store. This task had not been easy because the material was scattered between stores at six different locations and labels in many cases had been lost or removed. The team had found about twenty-two tonnes, which meant that about eighteen tonnes were missing.

*

In April 1995, we had another visit by the Israeli intelligence officer, Aaron. We met again in my apartment on Fortieth Street, where he told us about some mysterious components that a German company had supplied Iraq through TSMID. The bits and pieces comprised small electric motors, steel mesh cylinders and other miscellaneous components. What were they for? The problem resembled a puzzle in which one has to put the pieces together to form a geometric shape such as a cube. In this case I was not sure whether I had all the pieces, but sketched what I thought the end-product might look like: a rotating perforated cylinder, along the axis of which a "viscous liquid" was to be pumped, to be spun out through the perforations as a fine mist. I had not seen anything like this before and showed it to my Canadian colleague, Ken Johnson. He said, "Oh, that's an agricultural spray. There are a lot of those fitted to helicopters at the agricultural centre at Khan Bani Saad." But what I had was not for spraying agricultural chemicals but for something more sinister. Perhaps I had just identified an Iraqi biological weapon system. A visit to the supplier of these bits and pieces was now mandatory.

*

Rolf Ekeus was soon back in Baghdad at the invitation of Tariq Aziz for more talks. None of us was sure what to expect. Initially, when the talks were planned, we conjectured, somewhat optimistically, that Iraq might tell us about its biological weapons program. However, in the interim General Amer had hardened his stance, quashing any such hopes.

General Amer's approach to the biological issue was soon felt. He made it clear to Rolf Ekeus that Iraqi experts would not talk to Dick and me, and that we were not welcome; we would not even be permitted to attend the UNSCOM–Iraqi chemical talks that were taking place at that time.

Dick and I checked out of the Rashid Hotel on the morning of 31 May, but before we could leave, a demonstration by hospital workers was held against us. Doctors and nurses were in the lobby of the hotel, with some holding placards saying "UN kills babies". Even worse, some were actually holding very ill babies. I tried not to look as I walked through this phalanx to reach the car, accompanied by the cries of "lies". To say the least, it was intimidating and distressing. But that was not the end of it. Outside, in the hotel car park, another "spontaneous" demonstration of "ordinary" Iraqis had been organised. As our Iraqi government car nudged its way through the crowd, people hammered on the roof and windows. I recall one old lady tapping a dried crust on the windscreen while yelling, "This is all we have to eat!"

Once clear of the crowds, Dick and I, who were in the back seat, relaxed a little, while the Iraqi Foreign Affairs official in the front smirked: all this had, of course, been orchestrated. Once we had negotiated the crowded suburban streets of Baghdad, our Iraqi driver gunned the big old Chevrolet government car to speeds in excess of 150 kilometres per hour on the open highway to Habbiniyah airport. Just after Fallujah, a truck suddenly pulled out of a side road, and our driver swerved into the median strip, the car slewing sideways for a time before the driver could regain control. It was a near thing.

The Foreign Affairs official turned around, leaned over the bench seat and said, "That would have solved the biological problem!" I assumed what had just happened had not been planned, and that the comment was merely a throwaway line. But given Amer's attitude towards us, the demonstrations and now this comment, it seemed clear to Dick and me that the Iraqis saw their "biological problem" as one caused by a handful of UNSCOM inspectors: if they could just get rid of us, somehow the problem would go away.

Iraq's policy towards the biological issue was to backfire on it shortly after we returned to New York. UNSCOM reported to the Security Council every six months about progress on disarming Iraq, and so on 19 June 1995, Rolf Ekeus was scheduled to present his next report.[19] To emphasise the biological problem, Ekeus decided to play down the outstanding issues in the other areas while laying it on thick in the biological field.

He reported that:

The situation in the biological area remains blocked by Iraq's refusal to address the Commission's concerns. The evidence available to the Commission establishes that Iraq obtained or sought to obtain all the items and materials required to produce biological warfare agents in Iraq. With Iraq's failure to account for all those items and material for legitimate purposes, the only conclusion that can be drawn is that there is a high risk that Iraq purchased them and used them at least in part for proscribed purposes – the production of agents for biological weapons.

And concluded with the statement: "Iraq's failure to account for its military biological programme leaves one of its essential obligations unfulfilled."

The debate in the Council following this report did not go well for Iraq: even its sometime supporters, Russia and France, called for Iraq to come clean about its biological program. It seemed the game might be up. Shortly after the report was tabled, Rolf Ekeus was contacted by General Amer and invited back to Baghdad for the end of June. Amer wanted to make "a statement".

*

Dick and I were to accompany Rolf Ekeus, but first we had other business in Europe. On 25 June we caught an overnight plane for Copenhagen to see one of Europe's biggest manufacturer of industrial dryers, Niro. The senior company executives told us of a visit by Dr Taha's deputy, Abdul Rahman Thamer, in 1989. Thamer had brought with him a sample of bacteria, *Bacillus thuringiensis*, a bacterial insecticide, which he wanted the company to dry in a test of a special "leak-proof" dryer. Even then, it seemed remarkable to me that Thamer could board a plane with live, anthrax-like bacteria in his carry-on bag.

The company had vast experience in drying a range of products and had no difficulty dealing with the request. Thamer left more than satisfied, and shortly afterwards TSMID ordered the special dryer. Before the order could be filled, however, a Danish government official visited company officials to advise them that although there were no export controls on this sort of equipment, it would not be a good idea to proceed; Iraq might be up to no good. The company readily got the message and in spite of letters of protest from Iraq, refused to supply it.

Based on what we had already deduced about Iraq's biological program, the conclusion was unambiguous: Taha's group, as far back as 1989, was attempting to dry anthrax on an industrial scale. We also realised that even without help from Niro, by 1995 they had actually achieved this goal themselves by their experiments with the biopesticide BT. With some slight modifications, the process could be adapted to dry anthrax safely. Dried anthrax has a lifetime of hundreds of years. By contrast, the liquid form, depending on storage conditions, may have a use-by date of between one and twenty years.

We were in a hurry and therefore did not have time to enjoy Denmark. Our next stop was Zurich, and the following morning we drove out to Chemap, a manufacturer of fermenters. Pulling up in the vast car park, it was clear something was wrong: there were only three other cars parked there. Mr Salfati, the company's technical representative, soon informed us of the reason for the absence of cars: the company was closing its operations in Switzerland to concentrate on manufacturing in Germany. Except for a few security guards, our host was the last employee and even he was to retire in three days' time.

Fortunately Mr Salfati still had the files relating to Iraq and could provide us with the information we were seeking. He told us that the fermenter supplied to Al Muthanna in 1986 (Taha's "biopesticide" program) had not been used until at least 1988. He could be sure of this because as part of the sale agreement a technician had been sent to Iraq in 1988 to commission the fermenter, which was then at Salman Pak. The technician commented that it was still in pristine condition except for a few seals which had deteriorated with time. On the other hand, from 1988 onwards the company had supplied TSMID with a stream of spare parts for other fermenters. Obviously Dr Taha's agent production group had been busy.

*

We met up with Rolf Ekeus and the inner "blob" in Bahrain on 29 June. In Ekeus's suite at the Holiday Inn we discussed what we might expect in Baghdad. Was Iraq really going to "confess" or would we hear yet another story? Opinions were divided. Both Dick and I had seen enough of Amer and Taha to believe that Iraq would not really come clean. At the same time, we now had enough evidence to hang them, so we also believed they would be forced to say something.

General Amer had told Ekeus that Dr Taha would be giving a ninety-minute presentation the following morning in the Military Industrialisation Commission's headquarters. He did not give any hint of what might be in this presentation.

At 10 a.m. on 1 July 1995, we assembled in the MIC conference room in a state of great anticipation. As usual the Iraqi delegation was on one side of the table, with General Amer in the middle and Dr Taha sitting alongside him. The deputy Foreign Minister, Al Qaysi, was sitting quietly at the far end of the table. The eight-person UNSCOM delegation sat facing them. By now we had learned that Dr Taha had married General Amer, and for a fleeting moment I wondered whether they might be holding hands under the table.

General Amer gave a brief introduction before turning to Dr Taha to ask her to read the prepared statement she had on the desk in front of her. The tension showed on her face as, hesitatingly, she read her script:

> To clarify the beginning of the biological program, we state here that the program began at the end of 1985 at Al Muthanna State Establishment. At that time Dr Rihab Taha was working on biopesticides in the aforementioned establishment.

She continued on in this fashion for a brief time, giving background information and curiously referring to herself in the third person. We still could not tell whether this was a confession or merely another wriggle. Eventually she said:

> In the first quarter of 1988, and after the success of researches in relation to *Clostridium botulinum* (botulinum toxin) and *Bacillus anthracis* (anthrax), a decision was adopted to prepare the requirements for producing biological agents.

Before she could read on, Amer interrupted, and gently corrected her saying, "No, not biological agents. Biological *warfare* agents." Taha read the sentence again with the insertion. So, Iraq had confessed.

She continued with a description of the program. She talked about the unsuitability of Salman Pak for large-scale agent (or "biological *warfare* agent", as Amer again reminded her) production because of its proximity to residential and agricultural areas. As a consequence, the Al Hakam desert site was selected. She described the construction of this, including the acquisition of equipment and tonnes of bacterial growth media. She spoke of the failed attempt to acquire the Chemap fermenters.

Finally, she came to the quantity of agent they had produced. She stated that it had been 9000 litres of botulinum toxin and 600 litres of concentrated anthrax, both in liquid form. For botulinum toxin she told us, "The total batches of production consumed about fifteen tonnes, plus or minus a tonne, of culture media." But she did not give a figure for anthrax production. As to the fate of all this material, she went on:

> Due to the threats of bombing the economic and scientific facilities in the autumn of 1990, the superior authorities gave orders to dispose of the biological agents, the biological warfare agents, to avoid contamination of the environment. We destroyed the agents with chemical inactivation and with heat; it took months to damage. By October 1990 everything was clean and we stopped work.

So there it was: in twenty minutes Dr Taha had confessed to a secret biological weapons program. I now understood the incident I had provoked just over three months earlier. Dr Taha had broken down not because we were saying Iraq had a biological warfare program, but because we had hit on the very details of that program. She may even have thought we had an inside informant. She then found herself in the impossible position of defending the indefensible. Back in March, General Amer had jumped to her aid not so much to defend Iraq's honour but to defend his recent bride's honour. It all fitted into place now.

I felt a curious mixture of elation and depression. Elation because we had finally forced Iraq to admit to a biological warfare program: our assessment was correct. Depression because I could not believe that this was the complete truth. It did not make sense that they would destroy their entire agent stockpile in August 1990, shortly after Iraq's invasion of Kuwait. If war was coming, why destroy a major weapon system?

I was also disturbed about the lack of reference to a weapon delivery system. Biological agent sitting in storage tanks for years could not be used unless there were bombs, rockets or spray devices to distribute it. The question of weapons was in all of our minds, and thus it was Rolf Ekeus's first question. "What about the munitions?" he asked. Taha responded immediately, "No never. There was not time enough to carry on with munitions." Amer helped her out: "With the events of August 1990, we could not have possibly embarked on this course. We just wanted to prove that we could produce the agent, but weapons did not materialise."

That evening we had a workshop with Hossam Amin and Dr Taha. When we reached the heading "Weaponisation", Taha stated flatly that there was "none". Nikita, who was leading for us, remarked: "I cannot believe you had no weapons."

Amin replied for Taha: "We did not even think about weaponisation of the biological agent."

Nikita could not contain himself, and with cutting Russian wit argued: "It would be logical after several years of producing agent to *think* of weaponisation. If you did not think of it, there must have been an order not to 'think' of it. Who issued that order?"

Amin waved his hand and, looking slightly uncomfortable, said quietly: "You must understand Mr Nikita that this is political. It is all political."

The remark from Hossam Amin told us there was a lot more that they were not prepared to disclose. Unravelling the ball of twine was not that easy; it still had knots in it that we needed to untangle.

*

In mid-July Dick and I were on our way back to Baghdad to examine Iraq's draft of its new weapons declaration. On the way we stopped off in Germany to visit more of the suppliers of Iraq. We particularly wanted to follow up on the few leads in our possession that suggested Iraq had in fact weaponised its biological agent. Our first stop was in a pleasant and leafy Frankfurt suburb, where we met Mr Kobarian, the head of a small family export company, Mecran.* We knew through the intelligence we had received that Mecran had supplied Iraq with

---

*   I have used pseudonyms for obvious reasons.

the perforated cylinders that I had deduced formed part of a spray device. What made the deal even more suspicious was that payment had come in the form of a suitcase of dollars delivered by an Iraqi Embassy attaché. Kobarian was immediately evasive. Yes, he had been to Iraq on a number of occasions, and he had arranged for the supply of many printed circuit boards to TSMID, but he could not remember much of the detail. When pushed, he seemed vaguely to remember that he had provided the cylinders and somewhere he had the paperwork but could not lay his hands on it.

Mr Kobarian's evasiveness was in sharp contrast to the co-operation we had received from the representatives of large international companies. I figured there were three reasons for this. Firstly, the gains for a large company selling odds and ends to Iraq were small beer compared with the adverse publicity they might receive for such sales. Secondly, large public companies declare earnings to the tax authorities, but I suspect Mr Kobarian may not have declared his suitcase of money. And thirdly, the big companies had been duped. The items they supplied were dual-purpose and Iraq had requested them under the guise of legitimate agricultural or health requirements. On the other hand, Iraq had provided Mr Kobarian with sufficient detail to suggest that the cylinders were part of some kind of weapon system.

*

Our meeting with the Iraqis at the end of July did not go well. All four of us knew that Iraq had only told part of the story: it was evident that the biological agents had been weaponised. Dick summed up our position: "I must say now in the strongest of terms, that unless there is a fundamental shift from the present draft [of the weapons declaration] it will not be acceptable to us nor, we believe, to the international community."

Iraq would not budge. Dr Taha dismissed our concerns: "There should be a confidence and trust between us because if there is no confidence between us, why all these meetings and talks ..."

We could see another crisis looming.

True Confessions

Events took another dramatic turn. On 9 August we received news from Baghdad that Saddam's son-in-law, Hussein Kamal, together with his brother, had defected to Amman in Jordan. During our discussions with Iraq, we had heard Hussein Kamal's name mentioned frequently. He had been head of the Military Industrialisation Commission, the authority under which the chemical, biological and missile programs had operated. In this respect he had been General Amer Rashid's boss, and it was clear that Amer still reported to him on UNSCOM matters.

Iraq now put all the problems with its weapons' declaration squarely at the feet of Hussein Kamal. We were told that Kamal had given orders to both Tariq Aziz and General Amer not to disclose certain activities. Now both had more information to give us, particularly in the biological area, including "another BW facility that UNSCOM had inspected but not understood."

Kamal was not only being depicted as a traitor, but also as a common criminal. We were told that he had stolen millions of dollars from Iraqi banks before his departure and had fled to Jordan with this money in suitcases. General Amer was said to be "shocked". Apparently the Iraqi government had asked Interpol to arrest Kamal to recover the money. Ekeus dryly commented, "This is very optimistic."

General Amer wanted immediate discussions with Ekeus and requested that he catch the next plane for Baghdad. Ekeus also received a phone call from Tariq Aziz requesting that he come to Baghdad.

Ekeus and the inner blob arrived in Baghdad on 17 August to hear the "true confessions" of Aziz and Amer. A couple of days later, over dinner at the Holiday Inn, Rolf Ekeus told the UNSCOM biological team, the Gang of Four, about his remarkable visit to Baghdad. We listened in fascination as he described the panic and uncertainty among the leadership in Baghdad, and their admission of a much larger and more comprehensive biological program.

Firstly, we were right to be suspicious about their previous statements on weapons: Iraq had weaponised biological weapons by developing both bombs and SCUD warheads that could be filled with agents. These were ready to go during the Gulf War. Ekeus was also given a curious briefing from a Dr Zubeidy, who had developed some sort of weapon involving rotating perforated cylinders that sprayed out biological agent.

Amer's reference to "another BW facility" was a reference to Iraq's Foot and Mouth Disease Vaccine Plant, which had been converted at the end of 1990 to produce botulinum toxin. The program did not end there, however: other facilities producing other agents were involved. For example, the toxin ricin had been extracted from castor oil beans and tested in artillery shells. A fungal agent, aflatoxin, had also been produced and weaponised. They had even developed anti-plant fungal agents as a sort of economic weapon. Furthermore, just prior to the Gulf War, viral agents had been researched, but Ekeus was told that the work had not proceeded very far. Finally, he told us that Iraq claimed all the weapons and agents were destroyed unilaterally in the summer of 1991.

But the most remarkable part of Ekeus's story was that, as he was getting into his car for the trip to Habbiniyah Airfield, Hossam Amin had suddenly come to him with a message that his people had found a stash of documents near Haidar, west of Baghdad. They were located on a chicken farm that belonged to the "traitor" Hussein Kamal. Amin claimed it had come as a complete surprise to discover that these documents actually related to Iraq's WMD programs.

On hearing this, instead of going straight to the airport, Ekeus diverted to Haidar Farm to look at the documents himself. There, in dozens of steel trunks, were plans, records of experiments, designs and production figures, as well as reports, manuals, photographs and video-tapes, all relating to Iraq's weapons programs. One container was different, a small wooden box inside which were documents about the biological program. On top of the box there was, conveniently, a red photograph album. It appeared to be some sort of photographic record of part of the biological program; perhaps it had been part of a presentation for senior officials.

Nikita, who was with Ekeus during this "discovery", had been waiting for this part of Ekeus's story, and theatrically pulled out the red book from a bag under the table. As we ate our meal of kebabs and tabouli, we passed round the album, with its photos of dead dogs, dead sheep, dead donkeys, fermenters and rocket warheads. It was a taste of things to come. Ekeus told us that Tariq Aziz had promised him full co-operation.

The change in atmosphere was immediately apparent to us when we met with the Iraqis the following week. At the opening meeting we were greeted by Dr Ahmed Murthada, now the Minister for Transport and Telecommunications. We had interviewed Murthada on a number of occasions, but always in his office. He had formerly been the Director of the Technical Research Centre, and as such Dr Taha's boss. But as he reminded us many times, he was in charge of three different facilities and Taha's program was just a small part of one of these. Now he was here as our "host", resplendent in his honorary general's uniform, sporting a large and impressive Saddam Hussein badge.

Another honorary general, Lieutenant General Dr Amer Al Sa'adi, later joined Dr Murthada. We had not previously met Dr Al Sa'adi but soon discovered that he had been Hussein Kamal's deputy at the Military Industrialisation Commission. He was now the scientific adviser to Saddam Hussein.

The meeting started well. Holding up the previous biological declaration by one corner as if it were the homework of an errant student, Murthada claimed it to be now "null and void". He then told us that he had instructed all employees not to conceal anything: "This is an order. And I will personally supervise it."

We then began a long and exhausting series of interviews. We made a good team, the Gang of Four. David Kelly, with his vast experience and his systematic and probing style, led the questioning. His particular subjects were Iraq's research and production programs. Dick Spertzel, with his tremendous powers of recall, focused on imports of equipment such as fermenters. He impressed with his knowledge of dates, order numbers and sometimes even serial numbers of machines. Hamish, a military engineer, specialised in weapon systems: biological bombs, rockets and spray devices. He was also our expert whenever it came to interpreting blueprints or design drawings of everything from a SCUD warhead to a chicken house. And I, with my background with the Australia Group and intelligence, concentrated on import organisations and routes. Ekeus also referred to me as the "glue" that held the team together, and given my occasional mediation between Gang members, there may have been some truth in this.

From the first it was apparent that Iraq was at last providing us with substantive information. We were therefore anxious to vacuum up as much as we could while the going was good, always fearing that the mood or politics might change at any moment. Eventually, after nine days, we had conducted over fifty in-depth interviews, and had seminar-type interviews with many others. We now believed we had a reasonably good understanding of Iraq's biological program.

Even we were surprised at the size and extent of Iraq's biological warfare program. Production had focused on three agents: anthrax, botulinum toxin and aflatoxin. Iraq told us that some 8500 litres of concentrated anthrax, almost 20,000 litres of concentrated botulinum toxin and 2200 litres of aflatoxin were produced and stored. These had been tested in bombs and small rockets, using the same systems as those used to weaponise chemical warfare agents. We actually knew the man in charge of this quite well. He was Brigadier Mahmoud Bilal, a rotund and amiable man from Al Muthanna, who in another world could have been a clown at a children's party. In this one his job was to supervise weapon tests in which animals were exposed to exploding bombs filled with anthrax or other biological agents: he was Iraq's chemical and biological bomb-maker.

What we found disturbing was the admission that over 150 bombs and twenty-five SCUD warheads had been filled with agents just prior to the Gulf War. These were hidden at various locations, including

Airfield 37, ready to be used if the order came. We were told that the reason they had not been used was only because Iraq feared nuclear retaliation by the US.

Even more disturbing was a crash program to make a weapon that would kill most of the Israeli people. The origin of this was said to be an Israeli newspaper report from November 1990, which described how 98% of the population would be killed if Israel were attacked with anthrax. The article came to the attention of Hussein Kamal, who then instructed the weapon scientists and engineers to make it work. The system devised was based on remotely piloted MiG-21 aircraft equipped with drop-tanks modified to spray anthrax. The program had top priority, and development work continued on it throughout the Gulf War, the modified tanks being moved constantly to avoid Coalition bombing. We were told that a series of trials were held in January 1991 but the system was never completed, the components eventually being destroyed.

Now that we were hearing "true confessions", we thought it a good opportunity to explore a mystery that had been bugging us from the very start of our investigations. According to our intelligence, just south of the biological facilities at Salman Pak, some seventeen trenches had been dug at the end of the Gulf War and items buried. We had unsuccessfully investigated this area and now we wanted to know what was there. Hossam Amin answered, "Bodies." Dispassionately he explained: "During the war there were many dissidents, Iranians, who were doing bad things. They were shot and buried in the trenches. Later we dug them up and buried them elsewhere. It is of no concern to UNSCOM."

We wondered whether these "Iranians" were ever actually used in human experimentation. We were never to find out.

During the confessions, we were surprised to receive a visit from General Faiz Al Shahine, the former head of Iraq's chemical program at Al Muthanna. He had in tow another general, General Hathem El Shaybani, who told us about the development of a "dirty" nuclear bomb. This was a weapon that was filled with zirconium that had been radiated in one of Iraq's research reactors, and which on detonation would scatter radioactive particles to contaminate the surrounding environment. We were a little puzzled that they were confessing this to a biological team and not a nuclear team, but as Shahine explained, "We wanted to explain everything, no matter how small that may be."

Eventually we returned to biological programs. In particular, we were curious why Iraq had developed biological weapons and why the scientists had agreed to become involved. Some, like Dr Emad, who was in charge of developing fungal toxins and produced the aflatoxin, said he had been a mycologist in the Ministry of Agriculture and was "invited" to participate. In Saddam's Iraq, he knew that such invitations could not readily be refused. Dr Taha told us that her involvement came during the war with Iran and that she saw herself as helping to defend the country; perhaps she saw herself as a patriot.

On why Iraq had developed biological weapons, Dr Murthada told us:

> During the Iran–Iraq war, anyone who came to us with an idea of a weapon, we would study it and try to develop it. The fact is that during the Iran–Iraq war, there were masses of Iranians attacking Iraq. I have to say that these masses, if they did not die, they would have been unhappy, because they know that by dying, they go to heaven. So it was masses of people attacking Iraq. Any idea that was presented to us to find a solution to this problem on our border of 1200 kilometres was welcomed.

Even though the war with Iran had been bitter, it was difficult not to be somewhat shaken by the cold-blooded manner with which Murthada had described the Iraqi desire to kill masses of Iranians. It reminded me of an earlier statement by Saddam: "God made only two mistakes: he created flies and he created Iranians."

David asked Dr Amer Al Sa'adi about Iraq's treaty obligations. Dr Al Sa'adi was frank:

> What are treaties worth? When Israel hit our atomic reactor, it was a transparent program, a civil contract that was well known. Everything about it was well known. Our intention was to go about this in a legal way under international safeguards … and what

happened ... in front of the whole world the reactor was bombed. But instead of the world condemning it, they were cheering it. What are treaties worth?

That mission brought to a close a major chapter in the story of Iraq's weapons programs: the ball of twine had been unravelled. From when we had first started as a team, it had taken almost a year to unpick Iraq's story a strand at a time. The work that David and Hamish had conducted on the peculiar design of Al Hakam had initially set Iraq back on its heels, but it had been the uncovering of the imports of the bacterial growth media, and Iraq's clumsy attempts at covering these up, that had delivered the coup de grâce. When I thought about it, we had forced Iraq's confession using meticulous detective work to uncover a paper trail of letters of credit, proforma invoices and inventory cards. In other words, we had exposed Iraq's biological program through accountancy, in contrast to the popular image of weapons inspectors bursting through a door to discover a pile of anthrax bombs. Bookkeeping had proven better than bluster.

Verification

BACK IN NEW YORK, ROLF EKEUS briefed us on his meeting with Saddam's son-in-law, Hussein Kamal, who had defected to Jordan. Ekeus kept the report of his detailed discussions with Kamal quiet since it contained sensitive information that might compromise UNSCOM operations if it became public. But he did tell us that it had been a strange meeting. Kamal, in a rambling presentation, launched into a diatribe against the regime, condemning various individuals. Only he had the true interests of the people at heart and he had done his best for them.

Interestingly, he said that his defection had been prompted by the crisis following on from our investigation of the biological program. He blamed Tariq Aziz for Iraq's policy of non-disclosure of the program. When we got close to the truth, Kamal's plan was to disclose some details in return for the lifting of sanctions. Ekeus speculated that when it became clear that the sanctions were not going to be lifted, Kamal not only lost face but also favour with Saddam. This was the opportunity that Udai, Saddam's elder son and Kamal's arch-rival, had been waiting for, and he closed in to oust Kamal.

On the weapons programs, Kamal seemed vague and he could not, or perhaps would not, provide much detail. It was also evident that he had little understanding of the science of WMD and some of the things he said were technically impossible. He did say that everything was destroyed on his instruction in the summer of 1991, but again he was vague when it came to details. He professed no knowledge of the documents at Haidar Farm.

It was difficult to accept at face value anything Kamal had told Ekeus about Iraq's weapons programs. Perhaps what he said was true, but we were uncertain of his motivation. It seemed he thought that he could rally the support of Iraqi opposition groups to overthrow the regime and install himself as the new leader. If that was the case, he might be giving us a version of the truth that suited him. We also thought that his plan to return victorious to Iraq was highly optimistic: Kamal had far too much blood on his hands to rally the support of Iraqi dissidents.

*

Regardless of what Kamal had said about the destruction of the biological agents and weapons, we still needed to be satisfied that Iraq's new biological declaration was correct. We, the Gang of Four, therefore immediately began the task of verifying it. It was the start of a long, difficult and sometimes interesting investigation.

Now that Iraq had admitted to a biological program, we arranged one last trip to see Aaron in Tel Aviv, in order to re-examine the Israeli intelligence in light of what we now knew. Dick and I made the trip a side visit on our way to Baghdad in February 1996. On our arrival in Tel Aviv, Aaron stunned us with the news that Hussein Kamal was back in Baghdad. The next day, while on our circuitous trip to Baghdad, we discussed the pros and cons of a request for an interview with him. It turned out to be a moot point. By the time we reached Baghdad, Kamal was dead. According to Udai's newspaper, *The Baghdad Observer*,[20] he was killed by "his cousins and family members who sought to cleanse their name of the shame his defection has brought about".

One of our Iraqi contacts told me a different story. Apparently Kamal had been lured back with the promise that he would not be harmed: "How could Saddam harm the father of his grandchildren?" Kamal's punishment would be that he would lose his rank and position, and live in a minor mansion. On crossing the Iraqi border from Jordan he was met by Udai, separated from his wife (Udai's sister) and taken to one of Udai's interrogation centres. There he was tortured while being questioned about what he had told the CIA and the UN. When they were finished, he was killed "in the most brutal manner possible" and his body fed to dogs.

Was this chilling account true? Given what we knew about Saddam's Iraq it was certainly more credible than the official line. The comment that he died "in the most brutal manner possible" conjured up all sorts of images. I had already heard stories of death by chainsaw, where, bit by bit, pieces are hacked off until the victim dies of shock or blood-loss; my informant said that Udai would have considered this too quick for Kamal. Iraq truly had one of the most brutal governments of the twentieth century.

We also wondered how it would affect our task; after all, both Al Sa'adi and Murthada had been close associates of Kamal. Would the regime still trust them? Our first meeting with Hossam Amin began with great tension, with the conspicuous absence of both Al Sa'adi and Murthada. Eventually Al Sa'adi strolled in and everyone noticeably relaxed. A little while into the discussions Hamish asked about the role of Hussein Kamal. The room went quiet, but Al Sa'adi smiled and asked, "Do you mean the late HK?" From then on, the Iraqi side reduced "His Excellency, General Hussein Kamal" to these two initials; they could not bring themselves to utter his name.

That February mission was one of many. The major instrument of investigation was again interview. Much to Hossam Amin's consternation we would interview not only senior scientists and military officers, but also workers such as truck drivers. Amin was often dismissive of these "lower levels", but they provided a different perspective, sometimes supporting the official account and sometimes not.

We also heard some odd tales. We had been trying to confirm Iraq's story that empty biological bomb casings had been thrown into the Euphrates River. In the course of this investigation we interviewed a farmer who had found a bomb floating in the river downstream from Al Hakam. The farmer dragged it out of the water and, not knowing what it was, thought that it would be ideal as a bridge across one of his irrigation ditches. It served this purpose for several years until his neighbour pointed out that it was a bomb. The farmer panicked: he knew he would be in trouble for having a bomb. But instead of handing the bomb in to the authorities, he shot it! Noting that nothing had happened, he pushed the bomb back into the river, where we found it – complete with two bullet-holes. This was one story that was strange enough to believe.

Another bizarre tale came from General Nizar Attar, the one-time Director General of Al Muthanna and Taha's immediate boss. During the inspection of Al Muthanna we had noticed that some of the "animal" cages looked more like prison cells, complete with bench-type seats. Had Iraq experimented on humans? The answer was an emphatic no. The cages were built for chimpanzees, which they had trouble acquiring. General Attar then told us of the story of his attempts to acquire them. He had provided two officials with a suitcase of US dollars and despatched them to a central African country to purchase the animals. After considerable time they succeeded in making the appropriate contacts but just before finalising the deal were told that only the President could give the final authorisation. This would require more money. It was duly paid, but more delays occurred and they finally were told that the President had changed his mind. No chimpanzees would be provided. By now they had almost run out of cash and so returned to Iraq. In spite of the usual desert heat, their reception back at Al Muthanna was not a warm one. We were assured that they eventually repaid the debt, but just how was not explained.

The interviews also gave us an insight into the personalities and pecking order of those involved. During one mission we interviewed at length Dr Emad, the head of the fungal toxin program, but still part of Dr Taha's staff. We were not satisfied that he was telling us the truth about his experiments with aflatoxin, a view reinforced by his constant changes of story. Finally, with both sides exhausted, we called for a break, but Dr Taha, who throughout the interview had been sitting quietly alongside Emad, could no longer contain herself. She started with, "I have to tell you something about this man." For the next five minutes she continued with a vicious attack on Emad. She called his work unscientific and implied that he was corrupt. All this time, Emad sat silently, while we listened in astonishment. During the break we could hear shouting down the corridor as the invective continued. Taha, especially now that she was a Minister's wife, was not the meek and quiet person she had once seemed. Later one of her staff confirmed that the little tirade we had witnessed was in fact typical of her style of management.

Of course, not all of our investigations involved interviews. David and Hamish re-inspected each and every site, some dozens of them, that had been involved in the biological weapons program: everything from laboratories to railway tunnels where SCUD warheads filled with biological agents were hidden during the Gulf War. They also returned to Airfield 37, which Hamish and I had inspected four years earlier. Our intelligence had been correct: biological bombs had been buried there. However these had been recovered in July 1991 and, according to Iraq, destroyed. Our team in November 1991 had therefore missed them by a few months. If UNSCOM had acted on the intelligence when it first became available, maybe the history of Iraq would have been different.

Hamish also led a team to dig up the site at Al Azziziyah where Iraq claimed it had destroyed the 150 or so biological bombs and twenty-five biological SCUD warheads. These had been destroyed in pits by attaching explosives and detonating them. The remains were doused with diesel and burnt before being covered with earth. On top of this, conventional bombs were then detonated to make the site look like an ordinary ammo dump. Hamish's team had to pick their way carefully through the debris in order to work out what was what, the task being made all the more difficult by the occasional unexploded bomb. The result was that many biological bomb casings, although not all 150, were recovered, as well as the warheads, all of which were forensically sampled. This did not quite confirm Iraq's story but it came close, except for a few anomalies. Of course, it did not help to resolve the question of how many weapons had been produced in the first place.

*

After a few months of investigation it became apparent that the real problem with Iraq's declaration was not the general story but its detail. Iraq argued that all of this had happened a long time ago and what they declared had to be drawn from memory. If details varied, what did it matter? What was important was that in July 1991 they had destroyed all the biological agents and weapons.

As reasonable as Iraq's argument might sound, we saw problems with it. Iraq's declaration of November 1995 was the third major change in their story, not counting all the relatively minor changes that they had made. After each declaration they had sworn it was the truth, but it turned out not to be. It was like the boy who cried wolf. Could we believe them on this occasion? Given Iraq's past deception, we required more than assurances, we required hard evidence. We could not go to the Security Council with anything less.

We were also aware that small discrepancies or inconsistencies might turn out to be highly significant. For example, Iraq declared that all production of anthrax and botulinum toxin had concluded on 31 December 1990. This was inconsistent with the practice at all other military production establishments, which had continued work until the outbreak of the Gulf War on 17 January 1991. Taha insisted the date was accurate – and what did a couple of weeks matter anyway? A simple calculation showed that given the size and number of fermenters available at the two production facilities, many thousands of litres of agent could have been produced in those two weeks. We also had witnesses who said that there was activity at these plants in January 1991. So a couple of weeks' additional operation was of undeniable significance.

Although a myriad of small issues required resolution, the one causing the greatest concern by far was the verification of Iraq's claim that all of its biological agents had been destroyed. The story was that these had all been deactivated and dumped just outside the fence at Al Hakam. The soil there was certainly contaminated with anthrax spores, but we could not quantify the amount, and their presence could readily be explained by the wash-water from the anthrax fermenters, since Iraq admitted that it had been disposed of in the same area. Truck drivers at Al Hakam also had a different story. They told us that they had taken the anthrax in containers to a desert site somewhere and dumped it. The issue was crucial because unlike botulinum toxin and aflatoxin, anthrax, under the right conditions, could be stored almost indefinitely, with little loss of potency. Perhaps bulk anthrax still existed hidden away somewhere.

*

By early 1996 we were well into the investigation of Iraq's new biological declaration, although it was clear that many months of work remained. In March 1996 my contract with UNSCOM would expire, and I decided to return home to remind DIO of my existence.

Before leaving New York there was one major task I wanted to complete. According to Security Council Resolution 687, UNSCOM was required to supervise the "destruction or rendering harmless" of all the agents, weapons, materials and facilities associated with Iraq's WMD programs. There were no biological agents or weapons left to be destroyed, but there were certainly materials and facilities.

Iraq's biological warfare plant at Al Hakam was destroyed in May and June 1996. The equipment was removed and crushed by bulldozers, the bacterial growth media was mixed with water and dumped in pits, and the buildings spectacularly blown up. The rubble was then bulldozed into pits, covered with earth and capped with a thick layer of concrete. Even the roads, power lines, fences and other infrastructure were ripped out and the site returned to the desert it once was. There was no prospect that any part could again be used to make biological weapons.

One question disturbed me about the work UNSCOM was now doing. When would we know we were at the end? Because of Iraq's record of deceit, the standard of verification we required was very high. Would we always be seeking another interview, another document, another forensic sample? I asked Rolf Ekeus this question, and for a moment or two he was lost for an answer. Eventually he said thoughtfully, "I think we would *know* when we had reached the end of the process." I suspect that he had his doubts.

*

I returned to Canberra on 12 March wondering what job I would have in DIO, or indeed whether I would have a job at all. DIO had a new Director, Major General Jim Connolly, with whom I spent a pleasant time chatting about Somalia. But neither he nor anyone else there seemed to have any plans for me; perhaps I had been away for too long. There had also been a shift in the focus of DIO towards Australia's immediate region and away from global issues such as the Middle East and WMD.

The conversation I had had with Rolf Ekeus before leaving New York was still disturbing me. There seemed no end game for UNSCOM and I could see the situation continuing indefinitely. I decided to write a "think piece"[21] for the Australian Department of Foreign Affairs as a basis for discussion, in which I identified the core of the problem:

> UNSCOM has now been operating for over six years under UNSCR 687, but cannot yet verify Iraq's declarations. This has largely been because of Iraqi attempts at concealment and lack of co-operation, particularly in the early years of the investigation. Within UNSCOM this has resulted, probably justifiably, in an atmosphere of mistrust of Iraqi statements. The real problem now facing UNSCOM is recognising when the verification phase is complete. Inevitably there will be discrepancies between information held by UNSCOM and the detail in Iraq's declarations; UNSCOM's assessment of the significance of these discrepancies is critical to the question of Iraqi compliance with the Resolutions.

I added that the position of the US complicated any peaceful solution:

> The US is working to its own agenda. US policy appears to be to destabilise the Iraqi regime to bring down the President and the present regime. In this regard the US sees the imposition of sanctions as an important tool ... the US would not change its policy on sanctions while Saddam Hussein was in power. In pursuit of this policy the US also attempts to influence UNSCOM to keep pressure on Iraq, most recently through aggressive and intrusive inspections. The US is likely to continue to exploit the inherent uncertainty in UNSCOM's findings to claim that Iraq is not in compliance. Even if Iraq were to make further disclosures, it is likely that the US would change the goal posts, as it has on previous occasions, and point to Iraqi non-compliance in other areas such as missing Kuwaitis, return of property, or human rights.

The solution, as I saw it, was for UNSCOM to compromise on past weapons issues in return for a system of reinforced monitoring to ensure Iraq could not rebuild its programs. As unsatisfactory as any compromise might be, it was far preferable to the alternative, that is, not having any inspectors in the country. I suggested that Australia, through DFAT, could promote such ideas within the UN. The paper concluded:

> Without a plan for the end game it is likely that the UN will lose control of the situation in Iraq (as it may be doing now), which in turn would have serious consequences for the ability of UNSCOM to monitor Iraq's industries ... The End-Plan outlined above takes into account the risks inherent in concluding UNSCOM's work ... while at the same time providing Iraq with incentives for continued co-operation as well as promising penalties for non-compliance. It tempers the stick with the carrot.

I received a polite and somewhat interested reception from Foreign Affairs. I sensed, though, that they were not going to take any action; perhaps it was all too difficult.

*

I did not have long to muse over my new circumstances in Canberra, for I was soon to return to Iraq as part of the Gang of Four. I continued doing this for the next six months, coming and going as required. It was a strange situation; with no job in DIO, no-one seemed to mind my overseas absences and, except for the occasional spark of curiosity, no-one seemed particularly interested in what I was doing. After returning from one mission in May 1996, I bumped into General Connolly in the corridor. He asked me how it had gone. It had actually been a more than usually difficult mission, with many tensions following a "purge" of six generals by Saddam. I looked Connolly in the eye and said quietly, "You know that in Iraq, they shoot generals." He saw the humour and quickly responded, "Ah, but they were all Lieutenant Generals. I'm only a Major General!"

The honeymoon period with Iraq was well and truly over. The Iraqis were becoming more difficult, refusing now to change any part of their story even when we had documentary evidence to the contrary.

On one mission in July 1996 we conducted the shortest inspection ever – one day in the country – after Iraq refused to provide the people we wanted to interview.

I eventually retired from DIO in August 1996, after more than twenty-three years in intelligence. I left with some sadness because the work had been interesting and sometimes exciting, but I had now been on most of the rides at the funfair and it was time to leave. However, my participation in UNSCOM was to continue.

Most of the inspections were now routine, but one did stand out from the rest. In January 1997, as part of another interview mission, we asked for a meeting to discuss the activities of a front company, the Arabian Trading Company, which was used to import materials for the biological weapons program. Dr Taha was to attend this meeting, as was Dr Mahmoud Bilal, the man responsible for weaponising both chemical and biological agents. Both were conspicuous by their absence. Eventually, near the end of the discussions, Dr Taha, wearing a smart dark-blue suit and clutching a patent black leather handbag, entered the room. She looked as if she had just been visiting the President – and perhaps she had. We learnt later that the reason for her absence had been to attend a Science Day Presentation at the Military Industrialisation Commission's headquarters, where she was awarded a high honour for her work. Dr Bilal received a similar award. It seemed highly incongruous that as UNSCOM was trying to rid Iraq of its weapons of mass destruction, Iraq was rewarding its top scientists for making those very same weapons.

The Death of UNSCOM

UNSCOM HAD A CHANGE OF LEADERSHIP in 1997. Rolf Ekeus was appointed as the Swedish ambassador to the US and Richard Butler replaced him as UNSCOM's Executive Chairman. I knew Richard partly through his work as the Australian ambassador on disarmament in Geneva, but more so from his time as the ambassador to the UN.

His appointment coincided with a new phase in UNSCOM's relations with Iraq. After its disclosures following Hussein Kamal's death, Iraq had expected rapid progress towards the lifting of sanctions. Instead the verification process became bogged down in an endless morass of disputes over gaps in the supporting evidence and inconsistencies. Frustrations on both sides were rising. I recall Dr Al Sa'adi telling us more than once that he saw no point in proceeding further; he was only continuing discussions "for the sake of the Iraqi people".

In response to the impasse, Iraq became increasingly uncooperative, even obstructive. On several occasions access to sites was blocked and requests for interviews denied. Of course this only heightened UNSCOM's suspicions that weapons or equipment were being hidden. To counter this, Ekeus had started a new series of inspections using Scott Ritter, an aggressive and abrasive former marine. Scott, in his own words, was the "alpha dog" and on inspection protocol he would tell his team, "We're gonna raise our tails and we're gonna spray urine all over their walls – that's the equivalent of what we're doing. So when we leave a site they know they've been inspected."[22]

In mid-1997, Scott began a separate line of investigation into the concealment mechanisms used by Iraq to hide its remaining WMD assets. Often it involved attempts to search the headquarters of the Special Republican Guard, the Special Security Organisation and the Mukhabarat (Intelligence), where access was almost invariably denied.

I soon learned that Scott's objectives – like the man himself – were more complex than they appeared. Once when he told me where he was going on his next inspection, I commented, "You will never get in there." His response was telling: "That would be an even better result. The international publicity we will receive by sitting in the car park outside the building will be far more valuable than gaining access."

His logic was that it would force the Security Council, and perhaps the US, to take action against Iraq. Scott was very much a man of action and was contemptuous of the UN way of doing things, which he saw as pussyfooting. In that sense he was the right man for the job, but to me he seemed too much like a loose cannon and I decided very early on that I would never participate in one of his teams. Although I liked the man, his approach was not my style.

In fact the Security Council did take "action", although probably not in the way that Scott would have liked. In response to Ekeus's complaints to the Council about Iraqi intransigence, the Council passed (or in UN terms, "adopted") on 21 June 1997 a new resolution[23] that condemned Iraq for denying access to UNSCOM teams. By UN standards, the wording was tough. The resolution demanded "immediate, unconditional and unrestricted access" not only to Iraqi sites, but also to individuals.

It also required the Executive Chairman to report on Iraq's compliance in UNSCOM's next report, in October. In language peculiar to the UN, the Council decided "to remain seized of the matter", meaning it would review what progress had been made following the next report.

*

It was in this difficult environment that Richard Butler took charge. He was not the sort of person to back away from a challenge and, perhaps going back to his rugby days, he decided to tackle the Iraqis head-on.

One of the instruments for doing this was Scott Ritter. More aggressive and intrusive inspections were lined up.

Butler's first major task was to report to the Security Council on whether Iraq had complied with the June resolution. While conceding that some progress had been made in the missile and chemical fields, he did not pull any punches when it came to Iraq's biological declaration:

The September 1997 FFCD [declaration] fails to give a remotely credible account of Iraq's biological warfare programme ... This is an area that is unredeemed by progress or any approximation of the known facts of Iraq's programme.

He detailed some of the problems:

Bulk [biological] warfare agent production appears to be vastly understated by Iraq.

Iraq's biological warfare field trials are underreported and inadequately described to allow for proper verification.

Interview testimony generally does not support the account as presented in the FFCD.

And, probably most serious of all, "Iraq's account of the unilateral destruction of all its filled weapons and bulk biological warfare agent in summer 1991 is incompatible with facts known to the Commission."

On Scott Ritter's investigations, Butler wrote:

In the period under review, the Commission has encountered a pattern of Iraqi blockages and evidence of removal and/or destruction of documents and material at "sensitive sites" under inspection ... The Commission strongly believes that relevant materials and documents remain in Iraq and that there have been highly co-ordinated actions designed to mislead the Commission.

Butler's report concluded with a request to the Council: "The Commission is convinced of the need for the Council to insist that Iraq meet its obligation to disclose fully all of its prohibited weapons and associated programmes. There is no substitute for this whole truth."

It was a report that the Council could hardly ignore. In response, the US drafted a new, strongly worded resolution and, with the support of the UK, tabled it in the Security Council. It went nowhere. The other permanent members of the Council abstained from voting, and for the first time since the inception of UNSCOM, the Council was split. This was exactly the outcome that Iraq wanted and it was to have disastrous consequences for UNSCOM – Butler or no Butler.

Almost immediately after the failed vote, Iraq accused UNSCOM of being stacked with CIA agents and refused to allow into Iraq any UNSCOM team with an American inspector on it. Richard Butler was now in a difficult position. The Security Council had not backed him just a month earlier and he saw that his only option was to cease all inspections and withdraw staff from Baghdad, except for a skeleton crew. Throughout October and November 1997, various delegations were sent to Iraq to help resolve this latest crisis and at the same time there was a build-up of US forces in the Gulf. After almost a month, Iraq again accepted US inspectors, but not before realising that it could bypass UNSCOM and Richard Butler.

It was not long before Iraq engineered another crisis. In contravention of several Security Council resolutions, it announced that certain sites, such as palaces and intelligence headquarters, were off-limits to inspectors. Scott Ritter's team tested this in January 1998, only to find that Iraq meant what it said. Again Richard Butler was sidelined. This time it was Kofi Annan who went to Baghdad in February 1998 to negotiate directly with Saddam. Although this resolved a serious crisis, including possibly military action, it was another disaster for UNSCOM. It resulted in an agreement on modalities for inspection of sensitive sites: inspectors would be permitted under certain circumstances, and only if accompanied by international "observers". Annan appointed an arbiter to oversee compliance with the agreement by *both* Iraq and UNSCOM. Butler was becoming less relevant to the process.

On his return to the UN, Annan was hailed as a hero, but not by the UNSCOM staff. The mood among the inspectors was one of despondency; there was a feeling that UNSCOM's days were numbered. I did not speak to Richard Butler about this possibility, but clearly remember him trying to contain himself when asked by a news reporter what he thought of Kofi Annan's intervention. "Masterful," came his response, dripping with sarcasm.

UNSCOM lurched on through 1998. In the eighteen months following Iraq's declaration of its biological weapons program in August 1995, more than twenty-five biological inspections had been conducted in an attempt to verify the declaration. But the inspections had gone nowhere and none of the issues we had singled out back then were any closer to resolution. Although the situation in the chemical and missile areas was slightly better, serious problems remained here, too. If this was not bad enough, Butler also found himself facing problems on the home front.

After Ekeus's more consultative way of management, Butler's sometimes blunt, authoritarian style was viewed with resentment by some of UNSCOM's senior staff. They believed that Butler did not give full weight to technical issues, perhaps because he did not fully understand them. One senior inspector told me that Butler had said, "You handle the technical issues, and I will handle the political issues." The inspector observed that the technical issues *were* the political issues.

In June 1998, Richard Butler attempted once again to take the initiative by meeting with Tariq Aziz in Baghdad to work out a new "road map". I did not attend this meeting but shortly afterwards watched an Iraqi-supplied video of the meeting. His plan was to work from the "top downwards", that is, to start with the major issues such as the number of chemical and biological weapons Iraq had produced and try to resolve these before starting on "lesser" problems such as the purchase of chemicals and equipment. The problem with this approach was that all the levels were interlinked; one level could not be resolved without resolving all of the others. Most, if not all the UNSCOM specialists considered the road map to be empty proceduralism and unlikely to resolve anything. Tariq Aziz, being his usual arrogant self, took advantage of the situation and challenged Butler to explain the levels. Butler floundered and had to turn constantly to the UNSCOM specialists, who provided him with only minimal support. The meeting was not one of Butler's finest.

*

On 3 August 1998, Richard Butler returned to Baghdad for a three-day review of progress on the road map. But Tariq Aziz had other ideas. At the opening meeting he asked whether the biological issues had been resolved. When Butler told him what he already knew, Aziz announced that the talks were over. Except for monitoring, Iraq would no longer co-operate with UNSCOM. And unless the UN lifted sanctions at the next review in October, monitoring would also end. For two months all inspections to verify Iraq's weapons declarations were cancelled, although routine monitoring inspections continued.

Butler's problems were to multiply. He scarcely had time to sit down in his office on the thirty-first floor of the UN building when on 9 October, Scott Ritter handed in his resignation. Worse than that, Ritter went public, accusing the US of white-anting his inspections of Iraq's sensitive sites. He claimed that the US had lost its will to confront Iraq and was therefore no longer supporting UNSCOM. He quit because he did not want to be part of an ineffective organisation.

With no inspections to conduct, Richard Butler invited the Gang of Four to New York in mid-October, to help prepare a white paper that would detail for the Security Council the outstanding issues. While we were there, the crisis deepened. At the end of October, Iraq ended all co-operation with UNSCOM, so that even the monitoring teams stopped work. We now had no insight into Iraq's activities; for all we knew they could have resumed their weapons programs.

We completed the initial cut of the white paper in early November and before returning to Australia, I discussed with Richard Butler the future of UNSCOM. By this time the US and the UK were building up their forces in the Gulf. Butler believed that Iraq's stance was not a bluff and that this time, it would not back down. The future of UNSCOM looked bleak. He told me that he had on a couple of occasions dusted off my "think-piece" on an end game for UNSCOM, written a couple of years earlier. Perhaps if both sides accepted compromises regarding verification, monitoring could resume. I remarked sadly that it was all a bit late for that now.

As it turned out, Iraq did blink. On 14 November, with US strike aircraft reportedly in the air on their way to Bagdad, Iraq backed down and allowed inspections to resume. But Iraq was now on trial and

Richard Butler was required to report by mid-December on whether it was co-operating. To test this a number of inspections – of various kinds, in all disciplines – were organised for early December. I was on one of these missions.

*

It had long concerned me that not all of the bacterial growth media had been accounted for. Of the original forty or so tonnes, I judged that about two were still missing. In percentage terms this was not much, but if it had been used for agent production, it represented a significant amount of anthrax. I raised the issue on a number of occasions with Iraq and the explanation was always that some had been lost through wastage and some stolen. The theft story was particularly intriguing. Taha claimed that during the Gulf War some tonnes of media had been stored at a safe location, a schoolhouse at Al Asmara close to Al Hakam. After the war, thieves had broken into the schoolhouse and many items were stolen or damaged, including most of the media.

Much of the story was true. We found among the chicken farm documents a report by Iraqi security police that detailed the theft of Al Hakam equipment from the Asmara school. It described the scene of the crime and listed in detail the many items that were stolen. However, no mention was made of the media. The "theft report" was addressed to Murthada and signed not only by the head of security, but also by Taha and her deputy, Thamer. The investigation of this was to be the subject of my mission in December 1995.

My plan was not to disclose the fact that I had the report until I heard what Iraq had to say about the theft from the school. Two days of interviews covered the storage of the media, the crime scene, how much was missing and, most significantly, how there had been no police investigation or report. Dr Murthada was indignant that I had even asked the question: "How could you ask for an investigation when there was so much chaos in the country following the war?"

I deliberately left the disclosure of the theft report until late in the evening. After leading them on for two days concerning the theft of the media, I felt a bit of a heel pulling out a report that showed that everything they had said was a lie. But that was what I did. I asked yet again whether there was a report, and after hearing "No!" I said, "Well, perhaps I can help you," and showed them the front cover. I then said firmly that the report was completely inconsistent with what we had heard over the previous two days. I told them who the addressee and signatories were, and pointed out that Dr Murthada had annotated it in the margins, indicating that he had seen the report.

There was an embarrassed silence. Dr Taha, staring at her notes, looked as if she might burst into tears. Eventually Dr Murthada recovered his wits and, looking down the table to Thamer, said, "This man can explain." Thamer was the proverbial stunned mullet: his mouth moved up and down, but no words came out. Since the point of the exercise was not to humiliate them but to get at the truth, I indicated that as it was late, almost 11 p.m., we could re-convene the following morning.

On the following morning, Dr Taha opened for the Iraqi side: "We did not sleep much last night thinking about the report." I smiled. I hoped that overnight they had consulted with Tariq Aziz about whether to reveal more, and I listened anxiously as Dr Taha continued, "We have two possible explanations."

Thamer then picked up the ball, explaining his involvement in the investigation of the theft, and concluding: "The existence of the growth media was so sensitive, I could not put it in the report." This was clearly nonsense. Using one of my favourite expressions, one which avoided undiplomatic language but conveyed the sense that what I had just heard was a lie, I said, "Now I am puzzled." I pointed out that the report was classified "Top Secret" from the security services to a general in charge of the biological program and marked for his eyes only. Rhetorically I asked, "If you cannot put the information in this report, where can you put it?" Taha suggested that perhaps there was another explanation and launched into her alternative. It was one of her typically convoluted stories, as unsatisfactory as Thamer's had been, and I told her so.

We were all aware of the significance of this mission. Iraq was on trial for its lack of co-operation and we had just heard lies and equivocation. We told the Iraqis that we were not satisfied with their explanations and that we could only assume that the missing media still existed or, more disturbingly, had been used to make undeclared biological warfare agent. War was just around the corner.

The reports from the other UNSCOM teams in Iraq were no more encouraging. By the standard of the last few years, the co-operation was neither worse nor better. It was not what was required if the outstanding issues were to be resolved and Richard Butler reported this to the Security Council on 15 December 1998. Again he highlighted the problem with documentation: "It remains the Commission's strong view that, under the present circumstances, relevant documentation must exist in Iraq and that provision of such documentation is the best hope for revealing the full picture." Damningly, he concluded:

> Iraq did not provide the full co-operation it promised on 14 November 1998 ... Finally, in the light of this experience, that is, the absence of full co-operation by Iraq, it must regrettably be recorded again that the Commission is not able to conduct the substantive disarmament work mandated to it by the Security Council.

Military action was taken by the US and the UK the very next day. Operation Desert Fox lasted four days, hitting many of the facilities that the US judged could be used to support WMD programs. I thought it was a pointless and mean exercise. Although I believed Iraq had not co-operated, I also believed that force was not the solution. On 23 December, the *New York Times* published an article[24] I wrote expressing my feelings:

> The US has justified its military action by saying it had no choice. But of course it did. The problem for the US was that if it did not act, its warnings would lose their credibility not just with Iraq but with all errant states. After two very public threats earlier this year, it was almost inevitable that Iraq was to be bombed last week if it put a foot out of place.

I argued that the strikes did not even reduce Iraq's WMD capabilities:

The damage done to Iraq's weapons' capabilities is probably marginal. It is almost certain that no bomb hit hidden stockpiles of chemical or biological bombs. UNSCOM had been searching for years for such arsenals and if the inspectors had not found them, then it is unlikely that the US, even with its impressive intelligence resources, would know where they were.

Harking back to my end-game paper, I suggested a possible solution:

* President Clinton has not ruled out future bombing missions but this is no solution and no-one wants a permanent state of war … There are no easy solutions to the Iraqi dilemma. What is required is some creative thinking … It seems to me, however, that chances have to be taken with any solution and perhaps now is the time to consider the phased lifting of sanctions, say over a period of seven years. This is not to reward Iraq but to provide an incentive to accept a strict monitoring regime to ensure that its industries are not used to rebuild its weapons. Failure to comply would result in the freezing of sanctions at a particular phase and restrictions on the amount of oil it could sell. At the same time tough import controls would be applied to restrict what it could spend its vast oil wealth on. Through a combination of carrot and stick, it's possible, just possible, that Iraq could be brought back into the community of nations.

*

UNSCOM was finished in all but name. Our people had been pulled out of Iraq just before Desert Fox; we now had no presence there and little prospect of returning. Our sensitive information stored at the Canal Hotel had been burnt and the hard drives from the computers removed and destroyed. We did not want to leave anything behind that revealed our knowledge of Iraq's weapons programs.

The future for Iraq was grim. Without compliance with Security Council resolutions it was highly unlikely that sanctions would be lifted. However, its economy had recovered a little after Iraq signed up at the end of 1996 for the UN's Oil-for-Food deal, by which Iraq could sell oil to purchase food and other humanitarian goods. All of this was supposedly under the strict control of the UN, but UNSCOM inspectors, who worked alongside the Oil-for-Food monitors, had little faith in the competence of the latter.

The fatal blow for UNSCOM came in January 1999 with revelations that in July 1998, Richard Butler had authorised the instalment of a "black box" in our Baghdad headquarters at the Canal Hotel. The purpose of this device was to intercept Iraqi security communications about concealed weapons. The problem was that since the incoming material was encrypted, all the data had to be transmitted to the US for decrypting. This gave the US opportunity to collect intelligence on Iraq and, as it turned out, UNSCOM received none of the information.

In a sense, the black box was no different to the U2 spy aircraft operated by the US for UNSCOM. Both were surveillance systems operated by the US on behalf of the UN, and the US had access to the products of both. The only real difference was that, for obvious operational reasons, the black box was kept secret whereas the operation of the U2 was known and had Security Council approval.

Given Iraq's behaviour in hiding or removing WMD-related equipment, I believe it was reasonable for UNSCOM to have installed the black box in order to uncover this activity. But Richard Butler should have been aware that the US would use the black-box intelligence for its own purposes and should have insisted on tighter control over this information. In my view, not to do so was a serious error of judgment.

UNSCOM's death was now assured. With the end in sight, the Gang of Four was invited to New York to write a set of papers, some might say obituaries, on the key features of Iraq's biological weapons program. The objective was to document everything we knew on these subjects so that any successor organisation would have a set of "manuals" to refer to. Throughout 1999 we wrote a dozen or more of these manuals.

Such was the reputation of UNSCOM in 1999 that when I mentioned to some of my former UNOSOM colleagues that I was still working for UNSCOM, I received the response, "Oh, I am sorry to hear that." It was not altogether surprising. Kofi Annan had already referred to inspectors as "cowboys" and "UNSCOM" was now a dirty word in the corridors of the UN.

Richard Butler's contract finished in June 1999 and Charles Duelfer, his deputy, ran what was left of the organisation. With the skids under UNSCOM, the Security Council did not even bother to appoint a new Executive Chairman. The Security Council was now considering replacing UNSCOM with a new organisation that would be more accountable to the Council.

I returned to UNSCOM in New York for the last time in October 1999. During a coffee break in the UN canteen, I asked my colleagues in the Gang whether they would want to be involved in the new organisation. I pointed out that with all the controls that were being mooted by the Council, it was likely to be a watered-down version of UNSCOM. However, given our experience we might be able to make it more effective. On the other hand, if it was too constrained in its powers we might not want anything to do with it. No-one was enthusiastic. Predictably Dick Spertzel said he did not want to be involved with a sham organisation that was there only for political reasons. David Kelly said that if the British government backed the new organisation, of course he would work with it. Hamish Killip, like me, was guarded and decided he would "wait and see".

We planned to meet again in December to complete the last few manuals but events overtook us. On 17 December 1999, the Security Council "adopted" a resolution[25] establishing a new organisation, the United Nations Monitoring and Verification and Inspection Commission, or UNMOVIC. UNSCOM was dead.

Working with Blix

WITH THE CREATION OF UNMOVIC, interest in Iraq evaporated. Apparently everything had been fixed. There were of course the usual squabbles, including about who should head the new organisation. The US wanted Rolf Ekeus to return. They saw him as a man who would not let Iraq off the hook, but who also had the diplomatic skills to avoid crises. The Russians, however, believed Ekeus would just return to the issues of old, the very ones with which Richard Butler had grappled so unsuccessfully. The Russian objective was to have the sanctions lifted so that Iraq could repay the nine billion dollars it owed to the former Soviet Union for military equipment supplied during the Iran–Iraq war; they saw little prospect of this under Ekeus.

The compromise candidate, who was found by Kofi Annan, was another Swede, Dr Hans Blix, the former head of the International Atomic Energy Agency. Blix was actually on an Antarctic cruise ship enjoying retirement at the age of seventy-one when contacted. He was appointed as the Executive Chairman of UNMOVIC in March 2000, more than three months after the creation of that organisation.

I was watching all this from afar. Although I did not envisage working for UNMOVIC, I was interested to see how Blix would tackle the problem. I had considerable respect for him. An international lawyer by profession, he had been a distinguished Swedish public servant before entering politics and briefly becoming Sweden's Foreign Minister. I knew him from his time at the IAEA. Many UNSCOM inspectors had been critical of the way the IAEA inspectors had

conducted themselves; the term "gentleman inspectors" was sometimes used to deride them. Even the Iraqis had said to UNSCOM
inspectors, including the Gang of Four, "Why can't you behave like the
IAEA? They do not challenge everything we say."

It was true that Blix's IAEA inspectors had not been as confronta-
tional as UNSCOM's, but they had achieved their objectives nevertheless. Maybe this was the approach that was needed in the new millennium.
Or maybe the whole debate was academic, because Tariq Aziz had
already declared, "Iraq will never again accept UN inspections."

Blix surrounded himself with people he knew and trusted, bringing
in Demetrius Perricos, the experienced inspector from the IAEA, as
head of operations. There would be a core staff in New York of eighty
or so people, and a "roster" list of a couple of hundred trained inspectors who would be called on to go to Iraq at a moment's notice.

*

I found myself returning to the subject of Iraq's WMD like a bee to a
flower, or perhaps more appropriately, like a fly to something less
pleasant. In 2000 I appeared before parliamentary committees[26] in
Australia to argue for a way ahead concerning Iraq's WMD. I told the
committees that, while there were still issues to resolve, Iraq was effectively disarmed:

> Largely through the work of UNSCOM, much of Iraq's capabilities
> in these [missile, chemical, biological] fields have been eliminated.
> While it is not possible to be too definitive as to exactly what
> percentage of Iraq's capabilities have been eliminated, it is probably
> in the vicinity of 95%, or more.[27]

My judgment was that any weapons Iraq might have retained from
its pre-1991 programs now constituted no more than a "retaliatory capability", that is, they enabled it to respond to an attack by an adversary
such as Iran. I judged that Iraq could not possibly have sufficient weapons to initiate chemical or biological warfare. Whether they had started
to rebuild their programs since the end of inspections in December
1998 was another question. But even here I did not think much could

have been achieved in the intervening two years, especially given the parlous state of Iraq's industries. In other words, Iraq was not a threat.

Appearing before the inquiries had an unexpected consequence. I mentioned to the committee secretary that I would be in New York early in 2001, and she asked whether I would talk to Hans Blix while I was there. The invitation was fortuitous: I had written a paper outlining a way ahead for UNMOVIC, a sort of strategic plan, and I thought such a meeting would be a good opportunity to give a copy to Blix. So I readily agreed to the secretary's request.

*

I took an instant liking to Blix. He brought a lawyer's analytical mind to complex technical problems, and I found his new way of looking at old problems refreshing. He believed that only with a fresh start could the outstanding issues be resolved, and said that in recruiting staff, he looked for experts unsullied by the UNSCOM mantle, "new eyes" as he called them. He told me that the UNMOVIC staff had been analysing the outstanding problems in order to define each issue precisely. This had resulted in a list of over one hundred "Unresolved Disarmament Issues". The next step would be to work out exactly what was required of Iraq if it was to address these issues satisfactorily.

Up to this point in the meeting, I had been reluctant to give him a copy of my "Strategic Plan for UNMOVIC". While presenting it had seemed a good idea in Canberra, I wondered how Blix would feel about an outsider telling him how to do his job. But now I realised we were thinking along the same lines. My plan actually took the process he had started one step further, by proposing that the significance of each Unresolved Disarmament Issue should also be considered. For example, if a biological agent had deteriorated over time to become ineffective, then although the issue had not been officially "resolved", it could still be dismissed. I had actually taken this idea from Tariq Aziz: it had been one of his few helpful suggestions.

As I passed Blix a copy of my plan, he handed me a copy of a study done by his staff. We sat quietly for a few minutes, each reading the other's work. Eventually he looked up and said, "I like your paper. What do you think of ours?" I told him I could see some problems and explained briefly what they were. He responded, "That is exactly what I thought. Would you go and discuss this with [the author of the study]?" I was taken aback at this and told him that I considered it inappropriate for me to do so. At the same time, I was impressed that he would take such direct action to fix a problem.

My next stop was Washington, where I met with a former colleague from the CIA, "Henry". My reason for seeing him was a piece of old intelligence that I had been given in New York by a *New York Times* journalist, Judith Miller. Judy had been trawling for declassified intelligence on the Internet and had found "Document 62856". At first glance it seemed nothing special: an unidentified source spoke of biological warheads and bombs hidden in 1991 at various sites in Iraq, including Airfield 37. We already knew that weapons had been hidden at these locations, and this had been confirmed by Iraq when they declared their biological program in 1995. I also recalled the inspection that Hamish and I had conducted at the end of 1991 at Airfield 37, in which we had missed the hidden anthrax bombs by just a few months.

What was interesting about the document was the date of the information: "Early August 1991". At that time only very few people in Iraq would have known where hidden biological weapons were; it would have been one of the most closely held secrets in the country. Obviously this was a source who knew what he or she was talking about. But what made Document 62856 really exciting was the reference it made to other containers of biological agent hidden in sheds at "Electronic Warfare Unit 114". This was a site we had never heard of. And if all the anthrax in these other containers were tallied up, it far exceeded the quantity Iraq had declared.

Over lunch, I told Henry that because everything in the document that we already knew about was accurate, including the references to Al Hakam, then it was reasonable to assume that the new information about the containers was also true. It seemed to me to be damning evidence for Iraq, demonstrating that Iraq's last declaration to UNSCOM was false. What I wanted to know was whether the source was still available and, if he was, could more detail be obtained? Henry also saw the significance of the information in the document and realised that it had been overlooked by his agency.

Soon after this meeting, I received a call from Hans Blix, who asked me whether I would be interested in joining his staff. He told me that although he wanted "new eyes", he also recognised that experience from the past would be useful.

On the way home to Australia I travelled via the UK, largely to visit David Kelly at his old farmhouse near Oxford. In this beautiful and peaceful part of England, the problems of Iraq and its WMD seemed to belong to another time and another world. Nevertheless, he and I talked for a day and a half on the subject.

David thought that UNMOVIC was crippled by its lack of experienced staff. "You have to remember", he said, "that the same people in Iraq have been dealing with these issues since 1991. They know all the tricks and will run rings round UNMOVIC inspectors." I told him about the offer Hans Blix had made and David encouraged me to take up the job. Not long after this conversation, David's phone rang. It was Alice Hecht, UNMOVIC's Director of Administration. It seemed an omen; she told me that she had been trying to get in touch with me on behalf of Dr Blix and had called David on the off-chance. She told me more about the consultancy with UNMOVIC, and I accepted the offer then and there.

*

The main work of UNMOVIC at that time was to identify the Unresolved Disarmament Issues by analysis of the massive amount of data available to it – mainly from the chicken farm, but also other information that it had collected from a variety of sources.

In my first meeting with Hans Blix, he told me that he was disappointed that after a year his staff had not progressed any further. By now he felt that they should be close to finishing, but instead they were only at the start. I said, based on my experience as an intelligence director of analysis, that work of this kind was far from easy. The database contained a million documents, and for people unfamiliar with the subject it would take time to work through them and reach conclusions. I told him of the Gang of Four's efforts in 1999, which had taken months even though we were very familiar with the subject matter.

Over the next months I co-ordinated the work on the biological UDIs. The assessments were debated by the directors of all the divisions, and other senior staff, in meetings chaired by Hans Blix himself before final acceptance. The process therefore had not just been an academic exercise designed to train the inspectors or keep them busy, but a real attempt to grapple with the issues that one day UNMOVIC might take up with Iraq.

The meetings also gave me an insight to the personalities that shaped UNMOVIC. Blix was, as always, the arbiter, listening carefully to the arguments on both sides and taking a very balanced, if sometimes legalistic, approach. Demetri, on the other hand, was volatile, challenging the analysts with questions such as, "Why am I wasting my time with this? This is not important. What does it matter if a few bits of equipment are not accounted for?" These were good questions: not only did they make analysts think, but they also prepared them for what they might expect if they ever got to Iraq.

*

I left New York in August 2001 to return on another contract with Blix in October. In the interim, the course of the world changed. September 11 was not only a tragedy for New York and the US, it was also a tragedy for Iraq.

Initially not much changed in the work of UNMOVIC. The focus of the work was still the Unresolved Disarmament Issues and by October, we had narrowed down the number of Issues to about 100 and completed assessments of about eighty. I had reserved the issue of anthrax to research and write up. The core of the assessment would be Document 62856. Interestingly, the document was no longer on the Internet; someone in the CIA had realised its sensitivity and pulled it from the web-page.

The year of 9/11 finished sombrely for me. On 31 December 2001, I completed the Anthrax Assessment and realised that it was hard to escape the conclusion that Iraq had retained a stockpile of anthrax. The CIA document was like the central piece of a jigsaw; once it was in place all the surrounding pieces that had puzzled the Gang of Four made sense.

All of the information appeared to confirm my tentative earlier conclusion: Iraq's biological declaration was false. It seemed that Taha's group had produced more anthrax than she had let on; she had used the so-called "stolen" bacterial growth media for its production; the anthrax had been hidden at "Electronic Warfare Unit 114" (a place we had never heard of); it had not been destroyed at Al Hakam as claimed; and we did not know where the anthrax was now. Contrary to what Tariq Aziz had told us, these were not just minor discrepancies in Iraq's story, but major and significant breaches of Security Council resolutions. And that is what worried me.

In October 2001 "anthrax letters" sent to various prominent people in the US, including Senator Tom Daschle, caused a number of deaths and nationwide alarm. Copycat hoax letters had also sensitised many other countries to the issue. Evidence suggesting that Iraq probably retained stockpiles of anthrax would now be highly sensitive, and its revelation could have serious consequences. I therefore decided not to disseminate the assessment among UNMOVIC staff for comment without first talking to Blix.

Hans Blix read the assessment and the supporting evidence on 3 January 2002, and on the following morning he called me into his office. He started with a rhetorical question, "How do we handle it?" The evidence spoke for itself and he was convinced that Iraq was covering up a major capability. In fact, he thought that I had been too vague in concluding that, "The ultimate fate of the anthrax is unknown." Based on the evidence, he suggested that a better conclusion would be, "There must be a strong presumption that the anthrax still exists." Strong words, but I agreed.

We discussed whether the US analysts would have drawn the same conclusion. I thought it possible, but they did not have all the information that we had. In any case, it was one thing for the US to accuse Iraq of hiding stockpiles of anthrax, but quite another for the UN to do it: in a post 9/11 environment, the consequences would be explosive. Blix thought that we should hear the views of Demetri and a few select other senior staff before we came to any decision. In the meantime I was to keep the paper to myself.

The most difficult question was whether we should present the anthrax assessment to the Security Council straightaway. Blix's personal assistant, Jarmo Sareva, summed it up: "We are damned if we do, and damned if we don't." Demetri pointed out that if we published the finding by itself, we might be seen as a tool of the US; the spectre of UNSCOM sailing too close to the US was still with us. On the other hand, if we did not publish, we would be accused of suppressing important information. This is when Dr Blix, Doctor of International Law, stepped in. He explained that under Security Council Resolution 1284 that established UNMOVIC, we were only required to "*address* unresolved disarmament issues"; there was no obligation on us to *report* those issues to the Council. A nice legal ruling, I thought, but surely not in the spirit of the resolution: significant issues such as this should be brought to the attention of the Council. But I was happy with the final decision, which was that the assessment would be put through the usual "acid bath" of scrutiny by UNMOVIC experts and published along with the other UDIs when they were all completed, in a couple of months.

*

On Tuesday evening, 29 January 2002, President Bush gave his first State of the Union address after 9/11. Bush opened his speech with the words, "Our nation is at war ... and the civilised world faces unprecedented dangers." On Iraq he said:

> Iraq continues to flaunt its hostility toward America and to support terror. The Iraqi regime has plotted to develop anthrax and nerve gas and nuclear weapons for over a decade. This is a regime that has already used poison gas to murder thousands of its own citizens, leaving the bodies of mothers huddled over their dead children. This is a regime that agreed to international inspections, then kicked out the inspectors. This is a regime that has something to hide from the civilized world. States like these, and their terrorist allies, constitute an axis of evil, arming to threaten the peace of the world. By seeking weapons of mass destruction, these regimes pose a grave and growing danger.

It was a powerful speech. There was no doubt that terrorism was a major challenge to the US and the world, but the references to Iraq struck me as strange. For almost three years Iraq had been on the back-burner of American politics; while 9/11 had understandably caused a tectonic shift, it was not clear why the new emphasis on Iraq "flaunting its hostility" toward America. Iraq had no apparent connection with 9/11, nor was it a state with a history of exporting terrorism, except perhaps against some of its dissident expatriates. It was true that Iraq's non-cooperation with the UN was of concern, but Bush was talking about something on another scale altogether. His speech seemed to amount to a declaration of war on Iraq.

If anyone had any doubts about the meaning of his words, he rein-forced the message two months later, on the six-month anniversary of 9/11: "In preventing the spread of weapons of mass destruction, there is no margin for error, and no chance to learn from mistakes. Our coalition must act deliberately, but inaction is not an option."[28]

And when President Bush referred to action, I assumed he did not mean by this another UN resolution.

The new US stance made the publication of our Unresolved Disar-mament Issues even more problematic. The Anthrax Assessment may have been the most controversial of these, but other issues also caused us headaches. Foremost among these was VX, the most poisonous chemical known to humankind. Iraq initially denied making any of this, but after UNSCOM found evidence to the contrary, Iraq declared that it possessed a few kilograms. When this was shown to be incorrect, Iraq declared that it had produced about four tonnes, but that was it, absolutely all. However, both UNSCOM and UNMOVIC had trawled through all the figures on imports by Iraq of precursor chemicals for VX; a lot was unaccounted for. More disturbingly, traces of VX had been found by UNSCOM on some destroyed bombs, implying that Iraq had not only made the agent but had weaponised it. Iraq absolutely denied this. Publi-cation of our findings on this issue would also play into US hands.

The question was, would the timing get any better? I thought not. In fact, I was now close to certain that the US was on a headlong course for war; publication of the UDIs would make little difference and at least then we could not be accused of a cover-up.

*

Iraq too was slowly waking up to the new crisis that faced it. On 7 March 2002, Iraq's Foreign Minister met with Kofi Annan and Hans Blix. Although Iraq had not yet agreed to the resumption of inspections, it was interested in which disarmament issues UNMOVIC considered to be outstanding. The inclusion of Blix in this meeting was highly significant; it seemed to me that Iraq might try to take the wind out of the sails of the US by making various concessions. After all, this was the technique it had used in the past: push the world to the brink and then step back until interest dissipates. But this time I thought that the trick might not work: the mood in the US was much changed from earlier years.

On 2 May "technical talks" were held in New York between UNMOVIC and Iraq. I was not directly involved because as one of the "old guard of UNSCOM inspectors", it was thought my presence might be misinterpreted. The talks tiptoed around the main issues. Iraq's main concern was not so much to resolve issues as to define them. Blix, quite rightly, absolutely opposed this approach because, according to Resolution 1284, it was UNMOVIC's role to decide the issues, not Iraq's.

Even at the time, I thought Iraq's cautious approach to UNMOVIC, and its reluctance to accept inspections, was a major mistake. With war approaching, now was not a time to try to negotiate what was, and what was not, a disarmament issue. If at that time Iraq had unconditionally agreed to inspections, it might have defused the situation. But Iraq had a history of misreading the signals and making poor decisions; this was just the latest case.

*

At the end of my second contract with UNMOVIC in May 2002, I returned to Australia on the understanding that I would take up another contract later in the year. I did not want to miss the latest developments; I was convinced a crisis was looming. After the buzz of New York and rumours of war, Canberra seemed a backwater when it came to world affairs.

While in Canberra, I was asked by several government agencies to discuss events in the UN. What struck me as strange in these discussions was the rather relaxed attitude to the building crisis. If war was to come, it seemed inevitable that Australia would be involved, but in June 2002 there seemed to have been little preparation for a conflict that might be only a few months away. Perhaps Canberra, too, was misreading the signals. I asked a senior colleague in the public service what the general view was. He told me that in his opinion the prospect of war was less than 50%; others thought that full-scale war, i.e. invasion, was unlikely – the US did not have the heart for the military cost of a ground war. Perhaps it was me who was misreading the signals!

*

The US continued to apply the pressure. On 8 July President Bush reminded Iraq that it was the "stated policy of this government to have a regime change. And it hasn't changed. And we'll use all tools at our disposal to do so."[29] Similar aggressive statements followed, and by September, Iraq seemed finally to have got the message: there were hints that it might soon accept the return of inspectors. There were also signs a new tougher UN resolution on Iraq was being drafted; both the US and the UK were lobbying for this.

On 12 September President Bush addressed the UN General Assembly. Blix attended the speech while the rest of us gathered in the "bunker", UNMOVIC's secure conference room, to watch it on the UN's closed-circuit TV. Like Blix, none of us was sure what Bush was going to say, although we expected that he was going to be hard on Iraq: in that, we were not disappointed.

The theme running through Bush's speech was that unless Iraq disarmed, action would be taken against it. He began by reminding his audience that, "We created the United Nations Security Council so that, unlike the League of Nations, our deliberations would be more than talk, our resolutions would be more than wishes."

He listed Iraq's violations of Council resolutions and the WMD activities that it was still engaged in. I noted with surprise that on the subject of biological weapons he told the Assembly:

> UN inspectors believe Iraq has produced two to four times the amount of biological agents it declared, and has failed to account for more than three metric tons of material that could be used to

produce biological weapons. Right now, Iraq is expanding and improving facilities that were used for the production of biological weapons.

These words made us wonder whether Bush knew about our new assessment on anthrax, or whether it was a general reference to earlier UNSCOM reports. The statement that "Right now, Iraq is expanding and improving facilities," came as a complete surprise to us: we had no intelligence to support this and wondered what he could possibly be referring to, since all the capable facilities had been destroyed under UNSCOM supervision in 1996.

Bush continued:

As we meet today, it's been almost four years since the last UN inspectors set foot in Iraq, four years for the Iraqi regime to plan, and to build, and to test behind the cloak of secrecy … Saddam Hussein's regime is a grave and gathering danger. To suggest otherwise is to hope against the evidence. To assume this regime's good faith is to bet the lives of millions and the peace of the world in a reckless gamble. And this is a risk we must not take.

In an apparent jibe at the Security Council, Bush asked: "Will the United Nations serve the purpose of its founding, or will it be irrelevant?"

He implied that if the Council did not take action, the US would: "But the purposes of the United States should not be doubted. The Security Council resolutions will be enforced – the just demands of peace and security will be met – or action will be unavoidable."

The presentation seemed to me a clear threat of war. But not everyone saw it that way. Blix told me that he believed it was primarily a challenge to the UN to act, and that war was far from inevitable, especially if Iraq gave in. I did not see it this way. Even if, as we believed, Iraq retained a few old weapons, and now surrendered them, I did not think that this would satisfy the US, especially when "regime change" was on the agenda. I discussed the meaning of Bush's words with some of the senior UNMOVIC staff. The question we pondered was when war would break out, and each of us nominated a date. My date in mid-October was one of the earliest; others took dates up to late December. The weather in Iraq, as well as various political considerations, coloured our predictions, but none of us doubted the inevitability of war.

The Iraqi hierarchy too seemed to be thinking along similar lines. Just four days later, on 16 September, the Iraqi Ambassador delivered a letter to Kofi Annan accepting "unconditional" inspections. But as Blix pointed out to me, Bush had not just asked for the return of inspectors, he had demanded disarmament.

Barely two weeks after Bush's address to the Security Council, the British government published its own assessment on Iraq's WMD.[30] This document, soon to become known as The Dossier, contained further revelations for the UNMOVIC experts. It echoed Bush's address, in that it asserted in unequivocal terms that Iraq had continued to produce chemical and biological weapons, but added considerably more detail. Regarding biological warfare, for example, it claimed that Dr Taha had started to produce biological agents in mobile facilities. And regarding chemical weapons, it stated that old facilities had been repaired and that "Iraq has continued to produce chemical agent," although it was strangely vague about where this had occurred.

The Dossier left us bewildered. Its conclusions were at odds with our Unresolved Disarmament Issues document and we wondered what intelligence it was based on. Hans Blix asked me to help co-ordinate our own analysis of The Dossier. Some of its contents related to historical information that UNSCOM had uncovered and we considered this to be fairly presented. Thus we had no objection to the idea that some agents and weapons might have been retained illegally after the Gulf War, although officially UNMOVIC's position was simply that they "were unaccounted for". As Blix often reminded us, "We must not jump to the conclusion that they actually exist."

However, we had real difficulty with The Dossier's assessment of recent activity: it was not that we disputed this, rather that we had not seen any evidence that this activity had actually occurred. Privately we were sceptical because reconstruction of some of the facilities would have been difficult to achieve under sanctions, but we conceded it might just be possible. What also struck us as strange was the unqualified language in the report. The renewed production was not described as "possible" or "probable"; it was stated boldly that it *had* occurred. This was not the usual language of intelligence assessment.

One statement that particularly puzzled us was the claim that some of the chemical and biological weapons were deployable "within forty-five minutes of an order to use them". It was clearly a key statement in The Dossier, one mentioned first in the introduction by Prime Minister Tony Blair and then repeated several times. But what did it mean? We debated this among ourselves. Perhaps it referred to the time taken to fill an empty warhead or bomb after the instruction was given. This interpretation was based on our knowledge of Iraq's past practice of not filling weapons until shortly before they were to be used. But this did not make much sense: how many weapons were being filled and what type? Perhaps the forty-five minutes referred to the time for the command and control release mechanisms to filter down from the President to the field commander. This did not make much sense either: surely in a time of crisis it would not take that long? Someone suggested it was the time taken to fire a SCUD fitted with a chemical or biological warhead. This was a possible interpretation because every SCUD takes time to prepare for firing, but it was hardly a fact worth highlighting. In the end we advised Blix that we did not understand the claim.

The 45-minute claim so bugged me that I made a mental note to ask David Kelly about it on his next visit to New York. Over dinner in an Irish pub on Thirty-Fourth Street, I had a dig at him about it. "Tell me, David, why did you write that Iraq could use its biological weapons within forty-five minutes?" I assumed, of course, that he would not have written such a nonsensical statement. He looked embarrassed and, trying to distance himself from the statement, replied, "Well I made my contribution on The Dossier, and others made theirs." I knew better than to push it and changed the subject.

A week later we repeated The Dossier exercise with a National Intelligence Estimate on Iraq[31] published by the US. Our analysis of the unclassified version of the NIE more or less mirrored that for The Dossier. Its conclusions were also couched in unequivocal terms: "Baghdad *has* chemical and biological weapons as well as missiles with ranges in excess of UN restrictions ..."

The UK and US assessments posed problems for the publication of Unresolved Disarmament Issues. Our paper would not only cover outstanding matters from the UNSCOM days, but also what I referred to as the Dark Years, that is, the period during which there were no inspectors in Iraq, from 1998 to 2002. Blix left this to me and by October I had prepared a rough draft of the section. Although the lack of intelligence had made it difficult to write anything with certainty, it now appeared that the UK and the US had information that might help.

UNMOVIC had a section coyly named "Outside Information Sources", which was the UN euphemism for intelligence collection. It was headed by a former deputy head of the Canadian Secret Intelligence Service, Jim Corcoran, who had established good relations with many intelligence services, including those of the UK and the US. It was now Jim's job to see what he could elicit from the UK and the US after the publication of their assessments on Iraq. We awaited the result of his efforts with great interest.

In early October we also received considerable intelligence material from a surprising source: the Iraqi government. At the beginning of the month, Hans Blix had held talks in Vienna with Dr Al Sa'adi on practical matters that needed to be settled before inspections could be resumed. Discussions revolved around issues such as landing rights, security of personnel, accommodation and transport. At the end of the talks, Al Sa'adi handed Blix several CDs comprising "semi-annual declarations". Under former UNSCOM rules, Iraq was required to provide, every six months, declarations on all sites subject to inspection. The declarations were to list – in standard format – equipment, materials, activities, processes and products at hundreds of sites of interest. What Al Sa'adi had given us was the backlog from 1998 to 2002, equivalent to about 10,000 pages of information, providing us an insight into the Dark Years.

Of course the backlog of declarations could be a tissue of lies, but with impending inspections that would be a foolish move: it would not take long for inspectors to reveal them to be false. On the other hand, the declarations were unlikely to be the whole truth: if there had been prohibited activity, we did not expect them to declare it!

*

It was about this time that security concerns arose within UNMOVIC itself. The UN is staffed with people of all nationalities, and there are no such things as "security clearances" for staff: who would "clear" them and how? Blix was already wary that his office might be bugged; given the interest in Iraq, and the stakes, there were a number of candidates for this. He regularly had his office swept for listening devices and his apartment was similarly de-loused. But to play it safe, sensitive conversations were not held there and he would go outside or to a restaurant on confidential matters.

Blix's concern over security was not mere paranoia: one incident I experienced showed that we really did have a problem. I noticed one morning that the papers in my locked cabinet had been disturbed. On closer examination I discovered that a paper I had been writing in relation to the UDIs had been taken apart and re-stapled. The re-stapled papers clumsily included one photocopied page. I immediately went to Blix's office to suggest we should talk, but securely.

Hans Blix, Jim Corcoran and I met in one of the most secure locations we knew in the UN: the Vienna Café in the basement. We discussed the incident and what to do about it. The inspectors' area on the thirtieth floor was accessible by a swipe card issued to UNMOVIC personnel employed in that area. There were also a few other parties with access, including the cleaning and maintenance staff and a few others. We considered putting the area under secret camera surveillance, but issues such as human rights came up; we were the UN, after all. Instead we simply changed procedures to avert further attempts.

By late October, a new Security Council resolution transmogrified from rumour to reality. There had been almost two months of behind-the-scenes negotiation to get the resolution that far, the sticking point being whether force should be "automatic" if Iraq failed to comply. The result was a compromise, but unfortunately the differences between Council members were papered over rather than definitively resolved. On 21 October Resolution 1441[32] was tabled in the Security Council for debate and was formally "adopted" unanimously on 8 November 2002. We had entered a new world.

It seemed to me that the sole purpose of Resolution 1441 was to legitimise war with Iraq: Iraq had effectively been "set up". The resolution did that by putting requirements on Iraq that would be near to impossible for it to fulfil and at the same time declaring that it was "a final opportunity to comply". At the outset, the resolution stated as a fact "that Iraq has not provided an accurate, full, final and complete disclosure" of its former weapons' programs and in this regard "Iraq has been and remains in material breach of its obligations." It then demanded that Iraq lodge a new weapons declaration. The trap for Iraq was what to put in its new declaration. The disclosure of a few old weapons, if indeed it had them, was not going to be sufficient. In fact, nothing short of everything that the US and the UK had accused it of doing, including admissions to mobile BW plants and aluminium tubes for a nuclear weapons program, would satisfy the US and the UK. And what if these allegations were not true? What should Iraq do then?

In my view it was almost impossible for Iraq to write an acceptable declaration and hence it would remain in "material breach". The crunch for Iraq came at the end of the resolution: it would "face serious consequences as a result of its continued violations". This was UN parlance for military action.

The resolution did not allow for the possibility that at least on some disarmament issues, Iraq might have been telling the truth. Even though UNMOVIC had painstakingly developed a list of "Unresolved Disarmament Issues", they were just that: "unresolved". Perhaps Iraq really had destroyed all its weapons and agents in 1991, as it claimed. But unless it could prove this, it would remain in "material breach". And the resolution stated that any "omissions" in its new declaration would constitute a "further material breach". Judging from the earlier declaration of its nuclear, missile chemical and biological programs, any new declaration would be over a thousand pages long and in such a sizable document it seemed likely that "omissions", if only inadvertent ones, would occur. The problems for Iraq were also compounded by the time-frame. Just thirty days after the passing of the resolution, Iraq had to provide a new declaration, not only of its weapons programs but also of any civilian program of relevance, for example a chemical factory.

Of course, Iraq had brought much of this upon itself. It had not complied with previous resolutions, and according to both UNSCOM and UNMOVIC it had not provided adequate weapons declarations. The evidence also pointed to retained capabilities from 1991, possibly including chemical and biological weapons. But the Council now seemed to be deciding that Iraq's punishment would be war. Why else put in the phrase "serious consequences"? And although the resolution did not make it clear how, or who, would do the enforcing, given that this was Iraq's "final opportunity" and that, in all likelihood, it would remain in "material breach", war seemed the inevitable outcome. This seemed to me to be grossly unjust.

Resolution 1441 added new dimensions and new pressures to our work. According to the resolution, the Executive Chairman, Hans Blix (and his counterpart from the International Atomic Energy Agency, Mohamed El Baradei), would be responsible for reporting to the Council whether Iraq was complying. We could therefore be the trigger for war.

Pressure of another kind was also put on Blix. Although many Council members had expressed full confidence in him, it was clear that the US did not share this confidence. US officials unfairly harked back to the failure of Blix as head of the IAEA to discover Iraq's nuclear weapons program in the 1980s. But the US went further still. It conducted an investigation into Blix to get the "goods" on him, to discredit him. The investigation came up with nothing. There was also a campaign in the US media to belittle him and headlines such as "UN Blix-krieg: Inspection Chief's the Wrong Man for the Wrong Job"[33] abounded in the press. Blix, in his typical cool Swedish manner, shrugged all this off, but I felt that he was somewhat stung by the comments, although he did not express this outwardly. On the thirtieth floor many of the weapons experts pinned up such press headlines in their cubicles in a spirit of defiance.

The new resolution also coincided with a leak to the press of the "Anthrax Issue". Under the headline "US Says Baghdad is Hiding Anthrax," the *Washington Times*[34] reported:

> US intelligence agencies have told UN weapons inspectors that Iraq
> has hidden 7000 liters of anthrax but chief Hans Blix never reported
> the information to the UN Security Council ... The failure to inform

the council has raised questions about whether Mr Blix will report accurately on anticipated obstruction of weapons inspections.

It added, for good measure:

The failure to alert the Security Council to the anthrax stockpile has upset some Bush administration officials, who said the information might have helped persuade some members of the council to support tougher US action.

There was no doubting the accuracy of the information. It followed my assessment fairly closely and I could not help but wonder whether the raid on my cabinet had netted more than I originally thought. If so, the nationality of the culprit was now clear. Of course there were other possible sources, but there was nothing we could do about it now. Unfortunately the leak did not help the credibility of UNMOVIC, or Hans Blix, at a critical time.

Among my UNMOVIC colleagues, "betting" on the date of the war's commencement was again being debated. I now thought that the trigger would be Iraq's weapons declaration, which was due on 8 December, and I picked a date a week after that. Others thought that inspections due late in November would bring on the crisis and nominated dates late in December. But there were plenty of other potential triggers throughout early 2003 and all of us acknowledged that anything was possible, except peace.

We also wondered what Iraq would do now. In fact, it accepted the new resolution. Hans Blix arrived in Baghdad with an advance UNMOVIC team on 18 November and inspections began under the stewardship of Demetri on 27 November.

I have to confess that I shared with the US some reservations about the competence of some inspectors. Hamish and Nikita Smidovitch had run a refresher course, officially for team-building, involving the mock inspection of a warehouse in New Jersey. I helped with the scenario, which was not meant to be overly challenging but would nevertheless test the team's powers of observation. Hamish even constructed a mock biological bomb for the team to find. Depressingly, the team failed to achieve even one of their objectives. The inspectors did not notice that the building had a basement, they did not get the names of the key workers, the chief inspector lost his "confidential" UNMOVIC documents at the site, and the biological bomb was not discovered. They were probably not much worse than the first UNSCOM teams to Iraq in 1991, but UNMOVIC had had two years to prepare and the stakes were now very high. I could only hope that under the guidance and experience of Demetri, their performance would improve when they were in Iraq.

Iraq also met the deadline for its new weapons declaration. At 8.05 p.m. on 7 December 2002, under the gaze of the international press, Iraqi officials arrived at UNMOVIC's headquarters in Baghdad with several cardboard boxes and a couple of bags of documents and CDs. On the following evening, in New York, a small team of about eight gathered in anticipation in Blix's office to receive them. My diary recorded the historic moment:

> Blix asks me to go in at 8 p.m. We receive Iraq's declarations packed in a blue combination locked suitcase. They do not look much compared with the TV images. Ewen [Bucanan – UNMOVIC's media officer] suggests a photo but typically for UNMOVIC, no-one is prepared and there's no camera.
>
> At a quick flip of the docs, nothing new seems to be there – perhaps 160 pages of non-proscribed programs. We inventory the docs until after midnight.
>
> I lie awake until 3 a.m. thinking of the consequences. War?

As my notes record, we flicked through the pages of the documents scattered across Blix's conference table. Among us were experts familiar with Iraq's previous declarations to UNSCOM, and we could tell that much here was direct repetition, albeit slightly reorganised. The real test was the summary tables and a quick comparison of these with previous declarations soon established that things had not changed. Blix looked disappointed; we all were. Most of us believed that Iraq would make concessions, would reveal something new, in an attempt to ward off impending doom.

The next day I organised an initial assessment of the documents, which comprised almost 12,000 pages. Of course it would take weeks before we could analyse all the data, but it was important that Blix had something he could say to the Council immediately. The assessment confirmed my initial impressions: there was very little new in the declaration, and what there was was of little consequence. Therefore Iraq remained "in material breach of its obligations".

Our in-depth analysis of the declaration, which I was also co-ordinating, was interrupted by another time-consuming task. Security Council members quite reasonably sought copies of the declaration; after all, if "serious consequences" were to follow, members wanted to judge for themselves whether these were justified. Distribution, however, was immediately blocked by the US because, quite reasonably, they argued that Iraq's declaration resembled a how-to manual for WMD. In particular, the US did not want some countries – such as Syria, which was then a member of the Council – to get any ideas. The compromise was that the P5 members, who were already nuclear states, would receive the full declaration, whereas the other members would receive edited versions. UNMOVIC experts would do the editing on the advice from experts from the P5 countries. We were given less than a week to consider the suggestions from the P5 experts and then "edit" the whole 12,000 pages of declarations; there were a few late nights.

Now that members of the Security Council had received copies of Iraq's declaration, Blix decided that he would brief the Council on our assessment of it, particularly in regard to its adequacy. Was it "currently accurate, full, complete", as required? Were there "false statements or omissions"? Blix called me into his office on the afternoon of 17 December to ask me to draft the section of the report dealing with our assessment of Iraq's declaration while he drafted the other parts including his plans for the future. He told me, "We must get this right, and choose our words carefully. It will be tricky because of the different interests ... I think it will be the most important presentation that I have delivered to the Council." After impressing on me the gravity of the situation, he asked whether I could finish something by 5 p.m. because he had a meeting then and would like to take it home to study.

I delivered by the deadline, wondering how much of the fate of Iraq hung on my two hours of work.

On the morning of 19 December, Blix was still fiddling with the wording right up to the last minute, before delivering this "most important presentation" in his usual measured and convincing style.[35]

He spoke briefly about how many sites in Iraq had been inspected (forty-four) and some of the problems we had encountered, before moving on to our assessment of Iraq's weapons declaration. He noted that Iraq maintained the line that:

> There were no weapons of mass destruction in Iraq when inspectors left at the end of 1998 and that none have been designed, procured, produced or stored in the period since then.
>
> While individual governments have stated that they have convincing evidence to the contrary, UNMOVIC at this point is neither in a position to confirm Iraq's statements, nor in possession of evidence to disprove it.

I had deliberately made reference to governments not providing us with intelligence. Since the publication of The Dossier and the NIE, Jim Corcoran had received a few bits and pieces from the US and the UK, but none of these scraps identified what was the source of the information in the dossiers. We therefore could not assess whether it was credible intelligence or just marketplace gossip. In any case we had not seen sufficient of this material to be convinced, even in part, of the US and UK claims.

Blix therefore concluded that there were outstanding issues, but that:

> In most cases, the issues are outstanding not because there is information that contradicts Iraq's account, but simply because there is a lack of supporting evidence. Such supporting evidence, in the form of documentation, testimony by individuals who took part, or physical evidence, for example, destroyed warheads, is required to give confidence that Iraq's Declaration is indeed accurate, full and complete.

I had thought it was time that we said something about the "Anthrax Issue", especially as our assessment had been leaked to the press. The full publication of our Unresolved Disarmament Issues paper was also now unlikely in such a charged climate. And so Blix said:

> In a few cases, there is information in our possession that would appear to contradict Iraq's account. At this point, I will only mention that there are indications suggesting that Iraq's account of its production and unilateral destruction of anthrax during the period between 1988 and 1991 may not be accurate. On this matter, we shall certainly ask Iraq to provide explanations and further evidence.

No decision was made about whether or not Iraq was in "material breach", since we had not yet conducted an in-depth analysis of Iraq's 1200-page declaration. This however did not stop the US Ambassador, John Negroponte, asserting that there were "material omissions which represent further material breaches". Negroponte's point was that Iraq had not admitted to all activities it was accused of in the NIE. So inevitably Iraq was in "material breach".

I believe that Blix's presentation to the Council struck the right balance. He was frank about problems we saw with inspections and declarations but expressed no judgment about Iraqi compliance. He successfully walked the tightrope of interests without leaning towards one member of the Council or another. Afterwards he told me, with humour in his voice, "I like the way you think. It's very much like me!" I too felt an affinity. We both liked the precision and power of words, and were careful in their selection.

*

My fourth contract with UNMOVIC finished a few days after Hans Blix's presentation. I was in Blix's office saying my farewell to him when he asked me about my return. It was a matter to which I had given much thought. My previous frustrations with planning and management had not been assuaged, and now that inspections were surging ahead full-tilt, no-one seemed to have time to handle the routine things that are essential to the efficient running of any organisation. So I told Blix that I did not think that I would take up another contract.

There was, however, another reason for my reluctance to return. UNMOVIC had become increasingly irrelevant to the political process, which was now leading inexorably to war. To the US, we were no more than a nuisance and if necessary we, and the UN, would simply be bypassed. If there was no point in what we were doing, why should I continue?

Before I left New York at the end of 2002, Demetri, who had already heard that I might not return, said to me, "You cannot stay away. You would miss all the excitement." He was right: it was in my blood now. I had been involved since 1991, since even before that if my intelligence experience before the Gulf War counted. I could not stay away.

Another War, But Not Just

BACK IN AUSTRALIA THERE WAS NOW intense interest in what was going on in New York. I was curious to know what Australian analysts had made of this. I gained the clear impression that they were not as convinced of the case for war as their overseas counterparts.

On the evening of 9 January 2003, a senior intelligence officer brought extracts of the latest Australian government assessment to my house for comment. I agreed with the wording on Iraq's WMD capability: it stated as "highly likely" (or words to that effect) that Iraq had small stocks of chemical and biological weapons. Although this went one step further than UNMOVIC (we said only that some weapons and agents were "unaccounted for"), it corresponded with what many UNMOVIC experts believed. On renewed WMD production activities after 1998, it suggested that such activities could have restarted but the language was not as definitive as it was in the public versions of the US and the UK assessments. Overall, the assessment seemed reasonable.

What I saw included no judgment on whether Iraq posed a threat. If I had been asked about this, I would have said "only to its immediate neighbours and only then if attacked with WMD". I strongly disagreed with Bush's characterisation of Iraq as a "grave and growing danger".

*

I returned to New York on 12 January 2003. Although I had little confidence that UNMOVIC could make a difference now, I thought that even a remote chance made it worth returning. But mainly I was returning because, as Demetri said, I could not stay away at a time when events were converging.

My first day back in the office was spent vacuuming up information from inspectors who had recently returned from the field. There were many stories, good and bad. On the positive side, about 100 inspectors were now in Iraq and almost 150 sites had been inspected.

On the negative were the bungles born of inexperience. There were stories of inspectors getting lost and asking their Iraqi minders for directions to the facility they were about to inspect. Any element of surprise was lost, along with the inspectors' credibility.

One story concerned a chief inspector who saw a drum of burning paper at the entrance of an inspection site. When his team members wanted to investigate, he told them they had more important matters to attend to, and that he would raise it with the Iraqis at the end of the inspection. But by then there was nothing left to investigate and the Iraqis feigned anger at his questions: "Why did you not raise this at the start? We could have investigated this ourselves and resolved the matter. The papers were probably just old documents that the workers were burning to keep warm." The Iraqis were up to their old tricks and testing the new inspectors to see how they would cope. Any weakness they identified could be exploited later.

These seemed to be isolated incidents, though. The real question was whether the inspectors were up to the task. Would Iraqi deception tactics be too great a challenge? UNMOVIC was now receiving many leads about "hidden" weapons or proscribed activities. If the leads were credible, were the inspectors sufficiently experienced and alert to detect whether a piece of equipment had been moved? Would they know whether a chemical production line had been switched from nerve agent manufacture to detergent production? It was true that inspectors had missed some things. For example, one team had inspected a warehouse but had missed illegally imported rocket engines that had been stored there. Fortunately, a later team discovered their presence. How much else had been missed? It was a hard question to answer, but overall I felt that if Iraq had restarted its weapons programs, the teams were good enough to pick up at least some signs of this.

Finding weapons or agents that had been hidden since 1991 was another matter altogether. In all the years UNSCOM had been inspecting it had not found any significant caches of WMD, so it would have been remarkable if UNMOVIC, in a couple of months, had found any – if indeed such caches existed.

What did concern me was the lack of any concerted effort to investigate the Unresolved Disarmament Issues. Resolution 1441 had specifically given UNMOVIC the power to conduct interviews with any Iraqi official. We had the right to "conduct these interviews inside or outside of Iraq" and "without the presence of observers from the Iraqi Government". But by early January UNMOVIC had not pressed for this, and unsurprisingly no Iraqi had volunteered for interview.

*

Another deadline was also looming. Resolution 1441 required the Executive Chairman of UNMOVIC to update the Council on the progress towards disarmament, sixty days after the start of inspections. Inspections started on 27 November, so the deadline fell on 27 January, when Hans Blix would give what would undoubtedly be his most important presentation of all. War was in the air and the tone and flavour of what he had to say would be crucial. On 23 January, Blix asked me to draft the section on technical matters, including our assessment of Iraq's declaration, now that we had collected data from inspections of more than 150 sites in Iraq; as before, he would draft the sections on Iraqi co-operation and UNMOVIC's plans for the future.

On the following day, Blix invited me into his office to discuss our drafts. With typical humour he said, "You show me yours and I will show you mine." We swapped drafts and he said we would meet again tomorrow, Saturday, with the senior UNMOVIC staff and some of the experts. We had to be sure that we could justify all of our statements and that the balance was right. That Saturday afternoon we discussed every word, every expression and every section in the draft.

Significantly, Blix rejected a suggestion I had given him for his closing statement. Our inspections to this point had found nothing to support the US and UK claims of renewed WMD programs. This did not prove they did not exist, but given further time to investigate, we might be able to state with some degree of confidence that they did not.

I thought, therefore, that Hans Blix should give the Council some idea of how much time we would require before we had this confidence.

Blix crossed out my amendment, saying that he did not want to ask the Council for more time. He felt that if he asked for, say, three months, the Council would then have high expectations of what could be achieved by then and would want some definitive statement on Iraq's weapons programs that he would not be able to give. With an air of exasperation, he said, "I wish Mohamed was not going to ask for more time." He was referring to the presentation that Mohamed El Baradei, head of the IAEA, was to give to the Council. El Baradei's draft concluded:

> We should be able within the next few months to provide credible assurance that Iraq has no nuclear weapons programme. These few months would be a valuable investment in peace because they could help us avoid a war. We trust that we will continue to have your support.

With the world's eyes on him, Hans Blix made his presentation to the Security Council at 10.30 a.m. on 27 January 2003.[36] He soon got to the meat of the matter when he addressed the question of whether Iraq had co-operated with UNMOVIC. Quite cleverly, he had divided the subject into "Co-operation on Process" and "Co-operation in Substance".

On process he said: "Iraq has on the whole co-operated rather well so far with UNMOVIC in this field." But even this positive statement was qualified:

> I am obliged to note some recent disturbing incidents and harass-ment ... We must ask ourselves what the motives may be for these events. They do not facilitate an already difficult job, in which we try to be effective, professional and, at the same time, correct.

And with typical Blix tolerance he suggested: "Where our Iraqi counter-parts have some complaint they can take it up in a calmer and less unpleasant manner."

The crunch came with Blix's comments on "Co-operation on Substance" (which I had mainly drafted). On Iraq's weapons declaration he said:

> One might have expected that in preparing the Declaration, Iraq would have tried to respond to, clarify and submit supporting evidence regarding the many open disarmament issues, which the Iraqi side should be familiar with.

And with respect to these "open disarmament issues" he said:

> They deserve to be taken seriously by Iraq rather than being brushed aside as evil machinations of UNSCOM. Regrettably, the 12,000 page declaration, most of which is a reprint of earlier documents, does not seem to contain any new evidence that would eliminate the questions or reduce their number.

Blix then listed, in each field, the problems with Iraq's declaration. For example on the nerve agent VX he said:

> UNMOVIC, however, has information that conflicts with [Iraq's] account. There are indications that Iraq had worked on the problem of purity and stabilisation and that more had been achieved than has been declared. Indeed, even one of the documents provided by Iraq indicates that the purity of the agent, at least in laboratory production, was higher than declared.
> There are also indications that the agent was weaponised.

On biological weapons I thought that we should let the Council, and Iraq, know that we had information that contradicted Iraq's declaration. Blix said:

> Iraq has provided little evidence for [its production of anthrax] and no convincing evidence for its destruction.
> There are strong indications that Iraq produced more anthrax than it declared, and that at least some of this was retained after

the declared destruction date. It might still exist. Either it should be found and be destroyed under UNMOVIC supervision or else convincing evidence should be produced to show that it was, indeed, destroyed in 1991.

I thought that these words might persuade Iraq to tell us the truth about what it had done with its anthrax. Blix also had much to say concerning missiles. This is one area where we had irrefutable evidence that Iraq was not complying with UN resolutions. Iraq had developed two missiles that exceeded the permitted range of 150 kilometres and had imported components in contravention of sanctions.

Blix summed up our views on Iraq's "Co-operation in Substance":

Our Iraqi counterparts are fond of saying that there are no proscribed items and if no evidence is presented to the contrary they should have the benefit of the doubt, be presumed innocent. UNMOVIC, for its part, is not presuming that there are proscribed items and activities in Iraq, but nor is it … presuming the opposite, that no such items and activities exist in Iraq. Presumptions do not solve the problem. Evidence and full transparency may help.

Blix's presentation had been tough, but it also had balance. It told the good – what little there was of it – and the bad. He reported that while we had not found any evidence of WMD, Iraq had not been forthcoming in its declaration and had not co-operated on the areas that really mattered. The most damning thing he said was that, on a few issues, UNMOVIC had evidence that contradicted Iraqi claims of innocence. And although he had said, "Iraq appears not to have come to a genuine acceptance – not even today – of the disarmament which was demanded of it," he had not gone so far as to voice a judgment on whether Iraq was in "material breach": this he would leave for the Council to decide.

Not surprisingly, both the US and the UK jumped on Blix's report to show that Iraq was not complying with Council resolutions. The US Ambassador to the UN, John Negroponte stated:[37] "The declaration was a fundamental test of co-operation and intent and Iraq failed it resoundingly." He summed up the US position by saying, "In short, Iraq is not disarming ... Iraq failed the tests set out by 1441 and is close to squandering its final opportunity." The UK Foreign Secretary, Jack Straw, was even more cutting, describing Blix's report on Iraq as "damning and disturbing" and saying that it showed a "consistent pattern of concealment and deceit" by Iraq.[38] Straw said he had reached the "inescapable conclusion that Iraq is now in material breach of Resolution 1441".

My impression was that Blix was disturbed by the way his 27 January presentation was received by the US and the UK. While of course the report was for the Security Council, the audience was also Iraq. By being blunt, I believe he hoped to convince Iraq of the need to co-operate. But it seemed he had expected a more objective debate from the Council, including a consideration of the steps, which he had identified, that Iraq could take to meet its obligations. The US and the UK had simply used the report to edge closer to war. My view was that, short of declaring Iraq to be in "material breach", it made little difference what the report said, and so it was better to paint the picture as it was, warts and all.

*

The US Secretary of State, Colin Powell, picked up on Blix's presentation in his address to the Security Council on 5 February 2003. In a statement that must have stung Blix, he explained that he had asked for the hearing before the Council

> to support the core assessments made by Dr Blix and Dr El Baradei. As Dr Blix reported to this council on January 27, "Iraq appears not to have come to a genuine acceptance, not even today, of the disarmament which was demanded of it."

Most of the UNMOVIC experts, myself included, crowded into "the bunker" to watch Powell's presentation on the UN's closed-circuit TV. I was watching the screen; I was also watching the reaction of the other experts. There were occasional hoots of derision or guffaws of disbelief, but mainly they listened in silence. In spite of US claims that much intelligence had been provided to UNMOVIC, most of the detail Powell presented was new to us.

We were not surprised to hear about Iraq's efforts to hide its activities from UNMOVIC inspectors, but Powell's revelation that Iraq had set up a special committee to deny information to inspectors, and that Dr Al Sa'adi, Iraq's counterpart to Blix, was allegedly a member of the committee, was new to us. Powell said, "Al Sa'adi's job is not to co-operate, it is to deceive; not to disarm, but to undermine the inspectors; not to support them, but to frustrate them and to make sure they learn nothing."

Powell went on to detail all the things that Al Sa'adi had denied us information about. We had heard a little of this before, but much was completely new. Bush and Blair had both spoken of mobile biological production facilities, but we were fascinated by the detail that Powell showed in the slides. I recalled the questions that David Kelly had asked Dr Al Sa'adi in September 1995 about mobile facilities. Al Sa'adi told us that in 1987 he had suggested such a system to Taha who rejected it as impractical. But Powell seemed pretty certain of his intelligence so perhaps Iraq had solved the technical problems, or perhaps Al Sa'adi had been lying then and now.

Few of us were convinced that the intercepted Iraqi communications established that Iraq was hiding chemical weapons: other interpretations seemed possible. But the satellite picture of a chemical storage depot at Al Mussayib and the associated intelligence was more convincing. The design of the depot recalled the chemical storage depots that I had seen on inspections in 1991. One signature feature was a specially fenced-off area within an already secure ammunition dump, and Al Mussayib had just such a feature.

What Powell had to say about Iraq developing long-range missiles, possibly with a range of up to 1200 kilometres, was no surprise: we had come to similar conclusions ourselves. His comments, however, about the development of small Unmanned Aerial Vehicles with ranges of up to 500 kilometres, designed for the purpose of spraying chemical or biological agents, struck the UNMOVIC specialists as unlikely. These or similar UAVs had been inspected by UNMOVIC; although they had the range, they were far too small to deliver an effective load of chemical or biological agent.

My contemporaneous notes on Powell's presentation gave it 8 out of 10, qualified with the words "for the intended audience" (the members of the Security Council). Powell presented enough of the intelligence source material to suggest that his assessments were well and truly backed up. With George Tenet (the Director of the CIA) sitting just behind Powell during his presentation, it seemed to have, both figuratively and literally, the weight of the CIA behind it, and many of my UNMOVIC colleagues and I thought the talk reasonably convincing.

If what we heard was true, then over the past two months Iraq had effectively evaded our inspection efforts: we had not got even a whiff of what Powell was claiming. If, on the other hand, it was not true, then I could not see that there was anything we could do to convince the US of this: they would simply dismiss us as incompetent. Either way, the march to war seemed unstoppable.

Powell's revelations also posed problems for my assessment of Iraq's activities during the Dark Years. To this point, my draft stated that although Iraq had the expertise to restart its weapons programs after the exit of inspectors in 1998, it would have had difficulty obtaining some of the equipment and materials to make this a reality. We had no evidence that Iraq had restarted its programs, but (in Blix's words) "the possibility could not be discounted." Now, however, Powell's words and the certainty with which they were expressed, painted a very different picture. But, in spite of his assurance to the Council that, "we are providing all relevant information we can to the inspection teams for them to do their work," we had seen little evidence. In what we had seen, no sources had been identified, making any assessment of its reliability near impossible. Based on Powell's presentation, I drew up a long list of requests for further information and passed it to the US via Jim Corcoran. I would not change my draft until I had seen the evidence for myself.

*

Just a week after Powell's talk, Blix was due to give another update to the Security Council, but this time he would write it himself. He asked me for some short factual notes that he would incorporate in his report, and on the afternoon of 12 February I went into his office to hand him my contribution. Before I left, he shoved across his desk the draft he had been working on. "What do you think of this?" he asked. I was dismayed at what I read and it must have shown in my expression. Blix commented, "You think I've been too soft."

The text that he showed me stated that Iraq had made genuine efforts towards resolving some of the outstanding issues and this was indicative of real co-operation. In fact, all Iraq had done was to provide a series of papers that again argued its case, particularly in regard to the unilateral destruction of weapons and agents in 1991. There was no new evidence or any documentation to support the arguments. I told Blix that the Iraqi papers were close to worthless: mere rhetoric and not real co-operation. Blix disagreed and said that at least now Iraq was addressing the issues and that this must count for something.

Blix made his presentation on St Valentine's Day. He had toughened the language a little, but overall it left an impression that at last Iraq was co-operating where it mattered. For example, he said:

> The Iraqi side addressed some of the important outstanding disarmament issues and gave us a number of papers, e.g. regarding anthrax and growth material, the nerve agent VX and missile production ... the papers could be indicative of a more active attitude focusing on important open issues.

He also referred to two Iraqi committees that had been set up to look for chemical and biological weapons, and to hunt for lost documents. Again, I felt that these committees were mere window-dressing but Blix told the Council: "The two commissions could be useful tools to come up with proscribed items to be destroyed and with new documentary evidence."

He tempered this with, "They evidently need to work fast and effectively to convince us, and the world, that it is a serious effort."

On interviews with Iraqi scientists he was also overly positive:

> The Iraqi side confirmed the commitment, which it made to us on 20 January, to encourage persons asked to accept such interviews, whether in or out of Iraq ... Three persons that had previously

refused interviews on UNMOVIC's terms, subsequently accepted such interviews ... These interviews proved informative.

These statements seemed to me to misrepresent the situation. Assurances by Iraq meant nothing and the interview of three individuals scarcely seemed a breakthrough. In any case, the three were from Iraq's National Monitoring Directorate, Hossam Amin's outfit, and were all trusted and loyal party officials. The information we elicited after some "token" interviews provided nothing of any interest and only a mental contortionist could view them as "informative".

My diary recorded, "I'm disappointed in Blix. Presentation to SC [Security Council] is very equivocal, with a few misleading statements. Gives the impression of Iraqi progress – nonsense!" I believe that Blix's positive tone was adopted in an attempt to promote the idea that Iraq was now co-operating and that if the Council were to give him more time, disarmament might be achieved. Indeed, he concluded by saying: "The period of disarmament through inspection could still be short, if 'immediate, active and unconditional co-operation' with UNMOVIC and the IAEA were to be forthcoming," although he fell short of actually asking for more time.

Blix's St Valentine's talk was largely ignored by the US and the UK, with Britain's Foreign Secretary, Jack Straw,[39] claiming after the talk that Iraq had "failed substantively to meet the obligations imposed on them". Now there was a steady stream of ambassadors of all persuasions treading a path to Blix's office to present their views. Blix would listen to them politely as was his wont, but he was not going to be influenced either way to write or say anything that he did not believe.

The US media also picked up the pace of its attacks on Blix, but he now seemed immune to even the most vicious commentary, occasionally commenting good-humouredly on a particular item. Some of it was inventively witty, such as the dialogue I jotted down from a Fox News Commentary of 16 February:

If I was re-incarnated, I would want to return as Blix's son. Then when I hadn't done my homework, I would not be punished, he would just say "Look at the positive side – look at what you have done." [A reference to Blix's St Valentine's Day speech.]

In the meantime the New York UNMOVIC staff was busy trying to complete its own dossier on Iraq, the updated report on Unresolved Disarmament Issues, now renamed the Clusters Document. By mid-February we were close to a final version, which we passed to the members of College of Commissioners, UNMOVIC's guiding body, for comment. The Commissioners were due to meet for a special session in New York on 25 February to discuss it and the way ahead for UNMOVIC.

*

The Commissioners' meetings were usually staid affairs. Commissioners from the P5 would sometimes put forward opposing views as if it were a mini-Security Council, but since there was no vote (it was only an advisory body), matters would not proceed much beyond that. The 25 February meeting, however, turned out very differently.

A hint of what to come was given in the morning session. Hans Blix, as chairman, suggested that each delegate speak briefly on the Unresolved Disarmament Issues (Clusters) Document, so that there would be a basis for debate during the afternoon session. One by one the Commissioners spoke, and eventually the baton was passed to John Wolf, the US Commissioner and Assistant Secretary of Defense. He immediately pounced on the Dark Years section:

> The Cluster Document is eloquent testimony to Iraq's deceit, cheat and retreat. But you [Blix] said that that the Document includes all issues. I differ. We don't know what happened from 1998 to 2003. There are only two-and-a-half pages on new issues; for example, on mobile biological facilities, one paragraph. Are we to imagine that Iraqi cheating stopped in 1998?
>
> ... the Document is not complete, and not adequate for the period up to 2003. There is no reference to the material Secretary Powell provided in his presentation, for example, small UAVs.

I was sitting at the side of the room, quietly listening to the discussion and wondering what changes I could, or should, make to my draft concerning the Dark Years. In spite of our requests for more detailed intelligence from the US, we had received nothing of significance and it seemed unlikely now that we would. I was well aware that information about sources could be too sensitive to entrust to a porous body like the UN, especially if lives were at risk.

On the other hand, I also wondered whether there was a more sinister reason for the US not giving us source material. As a professional analyst, I was aware that intelligence is often open to interpretation. Perhaps we would not agree with the US. For example, on mobile facilities, UNMOVIC inspectors had already seen mobile health laboratories. Were the US sources mistakenly interpreting these as biological warfare production facilities? If we knocked a hole in any part of the US intelligence, the edifice could come tumbling down and the rationale for war might disappear.

After lunch the meeting resumed. I noticed that Wolf and the UK Commissioner, Bryan Wells, entered the room together and were engrossed in some intense discussion. Not long into the meeting Wolf asserted again that our treatment of the Dark Years was inadequate. This time, however, his tone was more accusatorial and his language less temperate. Pointing to Blix, he said:

> You have addressed the pre-1998 issues only, and an entire universe needs to be considered … The US government has shared information with you that shows gross violations by Iraq, that you have chosen to ignore. We have told you about UAVs that have a range of 500 kilometres but there is not one mention of this. We have told you about mobile labs that have recently produced biological agent, again no mention. You have not done your job.

Wolf continued on in this vein until Blix interrupted him. For the first and only time in my experience, Blix seemed upset and did not hide his feelings. He responded, perhaps a little unwisely, "We have heard what the US has said, but we can no more accept these statements without evidence than we can accept what Iraq has said without evidence."

The apparent (but unintended) comparison between the honesty of Iraq and the US sent Wolf into a spin. Like most at the meeting, I was stunned by the exchange. Wolf responded heatedly by defending the honour of his country, asking Blix how he could compare the US with Iraq, a country with a long record of lying and cheating. He then turned the attack back on Blix and accused him of following only Resolution 1284 while ignoring Resolution 1441. This last jibe was a cutting insult to Hans Blix, who as a top international public servant and international lawyer had spent many hours analysing exactly what he was required to do under the various resolutions. Everyone at the meeting understood that Wolf was really accusing Blix of being soft on Iraq, by focusing on the moderate language of 1284 rather than using the tough provisions of 1441 that started with the "fact" that Iraq was in material breach.

Blix snapped back, "I object to that. I am fully aware of my responsibilities. I act in accordance with both resolutions."

Blix was not yet clear of the sharks and after the exchange with Wolf, Bryan Wells, the UK Commissioner, immediately circled in for an attack. He was subtler but still probed the "inadequacy" of the Dark Years section, and the need to incorporate the intelligence that had been provided by both the UK and US governments.

Over the next few days we had intensive discussions on how to accommodate the Wolf–Wells views. Of course we could ignore them, but Blix was obliged under Resolution 1284 to take their counsel into account. Blix and I agreed that I would re-draft the Dark Years, mentioning examples from Powell's presentation and giving our assessment of them. Thus on mobile biological facilities I wrote:

UNMOVIC has not had direct access to the originators of these reports, some of whom are persons claiming to have been directly involved in the design and manufacture of mobile facilities in Iraq. In theory, such facilities are possible and, indeed, Iraq has acknowledged that in the late 1980s such facilities were seriously considered. Senior Iraqi officials informed UNSCOM that the concept was ultimately rejected because it was considered to be impractical.

This would satisfy neither Wolf or Wells, of course, but at least they could not say we ignored them. By this time, however, their governments were not interested: to them the UN had become irrelevant.

*

Blix finally presented the Clusters Document to the Security Council on 7 March 2003. Not surprisingly, it received little comment from Council members and sparse coverage in the press. Even Blix's observation to the Council that it "would not take years, nor weeks, but months" for Iraq to complete the key remaining disarmament tasks was ignored. Iraq and UNMOVIC were not going to be given more time to resolve anything. Less than two weeks later, on 19 March 2003, military action against Iraq was launched, coyly named by the US, Operation Iraqi Freedom.

My contract with UNMOVIC was also at an end. As I went to say my final farewell to Hans Blix on 21 March, I knew that this time he would not ask for my return. It was a sad occasion because it seemed that all the work we had done had come to nought: the peaceful disarmament of Iraq had not been achievable. I had enjoyed working for Blix; not only because he was one of the most agreeable bosses I have ever had, but also because he was a person who believed in what he was doing and that there was a peaceful solution to even the most intractable problems in the world.

Blix told me that he regretted that he had not published the Clusters Document earlier; I did not remind him that I had argued for this a year ago. He also surprised me by saying that he believed the US had been genuine when it tabled Resolution 1441, and almost until the end he had not believed that war was inevitable. He felt that the US and the UK required another resolution to go to war; a resolution that they had failed to get.

Blix was not naive, but he was too trusting in the good of people and of nations, and had too much faith in due process and legality. War is not about legality but about morality. Even if the US had managed to bludgeon members of the Council into adopting another resolution, it would not have made the war just.

On the plane back to Australia, I felt I was fleeing the scene of a crime, leaving New York and America to return to the sanctuary of home. Over the Pacific I asked myself a series of questions. As recorded in my notebook they were:

Did Iraq have WMD? Yes, some old ones, based on all the available evidence.

Was Iraq a threat to the US, UK and Australia? On the evidence I have seen, unequivocally, no.

Then did we go to war on a lie? This is a question I cannot easily answer. In the real world, issues are rarely that black-and-white. But US and UK intelligence analysts seem genuinely to believe their assessments. So it all depends on how much spin has been put on the truth.

The truth was something I would not learn for almost another year.

The Hunt for the Truth

EVEN BEFORE I LEFT NEW YORK, EVEN before the war broke out, I was approached by US authorities asking me whether I would be interested in returning to Iraq to hunt for Saddam's hidden weapons. For me this was an invitation to hunt for the truth as much as for WMD, and I readily agreed.

Since I was still a UN consultant and an adviser to Hans Blix, it seemed reasonable to inform him of the approach by the US. He asked me how I felt about it and I responded that I would have preferred that the UN would conduct the hunt but realistically this was not going to occur. He agreed and then wryly said, "So, you will be part of the Coalition of Willing Inspectors then!" He never seemed to lose his sense of humour.

The war was over more quickly than anyone had predicted and chaos came to Iraq more quickly than anyone imagined. However, the organised hunt for Iraq's WMD moved slowly. Initially, a group known as the 75th Exploitation Task Force, comprising US military personnel with little knowledge of WMD and a few technical specialists from the US Defense Department, was sent to Iraq. Everyone in the US Administration was so certain that weapons were there that the 75th ETF's instructions were simply to "search and find". No-one saw any need to conduct a more systematic investigation.

After a couple of months of searching, but no finding, squabbling broke out among several US government agencies, each of which believed it should take control of the hunt. Eventually in early May, plans were formulated for a new group, The Iraq Survey Group, which would be under the control of the Director of Central Intelligence, George Tenet. It would comprise experts from all the US intelligence agencies, as well as, by invitation, specialists from the UK and Australia, the idea being that former experienced inspectors from UNSCOM would form the core of the investigation. Lists of suitable candidates for non-US participation were drawn up: twenty from the UK and four from Australia. My colleagues David Kelly and Hamish Killip were on the UK list. I was one of the chosen ones for the Australian list, although for various reasons I did not join the ISG until some months later.

The first wave of the ISG set off for Iraq in mid-June 2003. If the 75th Exploitation Task Force had been short of expertise, the ISG fared only slightly better. Most of the experts were junior analysts from the CIA or DIA and, with very few exceptions, none had experience as weapons inspectors.

The UK people, especially David Kelly, would therefore play a senior role in the ISG. Kelly would bring not only his biological expertise to the ISG, but also his experience and knowledge of Iraq. It was recognised that the focus of the ISG would need to change from simply searching sites for hidden weapons to a more systematic investigation. Key to the investigation would be the Iraqi scientists and military personnel who had been involved in Iraq's former weapons programs. One by one, these individuals had been rounded up by US forces, or had handed themselves in, and were now incarcerated in a prison, Camp Cropper near Baghdad International Airport. Thus General Amer Rashid, the former Oil Minister, and the man whom I (and many UNSCOM inspectors) had crossed swords with years earlier, was now in jail. His wife, Dr Rihab Taha (the tabloids' "Dr Germ"), head of the former biological weapons program, was in the same prison, but not the same cell. So were Lieutenant General Dr Amer Al Sa'adi, (Blix's counterpart), Major General Hossam Amin (head of the National Monitoring Directorate), Major General Mahmoud Bilal (clown and Iraq's chemical and biological bomb-maker), Lieutenant General Dr Ahmed Murthada (Dr Taha's boss), Abdul Rahman Thamer (Dr Taha's deputy and anthrax specialist) and a few others. All were held in solitary confinement so that they could not exchange stories. David Kelly would want to interview all of these people to establish whether Iraq really had re-started its weapons programs after inspectors left in 1998.

*

I woke early on 19 July 2003 and turned on the radio to listen to the ABC news. The first item was about a UK government scientist, a former weapons inspector, whose body had been found the previous day in the woods near his home in Oxfordshire. His name was Dr David Kelly.

We had travelled, worked, and socialised together over the years for enough time for me to understand the man. On a personal level he was good company, a man with a wry sense of humour and a sharp wit. He liked to analyse complex situations and he was always quick to pick up on illogicalities in any argument. These attributes he brought with him to his job, and they made him the UN's top weapons inspector. Even tiny inconsistencies during an inspection would not escape his notice and he would demand an explanation from the Iraqis. On many occasions his quiet, systematic and logical questioning had demolished the stories that Iraq invented to cover up aspects of its weapons' programs. He was the elite of the inspectors.

Now he was gone. At first I could not believe the news. It was said that he had committed suicide, but I found this hard to believe or understand. He was the most sane, level-headed and rational person that I had known, and suicide seemed totally inconsistent with this. I was, however, aware that he had been under considerable pressure, from what should have been an unlikely source: his own government. For a man who had stood up to threats and intimidation from the Iraqis, it was a cruel twist.

The event that led to David's doom occurred on 29 May 2003, when a BBC journalist, Andrew Gilligan, stated on radio[40] that:

> Downing Street, our source says, ordered a week before publication, ordered it [the UK Dossier on Iraq's WMD] to be sexed up, to be made more exciting and ordered more facts to be discovered.

Gilligan's statement was an acute source of embarrassment for the Blair government, and there was a scramble within both the government and the media to discover the "source" of the leak. In the subsequent inquiry[41] into David's death, evidence showed that even before Gilligan's radio broadcast, David had volunteered to his civil service supervisors that he had spoken to Gilligan. Through the usual internal disciplinary procedures, David was reprimanded for indiscretions and there the matter would have remained – except that his government needed a scapegoat to deflect criticism from its own failings on The Dossier. In spite of commitments to the contrary, on 10 July 2003, the government deliberately disclosed to the media that David was the source of Gilligan's story.

David was now hounded out of his home by reporters. A few days later, on 15 July, he appeared before the Foreign Affairs Committee to face hostile and humiliating questioning about his role in the affair. His government had already abandoned him, dismissing him as "a middle-ranking technician". It was a gross insult to the man who was one of the world's leading WMD experts and a top weapons inspector who had led dozens of teams into Iraq. There was also the prospect of more public humiliation for David, with threats that he would face further inquiries.

Suicide seemed an improbable fate, but the betrayal by his own government for which he had worked so dedicatedly, presumably became too much.

David's death shocked not only the ISG inspectors, but also the Iraqis who knew him. Hamish told me that during an interview with Dr Al Sa'adi a couple of months later, he mentioned David's death. Al Sa'adi simply put his head in his hands and was silent for a time. Even though they were on the other side, the Iraqis too had great respect for the man.

*

The head of the ISG was Dr David Kay, the former senior International Atomic Energy Agency inspector who in 1991 had discovered a stash of secret documents on Iraq's nuclear weapons program. While Kay headed the hunt for WMD, Major General Keith Dayton was the military commander of the group.

The motto of the ISG was *"Find, Exploit, Eliminate"*, a reference to the weapons themselves. Although the organisation had evolved, its thinking had not; the weapons were there and it was just a matter of finding them. However, David Kay broadened the task from a simple hunt for weapons to a search for WMD facilities including laboratories, factories and storage sites.

I was watching all this from afar. Of course I was interested in the hunt and its outcome. Although weapons had not yet been found, it was still my view that some old stocks probably existed somewhere. The quantities would fit into a few basements, so it was unsurprising that they had not been located. On the other hand, if Iraq had the programs that the US claimed, it was surprising that not a scrap of evidence had been found, not only by the ISG but also by UNMOVIC before it. My experience told me that this was more than odd; it was beginning to point to the probability that the programs did not exist after 1991.

I was irritated by the continuing certainty with which politicians spoke about the existence of the weapons. Where were they getting their advice? If I had serious doubts, why did they not have doubts too? Yet on 13 May 2003, the Australian Foreign Minister, Alexander Downer, stated to Parliament:

> Mr Speaker, already we have seen evidence of what appear to be mobile biological laboratories, at two sites in Iraq, capable of producing biological materials for use in weapons of mass destruction. I know that it is disappointing to the Opposition to hear this, but I am afraid this is true.

Downer was referring to two trailers that US teams had found in Iraq and which superficially resembled the ones displayed in a slide by Colin Powell in his presentation to the Security Council on 5 February. Pictures of these trailers were posted on the CIA web-page, where I had carefully studied them. It was difficult to be definitive from the photos, but the equipment did not seem to be biologically related. The "fermenter" in particular was nothing like any fermenter I had seen in Iraq, or for that matter anywhere else. Other features also did not fit and it seemed unlikely that the trailers could have anything to do with anthrax production as claimed. I felt strongly enough about this to call a contact within ONA to voice my concern. I advised that the government should be more circumspect in its pronouncements, at least until further investigation had been conducted.

The first the world heard anything authoritative about how the search was going was in early October 2003. David Kay produced a highly classified "Interim Progress Report" and presented a public summary of the findings to Congress on 2 October.[42] Kay's report was equivocal. On the one hand he suggested that his teams had uncovered signs of WMD activity:

> We have discovered dozens of WMD-related program activities and significant amounts of equipment that Iraq concealed from the United Nations during the inspections that began in late 2002.

But when it came to the specifics, there was little concern. For example, he revealed that a scientist had stored biological reference strains in his home, but the list only included one bacterium with any relevance to biological warfare and even this only remotely. He spoke about the discovery of secret laboratories run by the Iraqi Intelligence Services but said nothing about the purpose of these labs. In the missile field he did reveal Iraqi activities that had been proscribed by UN resolutions but nothing that was surprising: UNMOVIC had uncovered similar activity. Overall the report was a damp squib, although Kay did caution that:

> We are still very much in the collection and analysis mode, still seeking the information and evidence that will allow us to confidently draw comprehensive conclusions to the actual objectives, scope, and dimensions of Iraq's WMD activities.

*

It was not long after the report was issued that the Australian Defence Department contacted me to ask if I was still interested in working with the ISG. During a visit to Baghdad by the Defence Minister,

Robert Hill, David Kay had asked for my services. The Deputy Director of the CIA, John McLaughlin, had sent a similar request to the Australian Embassy in Washington. With Hill supporting my attachment to the ISG, the bureaucratic wheels in Canberra began to turn, but slowly. I agreed to a new contract at the end of November, completed a short training course (what to do if kidnapped) in early December, and was on a plane to Baghdad on 16 December 2003.

I was keen to get there as soon as possible. I had heard via the inspectors' grapevine that David Kay had reached the conclusion that there were no WMD, nor programs to produce them after 1991. He was now planning a final report and aiming to wind up operations within a couple of months. Kay wanted me as part of his inner cabinet and as a special adviser, in much the same role as I had worked for Hans Blix. It also occurred to me that if Kay had really come to the conclusions that there were no WMD, he might want me for more than just advice. I suspected that he saw me as someone with strong credentials, who would eventually reach the same conclusions as he had, and say so. Being a non-American was also an advantage because I was less likely to be intimidated by the CIA.

I was also keen to get to Baghdad quickly because I had heard that David Kay was about to go on Christmas leave and I wanted to speak to him before he disappeared.

In the event I need not have bothered to hurry. By the time of my arrival in Baghdad, David Kay had left, not on Christmas leave but for good. I was now an Adviser with no-one to advise!

The British brigadier who headed the UK contingent to the ISG told me that in the last month, David Kay had appeared to be a greatly troubled man. Kay had been a strong believer that Iraq had WMD, but as he gradually came to the realisation that the weapons almost certainly did not exist, he became "like a man who had suddenly found there was no God".

*

Returning to Baghdad, the most obvious change from my last visit in 1998 was the new security measures. At strategic points throughout the city, roadblocks had been set up so that vehicles could be checked and identities confirmed, although I noticed that a flash of my Canberra driving licence usually got me through; my pale complexion was really my passport. Even more noticeable were the massive concrete blocks that lined many roads to protect buildings from car bombs. Otherwise the city seemed much the same as before, if perhaps a little more prosperous and busy than during the days of the sanctions. The markets were doing a good trade in air-conditioners, refrigerators and washing machines, items that were hard to obtain under the sanctions. The problem for the average Iraqi was the lack of electricity to run these appliances; every suburb, every day had its rotation of power outages.

The ISG's base, known as Camp Slayer, was located in the sprawling grounds of one of Saddam's palaces near Baghdad International Airport. The main building, the Perfume Palace, was a large circular building with a high domed roof. It had escaped Coalition bombing because it was thought from the shape of the building that it might be a mosque. Above the entrance was an inscription in stylised Arabic script that referred to Saddam Hussein's presence being as sweet as perfume – hence the name. This was the building where I was to work. Inside impressed with its elaborate marble Babylonian columns and mock-crystal chandeliers hanging from 20-metre-high ceilings. My office was more humble, with 7-metre high ceilings and just one chandelier, but it was still grander than any office I had ever worked in. It was located just off the central circular floor where a hundred workstations created the hubbub of a central railway station.

The person I was keen to see was General Dayton. Not only had David Kay left, so too had all the senior CIA staff. I wanted to meet the person who was now steering the ship.

General Dayton immediately impressed me. He was a lean man with a steely gaze and an upright military bearing. I soon learned he had a sharp mind and was careful but at the same time decisive. Some of his first words to me were, "You realise that you don't work for me." He went on to explain that he was about to return to Washington on leave, but that he would ask about David Kay's replacement. He pointed out that another report to Congress was scheduled for early February and the preparation of this would be a focus of the work of the ISG over the coming month. I offered to co-ordinate this and he gratefully accepted.

I spent the next week reading dozens of reports and talking to dozens of the ISG staff. Familiarisation tours of sections and units of the ISG were organised and over the coming weeks I gradually gained an understanding of its complex operation and the meaning of the myriad of acronyms so loved by the US military. The analytical laboratories that both the UK and the US had installed impressed me, as did a US mobile bomb exploitation unit. The latter could examine a chemical weapon using a variety of high-tech equipment, assessing its likely contents without ever having to open it up. All we needed now was a chemical bomb!

The ISG weapons experts were divided into six teams (nuclear, chemical, biological, missile, denial & deception and procurement), each comprising about seven specialists. These teams would organise site inspections that typically involved half-a-dozen armoured Humvees, three military personnel and three or four inspectors. A typical day might see three such teams sent out to sites around Baghdad.

There was also a unit (DOCEX) to exploit recovered documents. This was a major task: the ISG had found thousands of documents of various relevance and all of these had to be translated before their significance could be assessed. Much of this work was conducted in the safety of Qatar where most of the DOCEX staff were located.

Another unit of particular interest was the interrogation unit, known as the Joint Interrogation and Debriefing Centre or JIDC (pronounced "jidic"). The unit had around fifty interrogators whose task was to obtain information from the hundred or so prisoners held at Camp Cropper.

I was soon to find out more about the interrogation process. Just after Christmas the head of the biological team, a CIA officer, asked me whether I would interview General Dr Ahmed Murthada. He had been interviewed many times by the ISG, but the analysts were not sure whether he had told them everything he knew. They thought that because I knew him, he might be more forthcoming with me.

Of course I knew Dr Murthada very well. He had been Dr Taha's boss before 1991, and after the Gulf War had been promoted to Minister for Transport and Communications. He was one of the last Iraqis I had interviewed in 1998 shortly before Operation Desert Fox, and I recalled vividly how he had not told me the full story then. Murthada was now a "High Value Detainee" (HVD) at Camp Cropper. I was not sure how I would feel seeing him again in these different circumstances, and already I felt uncomfortable at the prospect.

*

Camp Cropper was situated near Baghdad International Airport just a short drive from Camp Slayer. A double razor-wire fence surrounded the cellblocks and an assortment of other single-storey concrete buildings. Two lines of metal portacabins inside the razor-wire fence formed the "Secure Interrogation Centre" or SIC. On the morning of the Murthada interview, we were shown by a guard to one such cabin. Accompanying me was Hamish, who that very morning had flown back from the UK after Christmas leave, as well as Murthada's case officer/interrogator and a note-taker. The small windowless room was simply furnished with a small table and five chairs. We sat and waited for Murthada to arrive.

There was a tap on the door. We opened it to see Dr Murthada dressed in an orange jumpsuit and behind him a guard who ushered him in and then stood guard outside. Murthada was thinner than when we had last met, but the significant change was in his demeanour. He was much subdued, not cowed but nevertheless someone whose spirit had been broken. This should not have surprised me. After all, he had been a Minister of State, a man of power, privilege and pride. Now, after eight months in prison in his orange jumpsuit, he was someone for whom I could not help but feel some pity.

In spite of our previous opposition, he seemed genuinely pleased to see me, a familiar face from other, and for him better, times. The interview deliberately covered old ground. I wanted to establish whether anything he had told us in the old UNSCOM days had changed. It had not. After two hours I suggested a break, and while the others wandered off, Dr Murthada smoked a cigarette outside the portacabin and we chatted, the guard all the time hovering in the background. When the others were out of earshot, Murthada grabbed my sleeve and said in hushed tones, "Mr Rod, you must help me get out of here. You know my family, my daughters, they need me."

Indeed I did "know" his daughters or at least their names. "Safah" and "Manal" were the names of two of Iraq's secret biological facilities where aflatoxins, botulinum toxin and anthrax were made before 1991. Murthada had named these places after his daughters as a sort of code. But I could not help Dr Murthada now, and although I was tempted to tell him I would try, I did not want to give him false hope. I simply told him, "I'm sorry, I cannot do anything."

After the break we gradually came to the subject of real concern – what Dr Taha and others had told the ISG about the disposal of the anthrax and other agents in 1991. According to Taha's new account, the anthrax had not been stored at Al Hakam during the Gulf War but rather hidden in a warehouse at "Electronic Warfare Unit 114". When this location became unsafe because of Coalition bombing, it was moved around the country on semitrailers. Eventually in July 1991, the instruction was given by Hussein Kamal to destroy it. At this time the anthrax was outside Radwaniyah Palace because this was where one of the semitrailers had broken down, and so the agent was deactivated there and simply tipped out onto the surrounding desert. Dr Taha could not declare this to UNSCOM or UNMOVIC because, to put it mildly, Saddam would not have been pleased. Hamish and I later visited the palace; as we stood at the steps to the entrance we could clearly see where the anthrax had been dumped.

Others confirmed Dr Taha's story. UNMOVIC's evidence, including Document 62856, had showed overwhelmingly that Iraq's story about the destruction of anthrax at Al Hakam could not be true. However, it was now clear that our conclusion, that "there must be a strong presumption that the anthrax still exists," had also been wrong. Now the ISG knew the truth: it had been destroyed outside one of Saddam's palaces.

I could not be sure whether Murthada had told us all he knew or not. For instance, he could not corroborate Taha's account. But I was certain now that it did not matter. The anthrax had been destroyed and his interview made little difference to our conclusions. I believed that Murthada should have been released. Before the Gulf War he had had minimal involvement in Iraq's biological warfare program, but even if his role had been greater he had committed no internationally recognised crime. And after the war he had been a Minister of State with no connection to WMD. There seemed to be no reason for his continued incarceration and I told the head of ISG's biological group this on my return to Slayer. My diary notes on Murthada concluded with: *"... so for the time being he stays. What a strange power we have – no such thing as natural justice here!"*

*

My interview with Murthada made me think about the interview process in general. There seemed to be a problem with co-ordination: it was not unusual for several teams to interview the same prisoner without consultation. Not only was this inefficient, but the prisoner could inadvertently be tipped off to areas of interest. I therefore called a meeting of all of the interrogators, at which the head of JIDC and I worked out new procedures. He also invited me to take a guided tour of Cropper.

The commandant led me through the various areas of the prison, showing me the medical centre, administration, shower blocks and of course the cells. My impression was that the prison was well run and the inmates well looked after, but a few things disturbed me, including the prolonged periods of solitary confinement many were kept in. My diary notes record my feelings at the time:

> Last week I went for a tour around the prison. A sombre place where 110 Iraqis now are incarcerated. I saw Murthada and some others from the old days but I did not like to stare. Huda Ammash, who I saw, is claustrophobic and is given her own room with windows. I felt a bit like a voyeur. It was difficult not to feel uncomfortable – I was part of a system that had put them there and most had committed no crime, at least none they could be tried for. On the other hand what choice is there for us?
>
> The detainees are well looked after except that they spend 23 hours a day in a two-metre box with a small metal flap half a metre from the ground for light and air. I vividly remember a face pushed to the hole looking up at me as I walked past – did I know him? He looked vaguely familiar, but I only saw part of his face for a fleeting

moment. I stepped inside one empty cell – four walls, a door, a bare light bulb, a toilet and water. Most prisoners have no writing or reading material.

During the tour I glimpsed Dr Al Sa'adi walking in a roped-off exercise area, more stooped now than before. I recalled our last meeting in 1998, when he said he thought we would not meet again. Although we did not quite meet this time, neither he nor I could have envisaged that we would arrive at circumstances like these.

*

I realised that if the ISG was to meet the deadline of February for the next report, drafting had to start immediately. That way David Kay's replacement, if and when he arrived, would have something to work with. Before General Dayton's departure, I had discussed with him what the report should contain. We both agreed that it should give some assessment of what had been found so far. David Kay had to a large extent ducked this in his Interim Report, but now, after six more months of investigations, something along these lines was required.

By the time Dayton returned on 17 January, drafting of the new report, which I optimistically titled the "Progress Report", was well underway. I went to his office to brief him on developments in his absence and he seemed pleased. Then he said to me, "Do you mind if I ask you something? You seem to have taken control here and I wondered whether that was just because you saw a vacuum or was there something else?" I wondered what else there could be; in the world of intelligence agencies anything was possible. But I had no other motive than that there was a vacuum and I told him so. He seemed relieved.

The ISG's relation to Washington was a curious one. The ISG was an independent body that reported to George Tenet, Director of Central Intelligence. While it did not take instructions directly from the CIA, it consulted with it before taking any major decision – such as the approach to be taken in the Progress Report, if not its actual content. On 20 January we hooked up for a video-conference with Washington to confirm with John McLaughlin, the CIA's Deputy

Director, that we were on the right track with the report. It was a relatively short discussion, for he was largely in agreement with our approach, including the section I had included on "Tentative Conclusions". Afterwards General Dayton and I agreed that no major changes were required; I would proceed on our present course and aim to produce the report by a new deadline of mid-March.

Although Dayton was in charge of logistical support for all the ISG operations, no-one was really captaining the ship. The teams were going out on daily inspections, but what were they looking for? It seemed to me that their focus was wrong. For example, team leaders, particularly in the chemical and biological area, were not addressing the fundamental question of Iraq's technical capacity to produce chemical or biological warfare agents. Did it have the equipment, materials and expertise to accomplish this? Teams were still looking for weapons without assessing the infrastructure required to produce them.

No-one was yet publicly contemplating the possibility that the weapons might not exist, that Iraq might not have rebuilt its capacity to produce WMD after the departure of UNSCOM in 1998. Even to suggest this was heresy. David Kay had come close to such heresy before his departure in early December, when he said, "We are 85% done," meaning that there were probably no weapons and that more searching would confirm this. But after his departure, it became a matter of honour to refute Kay's claim. I had failed this test when, shortly after my arrival, General Dayton asked me if I believed the ISG "was 85% done". I told him, yes, and I could tell it was not the answer he wanted to hear.

If the weapons were not out there, however, we still needed to know why not. But there was no-one to re-direct the effort and it was not clear whether Washington would even replace Kay. Dayton therefore asked me whether I would provide the guidance for the teams and I readily agreed. He observed what a strange situation had arisen, commenting, "This is an American operation, a CIA operation, but you're an Australian!" I agreed it was strange.

*

By late January the Progress Report was taking shape. Now I had some assistance in the form of Dr John Gee, the Australian who had been a prime mover in the early days of UNSCOM and was an expert on chemical weapons. By the time of John's arrival, over 150 pages of the report had been drafted, but I was encountering difficulties with both the chemical and biological teams. The leaders of these teams were reluctant to provide any assessment of what they had discovered, or to be more precise what they had not discovered, to date. Both had contributed to CIA assessments of Iraq's WMD capacity before the 2003 war and I wondered whether this was at the root of their present reluctance. Any assessment they wrote now would, after all, contradict their assessment of a year earlier.

One central issue was the two "biological" trailers that the CIA still maintained were for the production of anthrax. These trailers were parked at Camp Slayer and one of the British engineers had given me a guided tour of them. Now I had no doubt: the trailers had no biological role. The "fermenter" was not a fermenter but a chemical reactor, almost certainly for producing hydrogen for weather balloons. Sampling of the reactor had even found the chemicals used in hydrogen production.

The head of the biological group did not see it this way, however. She argued that because she was not an engineer, she did not know what they were for and therefore was not going to go against the prevailing CIA line that they were for anthrax production. This seemed to me a head-in-the-sand approach to assessment. Privately she conceded that she thought the CIA assessment was wrong but told me, "You just don't understand how difficult it is to say anything different." She was right, I did not understand.

The CIA was not about to let the ISG ship to sail rudderless for much longer. Towards the end of January we heard that Charles Duelfer was to be its new head. He had been deputy to both Rolf Ekeus and Richard Butler, and while somewhat overshadowed by these dominant personalties, he was a creative thinker and would leave his mark on the ISG. Most importantly he had the credentials within the US to report with authority to Congress.

Before he arrived, however, there was a dramatic shift in the politics of the hunt for WMD.

On 28 January 2004, David Kay appeared before the Senate Armed Services Committee and stated that with respect to the existence of WMD in Iraq, *we were almost all wrong.*[43] It was the first public acknowledgment by a person in authority that Iraq did not possess the weapons that had provided the justification for the 2003 war. However, the US administration was not going to concede as easily as that.

Within the ISG, Kay's statement caused little surprise. It was consistent with the "85% done" assessment he had made before his departure and so at first, it was business as usual. General Dayton gave a pep talk to the staff in the Perfume Palace to tell them that Kay's statement made little difference to the ISG's work. But things were soon to change.

Charles Duelfer arrived on 12 February. On the same day, George Tenet also paid an unannounced visit to Baghdad, including a lightning visit to the ISG to introduce his new man, Charles. The ISG headquarters staff were called together in the central hall of the Perfume Palace. George Tenet, still wearing his body armour (maybe he thought that that there was hostile intent inside the ISG), called up "Charlie" and wrapped an arm around him. Pointing to him with his free hand, he introduced the new leader of the ISG with the words, "This man is as weird as shit. But he knows a hell of a lot about Iraq." Charles understandably looked acutely uncomfortable. After this brief introduction, Tenet gave what he presumably saw as a rallying talk to the assembled mass, telling them there were weapons out there: we just had to find them. He finished with, "Are we 85% done?" The mass responded with a mumbled cry, "No." Tenet repeated the chant, now yelling, "Are we 85% done? I want to hear you!" "No," roared the crowd. And with that Tenet and his bodyguards departed.

I was standing next to the British brigadier Tim Tyler during Tenet's "speech". Afterwards we looked at each other in disbelief. Over coffee that evening, though, our discussion concentrated more on the sentiment than the spectacle. Did the CIA really still believe "there were weapons out there" to find? If so, the report that I was assembling would not be well received.

Charles naturally had his own ideas about the report. He explained that he did not want any assessment in the report, nor any conclusions

– some people would take them for our final views, which might make for awkwardness if we changed our minds. This evasiveness was going to cause problems. How, for example, could we say that we had found trailers with equipment on board and not mention our assessment of what that equipment was for? How could we say we had investigated the aluminium tubes that Secretary Powell said were for uranium enrichment and not mention that our assessment was that they were for rockets? Over a series of three long meetings John Gee and I tried to dissuade him from his evasive course. Charles argued that because he was new to the work, he could hardly present assessments to Congress in a month's time, when he would be insufficiently familiar with the issues to argue them out.

To John and I, this seemed a cop-out. We could sympathise with his difficulty, but the report could be delayed by a few weeks to give him time to become familiar with the complexities of the issues. After all, this was his job and given his extensive background, he had not exactly come into it cold. We both believed there was more to Charles's reluctance than concern about his preparedness. Charles was independent-minded, but on this we could not help but wonder whether the idea of avoiding assessment had come from Washington, especially given Tenet's recent rallying call to the masses.

To produce a report that deliberately omitted our assessments was misleading, and I told Charles this. What made matters worse was that political leaders in both the US and the UK (perhaps not Australia by this stage) were still claiming there was evidence of WMD in Iraq. We knew this was not true. If we were not to say so in our report, we would be complicit in a lie.

On 15 February, I wrote in my diary:

This report will say nothing – no "bad news" will be given – just the line that there is a lot more work to be done and we cannot draw any conclusions yet, (maybe true in some areas but not all). Our assessment of the trailers and the aluminium tubes etc will not be reported ... although we have done a lot of investigation, we have found no evidence [of WMD]. I believe we have a duty to report that, anything less is dishonest.

And a week later:

> The style and flavour of the report is set – no assessment, no
> annexes and no substance. Apart from suppressing our findings,
> which are mostly negative, Charles will be minced in Washington
> with a nothing report. He feels he can get away with it by saying he
> is new and there is still a lot of work to do. I doubt he'll succeed.

If I had any doubts about the origin of the new approach, they were
dispelled during a discussion with the senior CIA officer, effectively
Charles's deputy, who had newly arrived in the ISG. He told me that we
could not refer to the mobile trailers in the report, telling me, "I don't
care that they are not biological trailers. You cannot put that in your
report, it's politically not possible." I was rather stunned by this blatant
admission and told him (to no avail), "We are not political; we are
apolitical." Well, at least I felt I was! My diary recorded the event:

> The only reason we are going down this route is the politics in
> Washington. I recognise that they cannot be ignored but not at the
> expense of the truth.

Charles too did not want to know what the trailers were for, saying,
"I don't care about the stupid trailers. They are not important." Perhaps
he was right in the sense that the trailers were just one among a broad
range of issues, but, together with the aluminium tubes, uranium from
Niger, 45-minutes claim and chemical transhipment points, the existence of the trailers had been used to make the case for war. I wrote in
my diary that evening (15 February):

> I also discussed the trailers – Charles's attitude was he did not
> want to inspect them or know, then he could genuinely say in
> Washington that he doesn't know what they are for.

The new-style report was only part of the problem with the direction of the ISG. The chemical team had also conducted an exhaustive
investigation of a "chemical transhipment point" at Mussayib. Through
a series of exhaustive inspections, they had conclusively overturned

the evidence presented by Secretary Powell in his presentation to the General Assembly the previous year. The site was not a "chemical transhipment point": the "decontamination trucks" seen there were water carts to fill storage tanks located next to the shower blocks; the "chemical bunker" did not store chemical weapons but barbed wire, water bottles, mattresses and other innocuous items; the grading of the site was not to remove evidence of chemicals but was an annual event to remove vegetation which posed a fire hazard. The team had established this through three or four visits to the site, but even so CIA headquarters did not accept its findings and ordered it back for another look. My diary notes of 22 February noted that:

> Washington (i.e. CIA) demands a "higher standard of proof" before evidence that contradicts pre-OIF intelligence can be accepted. By this technique, nothing will be overturned.

In my view we had all the answers in Camp Cropper in the form of the HVDs: Iraq's former political and military leaders, and the former WMD scientists and engineers. Many had been talking freely, and even those who had not, had told us enough. The truth was that Iraq did not have WMD, or the programs to produce them, after 1991. There were therefore none to find at Mussayib or anywhere else.

But to propose this was to fight a losing battle. I now considered that remaining in the ISG was to be complicit in deceit. On the other hand, I had given a commitment to write the report; if I left now I would have to break that obligation. I discussed my dilemma with Tim Tyler, the British brigadier who had now become my confidant. He too had seen the political influences on the ISG, but he convinced me to stay, arguing, "If you go, then there will be no-one to keep them straight. And you might still be able to influence the report." It was the British version of "keeping the bastards honest", and it was a good point. I decided to see out the completion of the report.

John Gee, however, had had enough. He told me that he had "no confidence in the integrity of the process" and would leave as soon as it could be arranged. I admired his stance and began to wonder whether Tim was right. On 7 March I wrote in my diary:

This is my bleakest moment here ... John leaves tomorrow after explaining to Charles why he can't stay. I would like to leave too except that I feel obligated to complete the report. I am now finding it very difficult. I have not told Charles that I am going, but he might suspect. At the same time I am helping, even leading, the planning for the final report. I play a significant part in the strategy for the ISG. The problem is that these are just games – I have no real influence and the so-called strategy at best only touches the edges of what really happens. The actual investigation work is mostly aimed at supporting pre-OIF [Operation Iraqi Freedom] intelligence. No objectivity and no interest in the wider picture.

Hamish Killip too had had enough. He considered the investigation process had lost its objectivity and quit. With his departure, the ISG lost its most experienced and respected inspector.

But I did stay and the very next day after my "bleakest moment" Tim's words were put to the test. Charles's report, which he now called the "Status Report" (it certainly was not "Progress"!), was in its final drafting stages. Whereas the Progress Report would have run to about 200 pages, the Status Report had been reduced to a mere twenty-five. It said little. There was no mention of trailers, merely a brief account of our activities over the past six months and a list of vague promises concerning the next few months. I was ashamed of my involvement, but at least there were no outright lies: it simply did not tell what we knew. Now we sent the draft to the capitals, Washington, London and Canberra, for comment and the responses began to come back.

On 8 March Charles brought to my office the response from the UK and asked me to look at it. It was in the form of an email from John Scarlett, the chairman of the Joint Intelligence Committee. Momentarily I recalled my time as an intelligence liaison officer in London in the late 1980s and my attendance of the JIC under the then chairmanship of Sir Percy Craddock.

*

During that time I attended many JIC meetings, and it was one aspect of British intelligence that had impressed me. The meetings were held in offices adjacent to the chambers of the Privy Council on Whitehall. The room itself was oak-panelled with subdued lighting and plush carpets. Sombre portraits of long-forgotten dignitaries stared down. The seating order was precise, with the Chairman of the JIC sitting at one end of a large rectangular table with his back to the only window. At the opposite end to Sir Percy were "The Allies" with, from the left, representatives from the CIA, DIA, Canada and Australia, perhaps indicating our relative importance. The heads of all the intelligence agencies sat in assigned places around the table, with the Chief of Defence Intelligence, as deputy chair, sitting next to Sir Percy.

The discussion of intelligence assessments usually revolved around the question of whether the findings were fairly based on the evidence available. Rarely in the intelligence world does absolute proof exist. In any assessment, the considerations relate to the reliability of sources, consistency between various types of sources and the existence, or otherwise, of contradictory evidence. The JIC debated these. The overall interpretation was then discussed. Finally, Sir Percy would sum up and suggest some word changes, some nuances, to reflect more accurately the nature of the evidence and to show the level of confidence the committee had in its conclusions.

*

The real strength of the JIC process I had observed was the close involvement, objectivity and professionalism of its members. It may have been a relic of the British Empire, but at least in the 1980s its deliberations were not superficial and it was not merely a "rubber stamp" committee.

Sadly, under Scarlett standards seemed to have declined. What he was suggesting for the ISG's Status Report, I could not imagine Craddock considering for a moment. Scarlett felt our report was light on impact. I could not argue with this! He suggested that we needed to show that Iraq had breached various Security Council resolutions by developing WMD. To do this, he picked out nine or ten "nuggets", as he called them, from David Kay's Interim Report of the previous September and suggested we insert these into our report. The list included Iraq's work on ricin (a toxin from the castor oil plant), its work on cluster bombs, and developments at various research centres. The purpose of his suggestions was to sex up our report to imply that there was evidence of WMD yet to be found. It seemed that he had not heard David Kay say, "*we were almost all wrong*", and that there was no substance in any of the findings of his Interim Report.

Scarlett's suggestions for the report would have shocked me if I had not been aware that he had done this before. By now the Hutton Inquiry concerning the circumstances surrounding David Kelly's death had published its findings. Scarlett had been identified as one person responsible for sexing up the UK dossier on Iraq. Now he was at it again. It seemed to me he was not a fit person to head any intelligence organisation. I told Charles that we should not accept any of Scarlett's suggestions, and after some consideration he agreed.

Having repelled boarders from the UK we went through a repeat exercise with the US. The CIA sent comments a day or two later and while most of these were constructive, there were also two blatant attempts to modify our report for political reasons. While the report did not mention trailers, it did briefly mention the ISG's investigation of reports of an Iraqi mobile biological program from a source known as "Curveball". The claims that Curveball had made turned out to be wrong and we reported this factually, without comment. The CIA wanted us to change this because "it did not track with comments made by DCI at Georgetown University." What we had found did indeed contradict Tenet's statement to students at Georgetown University on 5 February. But we could not change our findings because of that.

The second suggestion for change concerned the aluminium tubes. Powell had argued in his presentation to the UN that because the tubes had exacting specifications, they were for uranium enrichment. Our investigations, however, unambiguously established that they were for the manufacture of small artillery rockets.

The CIA did not want us to reveal these findings.

On 18 March 2004, John Scarlett made one more attempt to insert his "nuggets" into the report. During a video link between Washington, London and Canberra to discuss the report, Scarlett asked Charles what he was doing about inserting the nuggets. We had been prepared for this and Charles simply deflected the enquiry, throwing it back at him by asking for his suggestions on how to select the nuggets. It was the last we heard from Scarlett on this matter.

The final version of the Status Report was scheduled for publication on Monday, 23 March and I arranged to catch the first RAAF flight out of Baghdad after that. My diary records my feelings at the time:

> Tomorrow I go home. Last Friday night I told Charles – just as I had planned to do. He was visibly upset and of course I felt bad. I told him why I couldn't continue, and he repeated his case. He said he thought that I had come round to some sort of acceptance of the way he was reporting. I told him no, and that the reason I was finishing the report was because I had felt I had a commitment ... My sole product was a report that was unbalanced and non-objective (and dishonest?). I asked him not to make my farewell public at the [daily briefing], because it would be difficult for me not to respond by saying things I might regret later.
>
> Next morning I told the General. He said he was not surprised and understood. He said he had argued with Charles but he would not listen.
>
> So I feel a bit like a rat – perhaps leaving a sinking ship. On the other hand I have no choice, and although in one way I feel as if I've left them in the lurch, it's better than continuing on with no belief in what I'm doing. I now look forward to going home. I don't expect them to embrace me either so my little protest will be a lonely one. I suppose though that there are a lot in the ISG who support me.

I could not understand Charles's behaviour; it seemed out of character, and I found it hard to believe that the decisions were entirely his. Many in the ISG did not understand the course he had adopted either, and there were even some who felt as strongly about it as I did. My notes of 24 March commented:

> I believe Charles is honest but complex in the way he views things. I am not sure what influences are on him – he says none, then hints at some. He says the course he has chosen was his, and that it was supported by others. Could it have been the other way around?

Truth Uncovered

ON 23 MARCH 2004 I WAS BACK IN Canberra where I immediately arranged to meet with the First Assistant Secretary of International Policy, Myra Rowling in the Defence Department.

I explained to her the reasons for my resignation and the lack of objectivity of the ISG. Another matter had also been worrying me. During the daily briefings in Iraq, slides of prisoners (the HVDs) were shown in a sort of prisoner-of-the-week briefing. The photographs displayed were mugshots of the prisoners as they were inducted into Camp Cropper. During two briefings in January, prisoners were shown with abrasions on their face. General Dayton asked about this, and the director of JIDC replied that they had resisted arrest. I did not think much more about this until Hamish told me about Purgatory. This was a practice whereby prisoners were disorientated and questioned for seventy-two hours before being jailed in Cropper. The question troubling me was this: did Purgatory involve beatings and other mistreatment as well?

The more I thought about whether the prisoners had been abused, the more likely it seemed. By the time of my return to Australia, I believed I had enough information to raise my concerns with Myra, which I did. I also recommended that we, Australia, should have nothing further to do with the prisoners. Myra did not comment and, regrettably, I did not push the issue.

Any doubts I had about the occurrence of prisoner abuse were dispelled at the end of April when graphic pictures were shown of prisoner abuse at Abu Ghraib. What I had seen in the mugshots, and heard about Purgatory, was consistent with such behaviour, and it now seemed likely it was part of a pattern. But Purgatory was an official policy, and not the result of a few undisciplined soldiers, and in that regard it was more disturbing.

The images from Abu Ghraib sparked off a series of inquiries in May and June within the Defence Department. Although I had now resigned from Defence, I volunteered to become involved in these. By now I was even more disturbed about the shape of events. On 28 May, a US press article[44] referred to the death of an Iraqi WMD scientist, Dr Munem Al Azmerli, who had been in US custody at Camp Cropper. The family had recovered the body some weeks after his death; an autopsy showed that Azmerli had died from "blunt force trauma". He also had abrasions about his face.

Azmerli was well known to the analysts in the ISG. He had been in charge of a unit within the Iraqi Intelligence Services responsible for developing poisons for the purpose of assassination. Azmerli had experimented on prisoners and by his own admission had caused the death of at least twenty people; others put this as at least 100. He claimed that such experimentation had occurred in the 1970s, but other evidence suggested it might have continued until the mid-1990s. Azmerli did not consider himself to have done anything wrong: the prisoners had all been guilty of political crimes and were condemned to death, so he was just carrying out the death penalty. Anyway, he said, it had all happened a long time ago.

According to the head of JIDC he had died of natural causes, a brain aneuryism, but the autopsy contradicted this. Azmerli might have been the scum of the earth, but he should have been charged and tried for his crimes, not beaten to death, if indeed that is what happened. What I now asked for was that his death be investigated.

The head of the Defence inquiry into prisoner abuse, Mike Pezzullo, interviewed me early in June and I provided him with all the information that I had on prisoner abuse. Pezzullo was the adviser to the Defence Minister, Robert Hill, and I was therefore angry when Senator Hill told Parliament on 16 June:[45]

Mr President, Defence has thoroughly reviewed the information available to it and has confirmed the key facts in this issue. Australia did not interrogate prisoners. Australia was not involved in guarding prisoners at the Abu Ghraib prison or any other Iraqi prison.

He went on:

It was only with the release of the horrific photos in late April of this year that I became aware that abuses had occurred and the extent of those abuses.

I called Pezzullo the next morning to register my dissatisfaction. I had interrogated an Iraqi prisoner, Dr Murthada, and I was aware that DIO analysts serving with the ISG had been involved in other interrogations. I had also been involved in reorganising procedures for interrogations. And I had even, in a minor way, been involved in the arrest of one prisoner. So Hill could not say Australia had no involvement. Even more significantly, I had informed the Defence Department of abuse in March. Hill's statement was misleading because it distanced Australia from the treatment of prisoners in Iraq by implying that we had nothing to do with them. It was true that Australians had not been involved in abuse, but they were involved with the incarceration of prisoners and their interrogation, and Hill should have told Parliament the full story.

Pezzullo told me that he believed I had conducted an "interview" and not an "interrogation". It seemed an overly fine distinction, especially if the prisoner in question had little choice about whether he was "interviewed". On the issue of abuse he said that he had given Hill all the information I had provided. However, Pezzullo, sensing my irritation, said that he would make Hill aware of my views.

Towards the end of June, Pezzullo called me back to tell me that two lines of inquiry had been set up. One to find out what had happened within the Defence Department in response to my report of abuse, and an external one to ask the US to look into the concerns I had raised, including the possible beating to death of Azmerli. Pezzullo's call was followed by a call from the Deputy Secretary of Defence, Ron Bonighton, to tell me that he had written to the US Ambassador in Canberra, Tom Schieffer, on the matter. And then in mid-August a US military police officer from the Criminal Investigation Division visited my house to interview me. I was pleased that my suspicions of abuse were, at last, being investigated.

*

After my resignation from the ISG, I believed that my involvement with Iraq had come to a sad end. But I was wrong. In late July, Charles Duelfer emailed me to ask if I had "the slightest interest" in returning to the ISG to help with a review of a "substantive" report he was putting together. I had told Charles during a visit he made to Canberra in late March that I would need to be convinced the process was objective before I would contemplate becoming involved again. Charles now suggested that I contact Hamish or one of the other inspectors and ask them about the legitimacy of the ISG's work.

The reports from trusted colleagues in the ISG were positive, and so I decided to participate in the review, which was held in London at the end of August 2004. Charles recruited Dick Spertzel to help with the biological section and other old UNSCOM hands were also involved, including Hamish, who had drafted much of the biological section, although it was still far from complete. The entire report was now over a thousand pages long, but a number of sections were still incomplete, and considerable time in London was spent not reviewing, but writing.

The "Comprehensive Report" could not have been further in style and content from the March report. In a briefing note to Canberra I wrote:

> [The report] as far as I can judge is accurate and honest. There does not appear to be any bias towards presenting the information in a particular way to support certain interests …
>
> The ISG has found no evidence to suggest that Saddam had active WMD production programs pre-OIF. Some facilities had dual-use application as did some research projects. Some of this was deliberate, some we are not sure about, and some was probably

incidental. The situation in the missile field is different. Here Iraq had programs to develop long-range delivery systems, which perhaps at some future date would have had WMD warheads. We however have found no evidence of a clear and defined plan of this.

The writing-up of the report continued in Baghdad and I joined the ISG there for a couple of weeks to help with the process. Dick Spertzel and Hamish Killip were there too; sadly, without David Kelly we formed the Gang of Three. There would be only one version of this report, and as much as possible would be released to the public (in fact, over 95% of the report was eventually declassified).

There was no interrogating – or interviewing – of prisoners, at least not by us. After Iraq had regained its sovereignty by forming a transitional government at the end of June, the status of the prisoners changed. Before they had been prisoners of war or the civilian equivalent; now they were officially prisoners of the new government of Iraq. Of course in reality they were still American prisoners, and the legality of that was questionable. In fact the UK government became so concerned that it prohibited British members of the ISG from having anything to do with the prisoners; even the information from interviews conducted by the US after June would not be used by the UK. I could not establish precisely what the Australian rules were, but decided too that the prisoners were now being illegally held and in spite of being asked by Charles, decided to have no contact with them whatsoever. I declined even to write questions for others to ask.

Even though there were some rough edges the final product was a pleasing one. The opening chapter discussed Regime Strategic Intent. The key finding was that Saddam never gave up his ambitions for the weapons and would have resumed his programs when the opportunity arose. However he had no definite plans and nothing was in place by the time of the 2003 war.

The chapter also made the point that the Regime was Saddam, and Saddam was the Regime. This answered many of the apparently strange and contradictory signals that came out of Iraq before the war, including sometimes ambiguous messages about possession of WMD. Saddam encouraged this ambiguity: he wanted his enemies, particularly Iran and Israel, to believe that he had the weapons, but also wanted the UN to believe that he had disarmed. Just as importantly, he wanted to impress on his own generals that he was the strong man and had stood up to the UN by keeping his weapons. One general told the ISG that as the 2003 war was about to begin, he and his colleagues fully expected Saddam to reveal his plans for the use of WMD, only to be severely disappointed when they realised there were none.

No major decision was made without Saddam, but rarely did he set out clear policies or give specific, clearly defined instructions. Rather he left it to his inner circle to interpret his musings. One can only imagine how difficult it must have been for his lieutenants to get it right.

Understanding how the regime worked under Saddam was also the key to assessments prior to the 2003 war. Unfortunately the CIA and other intelligence agencies never achieved such an understanding: their interpretation of developments in Iraq was based on Western thinking. It was a fundamental failing. Now, with the advantage of the work of the ISG, it was clear where many of their assessments had gone wrong. I could only wonder what advice Bush, Blair and Howard would have received if the analysts had followed their tradecraft.

UNMOVIC assessments, too, had been wrong in three important areas, and as an adviser to Blix I felt some responsibility for this. David Kay's words rang in my ears: *"we were almost all wrong."*

UNMOVIC had been right to request documentation from Iraq, but the assumption that such documentation existed was incorrect. Iraq had destroyed all its weapons unilaterally in July 1991, but UNMOVIC had not believed it when it claimed no record had been kept of this. Blix had said that "this is not marmalade," meaning that a country would not destroy something as important as WMD, which it had spent billions of dollars to produce, without documentation. But in Saddam's Iraq, an order from the leadership was not questioned, and written authorisation was not requested.

Secondly, UNMOVIC's anthrax assessment was wrong. The story that Taha had told UNMOVIC about her production and disposal of anthrax was false, but UNMOVIC's conclusion that "there must be a strong presumption that it might still exist", however reasonable at the time, was incorrect.

Finally, UNMOVIC's conclusion that Iraq had weaponised the nerve agent VX was also wrong. Traces of the agent had been found on the remnants of weapons that Iraq had unilaterally destroyed in 1991, thus creating suspicion. Iraq did not explain the presence of VX, instead accusing the UN of falsifying the results. The ISG later discovered that four bombs had actually been filled with VX and dropped on Iran during the war with that country in the 1980s. My guess was that the pump used for filling those bombs had also been used for filling other chemical bombs, resulting in cross-contamination. Because Iraq had omitted to declare its VX attack on Iran, UNMOVIC had no explanation for the traces of the agent on the discarded bombs and again had come to a reasonable, but wrong, conclusion.

So had Iraq brought the war on itself? The declaration to UNMOVIC it made in December 2002 was certainly not "Currently Accurate, Full and Complete". The findings of the ISG showed that the declaration included false statements, such as the account of Iraq's production and disposal of anthrax. It also showed there had been significant omissions, such as the use of VX chemical bombs against Iran and the dropping of Sarin bombs on Shias in April 1991 (after the Gulf War) to quell an uprising. Thus, based on the wording of Security Council Resolution 1441, Iraq was in "material breach". But in my view Iraq should never have been judged a threat to the Coalition countries. There was no justification for war based on its WMD capabilities.

*

On completion of the report,[46] Charles invited me to Washington in October to help him prepare for Congressional hearings. The preparatory meetings were held at Langley, the CIA's headquarters, where one senior analyst told me that my quitting in March that year had been a good decision because, "after that, Charlie found religion. No-one could give him advice; he did his own thing." Another analyst told me that she thought the final report was excellent but "most of it could have been written at the beginning of the year." No doubt David Kay would have agreed with that.

The US would hold its presidential elections in just over a month's time, and so I expected that Charles would receive a tough reception.

The timing had, in fact, been Charles's decision. He did not want to be accused of being a political animal by delaying the report until after the elections and I admired him for this.

As it happened, though, the hearing proved uncontroversial – by this time the findings came as no great surprise. In addition, both sides of politics could find something in Charles's report to draw on. For the Republicans, it was Saddam's intention to re-acquire WMD; this was confirmed by Tariq Aziz's statement that "Saddam never lost his ambition for nuclear weapons." For the Democrats, it was the fact that the intelligence agencies had got it wrong. There were no WMD in Iraq after 1991.

Senator Edward Kennedy made the point that, "We did not go to war over intent. But that he [Saddam] *had* WMD." Kennedy then asked Charles to comment on Defense Secretary Donald Rumsfeld's support for the war, based as it was on the weapons that Saddam "had". Charles refused to be drawn on the subject of the rationale for war and replied, "I spent more time with the Iraqi Secretary of Defence than the US Secretary – ask me about him!"

Kennedy also asked Charles about the hunt for WMD, and whether it was a wild goose chase. Charles's response was, "My task was not to find weapons of mass destruction, but to find the truth." And now we knew the truth. It had been a long journey.

Epilogue

HAD WE GONE TO WAR ON A LIE? That is a question that is still being argued today. We now know that Iraq did not have Weapons of Mass Destruction but in 2003 it was less certain. Even UNMOVIC believed then that the existence of some remnant weapons was a possibility. Blix had told the Security Council that "there must be a strong presumption that the anthrax still exists."

I do not believe that the CIA deliberately set out to mislead its government about Iraq's capabilities prior to the war. Many CIA analysts whom I have spoken to genuinely believed their assessments. This, however, does not absolve them of culpability: if they had been following the fundamentals of their trade, they would not have got it so wrong. There should have been more questioning of the intelligence, more caution in their assessments and more review of their reporting. The CIA gave its political leaders what they wanted. No doubt the feedback that President Bush gave the agency only encouraged George Tenet. If there had been any objectivity among the analysts up to then, it was crushed in the rush to offer more of the same.

In the UK and Australia, the situation was different. In both countries the intelligence agencies judged only that there was a possibility that Iraq had retained old munitions, and a possibility that Iraq might have started new programs to produce further stockpiles. Of course that did not stop John Scarlett and others sexing up these assessments to turn possibilities into certainties. There is no question that Tony Blair would have known the truth, but he did not hesitate to use Scarlett's Dossier of Deceit to convince Parliament to vote for war.

Australia's Prime Minister, John Howard, also misled the electorate. I was reliably told that when Howard saw Australia's intelligence assessment in late 2002, he exclaimed something along the lines of "Is that all there is?" Subsequently he applied almost as much spin to the intelligence given him as Shane Warne to a wrong 'un. Never in presenting his justification for war did he exhibit any uncertainty: if he had, there would have been even less support for Australia's participation.

Nor can the leaders of the Coalition of the Willing hide behind intelligence assessments indicating that there was a possibility that Iraq might have had stockpiles of WMD prior to the 2003 war. The question our leaders should have been honestly addressing was, is Iraq a threat, is there an imminent danger from Iraq's WMD? We now know the nonsense of the "forty-five minutes from doomsday" claim and other misrepresentations. The possibility that Iraq might have had small, ageing stockpiles of chemical and biological weapons did not justify the war. Our leaders knew the truth but chose for various reasons to mislead us. We did go to war on a lie.

*

We live in a democracy and leaders can be voted out. But we do not vote for our intelligence agencies. Can we trust them in the future? Have they learnt anything from their mistakes? Will there be changes?

Inquiries into performance of the intelligence agencies in all the Coalition countries were conducted in 2003 and 2004. The most probing of the intelligence inquiries was President Bush's "Commission on the Intelligence Capabilities of the United States regarding Weapons of Mass Destruction". Its findings, delivered in March 2005, were blunt. The agencies were "dead wrong" in almost all of their pre-war judgments; a culture of "group-think" prevailed in which there was no challenge to set views. But that sort of frankness was rare among the reviews. In the UK, for example, the Joint Intelligence Committee, in a self-assessment[47] issued early in 2005, simply noted that many of its pre-war claims have "not been substantiated", implying that its judgments might still be proven correct.

The best that could be said of the two inquiries[48] held into the performance of Australian intelligence agencies was that they were a good start. Neither had terms of reference that would allow thorough examination of why things went wrong.

I fear that the agencies in all three Coalition countries will not learn the lessons of the Iraqi WMD debacle. Many of the analysts and the senior staff have moved on and the new generation will think that the lessons do not apply to them. There is a parallel with the Yellow Rain saga of two decades earlier, after which no lessons were learned and no changes implemented.

*

We may have gone to war on a lie, but the clock cannot now be wound back. Undoubtedly the Iraqi people are better off without Saddam, but they are presently paying a high price for his removal. And so is the Coalition, with more casualties occurring after the war than during it. The solution, however, is not for the Coalition to pull out of Iraq, for that would rapidly lead to anarchy. I have seen anarchy in Somalia, and as bad as Iraq is now, it is a long way from that. The Coalition is the cause of the mess that Iraq is today, and it now bears a responsibility for the Iraqi people. I believe we have little choice but to remain there until Iraq can fend for itself, however long that might take. This is a far better, and a far more just, "exit strategy" than any timetable that would simply pull out the troops whether Iraq was ready or not.

*

On 14 February 2005, my views on Iraq and the events that led up to the war were broadcast by the ABC in a *Four Corners* documentary entitled "Secrets and Lies". It was a difficult program for me to make. After a lifetime working in the secret world of intelligence, becoming a whistleblower was not easy. I also knew there would be consequences for such action. But Australia and the other Coalition members had gone to war and many lives had been lost; the public had a right to know the events behind the decisions. I also wanted to make it clear to the government that it was accountable and that politicians cannot simply mislead people with impunity.

I was also motivated by concern for the fate of the prisoners at Camp Cropper. I had tried official channels when I reported my suspicions of abuse of prisoners to the Australian government. But although an investigation had begun, nothing came of it. Late in 2004, the Deputy Secretary of Defence contacted me to tell me that he had been informed that the US could not proceed further because, *"Barton had not witnessed prisoner abuse nor had direct knowledge. Therefore the investigation could not proceed further ..."* I was outraged. I had never claimed that I had witnessed the abuse myself, but the evidence was certainly strong enough for a serious investigation to be conducted. The Deputy Secretary agreed with me, but I heard no more and I sensed that once the heat was off, the inquiry would once again fall into a hole.

I was concerned, too, about the continuing incarceration of the scientists and engineers who had been involved with Iraq's WMD programs before 1991. They had not committed any crime, at least not as recognised under international law, and should not be languishing in jail. Alternatively, if it was believed that they had committed a crime, then they should be charged. In that case all of the others who had been involved with these programs, some thousands, should also be in jail and not just the half-dozen that were there now.

After my views were aired on Australian television, the Australian Senate agreed to an inquiry[49] into the issues I had raised on the *Four Corners* program. It was possibly unique in the history of government inquiries in that only one witness testified. That was me. It was clear from the Senate Estimates inquiries earlier in the year that there were others with knowledge, but these public servants and military officers were "discouraged" from coming forward. It seems a strange democracy where the truth is discouraged.

I expected, and received, the roughing-up characteristic of such inquiries. For example, in an attempt to discredit my suspicions of prisoner abuse, the Liberal Senator David Johnston asked in bullying tones:[50]

SENATOR JOHNSTON: Did you ever come across the concept of hearsay?

MR BARTON: Yes.

SENATOR JOHNSTON: Do you understand the meaning of the word "rumour"?

MR BARTON: Yes.

SENATOR JOHNSTON: Do you understand the meaning of the word "gossip"?

MR BARTON: I do.

SENATOR JOHNSTON: Where, in terms of your allegations about abuse, does your understanding fit in that spectrum – hearsay, rumour or gossip?

MR BARTON: It does not fit any of those. I am an intelligence analyst. I have collected intelligence over many years. There is rumour and gossip, but you have to assess sources. If I believe the source is reliable, then I put that for what that is.

I was annoyed at the line of questioning but resisted the temptation to show my feelings. I felt that the issues were too important to let them be caught up in the politics of the Australian Senate, and instead I asked the Committee to consider Australia's responsibility for the prisoners:

Australia has some responsibility for the prisoners at Cropper: we were part of the Coalition, we were part of the ISG and we were involved with the prisoners. I believe that the Australian government should formally request the US, and the new Iraqi government, to release from Cropper those prisoners who are not to be charged with any crime.

The findings of the Senate Inquiry were tabled in Parliament on 18 August 2005. Neither the Minister of Defence, Robert Hill, nor his department came out well. Contrary to Hill's claims, the Committee's views on interrogations were that "given that those interviewed were being forcibly detained, the meaning of the terms 'interview' and 'interrogation' appear to merge." The Defence Department was also admonished for its lack of internal communication about the issues I had raised with it.

While these were important matters, they were not central to my concerns. Unfortunately the issue of the prisoners and what should be done about them was overlooked. Perhaps it was all too difficult. It was ironical that close to where I gave evidence to the Senate Inquiry in Parliament House is a copy of the *Magna Carta* of 1215, a gift of the British government. This was the first great charter of liberty and on a visit to Parliament House you can read:

No man shall be imprisoned except by lawful judgement of his equals. To none shall justice be sold, denied or delayed.

These great principles seem to have been forgotten by all members of the Coalition.

The obsession of Australian politicians with themselves and with scoring political points against each other, resulted in a handful of Iraqis becoming yet another casualty from an unjust war. In December 2005, the US announced the release of some of the former WMD scientists, including Dr Taha. After two and a half years without charge, this was good news. But such is the secrecy of the US incarceration system in Iraq, we may never know whether all of the former scientists have been released.

I will not forget Iraq, I will not forget the Iraqi people, and I will not give up on the fight for the release of the former scientists still imprisoned at Camp Cropper.

Cast of Characters

Lt Colonel "Aaron" Israeli military intelligence officer.

Major-General Hossam Amin Head of Iraq's National Monitoring Directorate (responsible for WMD disarmament); prisoner in Camp Cropper – reportedly released December 2005.

Tariq Aziz Iraqi Foreign Minister; Iraqi Deputy Prime Minister; prisoner in Camp Cropper.

Lt General John Baker Director Defence Intelligence Organisation; Chief of Australian Defence Force.

Dr Maurice Barton Director Scientific and Technical Intelligence, Joint Intelligence Organisation.

Rod Barton Director Strategic Technology, Defence Intelligence Organisation; weapons inspector; member of the "Gang of Four" investigators.

Dr Hans Blix Director-General of the International Atomic Energy Agency, Executive Chairman of the UN Monitoring, Verification and Inspection Commission (UNMOVIC).

Richard Butler Australian Ambassador to UN; Executive Chairman of the UN Special Commission (UNSCOM).

Sir Percy Craddock Chairman of the UK Joint Intelligence Committee; Policy Adviser to British Prime Minister, Mrs Thatcher.

Dr Hugh Crone Senior Principal Research Scientist (chemical defence), Material Research Laboratories, Melbourne.

Lt General Keith Dayton Military head of the Iraq Survey Group.

Charles Duelfer US State Department official; Deputy Director UNSCOM; Head of Iraq Survey Group.

Dr Peter Dunn Superintending Scientist, Material Research Laboratories, Melbourne.

Rolf Ekeus Executive Chairman of the UN Special Commission (UNSCOM); Swedish Ambassador to the US.

Dr John Gee Australian diplomat; UNSCOM Commissioner; Deputy Director-General UN Organisation for the Prohibition of Chemical Weapons.

Annick Paul-Henriot UN lawyer; co-ordinator for UNSCOM biological group.

Hussein Moalim Iman Somali agronomist; Manager of Bon Kai demobilisation farm.

Lt General Hussein Kamal Saddam's son-in-law; Minister of Military Industrialisation (responsible for WMD programs).

Dr Leonard Kapungu Head of Political Division of the UN Operations in Somalia (UNOSOM).

Dr Doug Kean Nuclear Intelligence analyst; Deputy Director Office of National Assessments; Deputy Director Defence Intelligence Organisation.

Dr David Kelly Microbiologist; Senior Adviser on biological weapons to UK government; weapons inspector; member of the "Gang of Four" investigators.

Hamish Killip Colonel in British Royal Engineers; weapons inspector; member of the "Gang of Four" investigators.

John McLaughlin Deputy Director CIA.

Robert Mathams Director Scientific and Technical Intelligence, Joint Intelligence Organisation.

Dr Ahmed Murthada Engineer; Dr Taha's boss; Minister for Transport and Telecommunications; prisoner in Camp Cropper.

Demetrius (Demetri) Perricos International Atomic Energy Agency Inspector; Deputy Executive Chairman & Director Operations (Inspections), UNMOVIC.

Lt General Amer Rashid Head of Iraq's SCUD program; chief negotiator on Iraq's WMD; Oil Minister; prisoner in Camp Cropper – status unknown.

Scott Ritter US Marine; weapons inspector.

Lt General Amer Al Sa'adi Chief Scientist for Iraq's chemical and biological weapons programs; chief negotiator on Iraq's WMD; Saddam's Scientific Adviser; prisoner in Camp Cropper – status unknown.

John Scarlett Chairman of the UK Joint Intelligence Committee; Head of MI6.

General Faiz Al Shahine Director of Al Muthanna chemical weapons plant; deputy Oil Minister.

Nikita Smidovitch Russian diplomat; UN weapons inspector (head of missile group); Head of Training, UNMOVIC.

Dr Richard (Dick) Spertzel US Army Colonel; veterinarian; weapons inspector; member of the "Gang of Four" investigators.

Dr Rihab Taha Microbiologist; Head of Iraq's biological weapons program; prisoner in Camp Cropper – released December 2005.

George Tenet Director of Central Intelligence; Director CIA.

Abdul Thamer Biologist; Dr Taha's deputy; prisoner in Camp Cropper – status unknown.

Harry Turner Head Nuclear Intelligence, Joint Intelligence Organisation.

Notes

1 *Sub Rosa: Memoirs of an Australian Intelligence Analyst*, R. H. Mathams, 1982, p. 88.
2 Soviet Military Power 1985, US Department of Defense, p. 134.
3 Pine Gap was the prime target, for reasons which have been written about extensively by others. See, for example, *A Suitable Piece of Real Estate*, Sydney, Hale & Iremonger, 1980, by Desmond Ball.
4 Special Report No. 98, "Chemical Warfare in Southeast Asia and Afghanistan", Report to the Congress from Secretary of State Alexander M. Haig, Jr, 22 March 1982.
5 "The examination of 'Yellow Rain' specimens received at MRL in April 1982", Technical Report, Hugh Crone, August 1982.
6 Special Report No. 104, "Chemical Warfare in Southeast Asia and Afghanistan: An Update", Report to the Congress from Secretary of State, George P. Shultz, November 1982.
7 American Association for the Advancement of Science, Detroit, M. Meselson et al., 31 May 1983.
8 "A study of the origin and the Pollen Analysis of 'Yellow Rain' in northern Jiangsu", Chang Tsung et al., Nanking University Science Bulletin, September 1977.
9 UN Security Council, report S/16433, 26 March 1984.
10 United Nations Security Council Resolution 660, August 1990.
11 United Nations Security Council Resolution 661, August 1990.
12 United Nations Security Council Resolution 687, April 1991.
13 UN Security Council Resolution 707, August 1991.
14 UN Security Council Resolution 707, 15 August 1991.
15 UN Security Council Resolution 715, 11 October 1991.
16 Letter from Iraq's Foreign Minister, Ahmed Hussein to President of the Security Council, 19 November 1991.
17 Letter from Iraq to President of the Security Council, S/26811, 26 November 1993.

18 "Iraq's Ton of Germs", William Safire, *New York Times*, 13 March 1995.

19 S/195494 of 19 June 1995.

20 "Hussein Kamil, brothers killed by Family Members", 28 February 1996, *Baghdad Observer*.

21 Discussion Paper (DFAT), "UNSCOM: Establishing an Endgame", Rod Barton, 26 July 1996 (Revised 14 May 1997).

22 "Scott Ritter's Private War", Peter Boyer, *The New Yorker*, 9 November 1998.

23 UN Security Council Resolution 1115, 21 June 1997.

24 "Iraq is Down but Not Out", Rod Barton, 23 December 1998, *New York Times*.

25 UN Security Council Resolution 1284, 17 December 1999.

26 Australia's Role in United Nations Reform, Joint Standing Committee on Foreign Affairs, Defence and Trade, June 2001.

27 Ibid, p. 99.

28 President George W. Bush press conference, South Lawns of White House, 11 March 2002.

29 President George W. Bush press conference, James S. Brady Briefing Room, 8 July 2002.

30 Iraq's Weapons of Mass Destruction, An Assessment of the British Government, 24 September 2002.

31 National Intelligence Estimate, Iraq's Continuing Programs for Weapons of Mass Destruction, 1 October 2002.

32 UN Security Council Resolution 1441, 8 November 2002.

33 "Post Opinion", *New York Post*, 3 October 2002.

34 "U.S. says Baghdad is hiding anthrax", Bill Gertz, *Washington Times*, 8 November 2002.

35 Briefing to the Security Council, Inspections in Iraq and a Preliminary Assessment of Iraq's Weapons Declaration, The Executive Chairman of UNMOVIC, Hans Blix, 19 December 2002.

36 Briefing to the Security Council, An Update on Inspections, The Executive Chairman of UNMOVIC, Hans Blix, 27 January 2003.

37 Senate Foreign Relations Committee, Statement by the Honorable John D. Negroponte, 30 January 2003.

38 Press Statement by Foreign Minister Jack Straw, "Iraq is in 'Material Breach' of 1441", 28 January 2003.

39 British government press release, "Foreign Secretary's response to weapons inspectors' report", 14 February 2003.

40 "Today" program, BBC Radio 4, 29 May 2003.

41 Lord Hutton's inquiry into the circumstances surrounding the death of Dr David Kelly. Report issued 28 January 2004.

42 Statement by David Kay on the Interim Progress Report on the Activities of the Iraq Survey Group, House Select Committee on Intelligence, 2 October 2003.

43 Hearing of the Senate Armed Services Committee, Iraqi Weapons of Mass Destruction, 28 January 2004.

44 "Suspicion Surround the Death of Iraqi Scientist in US Custody" Alissa Rubin, *Los Angeles Times*, 28 May 2004.

45 Statement to Senate by Senator Robert Hill, 16 June 2004.

46 Comprehensive Report of the Special Adviser to DCI on Iraq's WMD, 30 September 2004.

47 Intelligence and Security Committee Annual report 2004–05, April 2005.

48 Intelligence on Iraq's weapons of mass destruction, Parliamentary Joint Committee on ASIO, ASIS and DSD, December 2003; Report of the inquiry into Australian Intelligence Agencies, 22 July 2004.

49 Duties of Australian Personnel in Iraq, Foreign Affairs, Defence and Trade References Committee, 2005.

50 Hansard, Duties of Australian Personnel in Iraq, Foreign Affairs, Defence and Trade References Committee, 29 March 2005.

Note for researchers

The original version of *The Weapons Detective* under the title *The Adventures of an Ordinary Man* will be accessible from the Australian National Library, Canberra, in late 2006. *The Adventures of an Ordinary Man* contains additional chapters and material that may be of interest to researchers and historians. The author may be contacted at <rod_barton@hotmail.com>.

Index

The following abbreviations have been used in the index. BW for biological weapons and RB for Rob Barton.